KNOWLEDGE AND POWER IN PUBLIC BUREAUCRACIES

Ever since Max Weber and Frederick Taylor, public organizations have been told that effective practice lies in maximizing rationality through science. Yet science-based management reforms have had only marginal impact on performance. People in entry-level positions possess knowledge from direct experience of the work, management knowledge is often science-based and distanced from the work, and appointed top executives struggle to join bureaucratic rationality with political exigencies. *Knowledge and Power in Public Bureaucracies: From Pyramid to Circle* offers fresh thinking about public organizations, arguing that conflicting forms of knowledge may be found within the bureaucratic pyramid.

Answering the question of why management reforms over the past century have failed on their own terms, this book examines the existence of conflicting forms of knowledge within public bureaucracies, how these contradictory perspectives interact (or fail to interact), and the ways in which these systems preserve managerial efforts to control workers. Authors Carnevale and Stivers argue that bureaucratic rationality is not the "one best way," as Taylor promised, and indeed, there is no one best way or model that can be deployed in all situations. The bureaucratic pyramid can, however, be made more effective by paying attention to circular processes that are widespread within the hierarchy, the authors argue, describing such circular processes as "facework." This book will serve as an ideal supplement to introductory public administration and organizational theory courses, as well as courses for mid-career professionals, helping to frame their work experiences.

David G. Carnevale is a professor emeritus from the University of Oklahoma. He is former international union director for AFSCME-AFL-CIO, operations administrator of the California State Employees Association, and executive director of the Maine State Employees Association. He is author of *Trustworthy Government: Leadership and Management Strategies for Building Trust and High Performance*, and *Organization Development in the Public Sector*. Dr Carnevale is a practiced mediator and a Vietnam veteran.

Camilla Stivers spent two decades as a staff member in community-based publicly funded organizations. She taught public and nonprofit administration at The Evergreen State College, Olympia, Washington, and the Levin College of Urban Affairs at Cleveland State University, where she held the Albert A. Levin chair in public service and urban studies. She is the author or co-author of six additional books. She is a fellow of the National Academy of Public Administration and a former associate editor of *Public Administration Review*.

KNOWLEDGE AND POWER IN PUBLIC BUREAUCRACIES

From Pyramid to Circle

David G. Carnevale and Camilla Stivers

NEW YORK AND LONDON

First published 2020
by Routledge
52 Vanderbilt Avenue, New York, NY 10017

and by Routledge
2 Park Square, Milton Park, Abingdon, Oxon OX14 4RN

Routledge is an imprint of the Taylor & Francis Group, an informa business

© 2020 David G. Carnevale and Camilla Stivers

The right of David G. Carnevale and Camilla Stivers to be identified as author of this work has been asserted by him in accordance with sections 77 and 78 of the Copyright, Designs and Patents Act 1988.

All rights reserved. No part of this book may be reprinted or reproduced or utilised in any form or by any electronic, mechanical, or other means, now known or hereafter invented, including photocopying and recording, or in any information storage or retrieval system, without permission in writing from the publishers.

Trademark notice: Product or corporate names may be trademarks or registered trademarks, and are used only for identification and explanation without intent to infringe.

British Library Cataloguing in Publication Data
A catalogue record for this book is available from the British Library

Library of Congress Cataloging-in-Publication Data
Names: Carnevale, David G., 1945- author. | Stivers, Camilla, author.
Title: Knowledge and power in public bureaucracies : from pyramid to circle / David G. Carnevale and Camilla Stivers.
Description: Abingdon, Oxon ; New York, NY : Routledge, 2019. | Includes bibliographical references.
Identifiers: LCCN 2019000114 (print) | LCCN 2019010405 (ebook) | ISBN 9780429266485 (eBook) | ISBN 9780367210809 (hbk : alk. paper) | ISBN 9780367210793 (pbk : alk. paper) | ISBN 9780429266485 (ebk)
Subjects: LCSH: Bureaucracy. | Organizational behavior. | Administrative agencies--Management. | Executive departments--Management. | Communication in organizations. | Knowledge, Theory of.
Classification: LCC JF1501 (ebook) | LCC JF1501 .C44 2019 (print) | DDC 302.3/5–dc23
LC record available at https://lccn.loc.gov/2019000114

ISBN: 978-0-367-21080-9 (hbk)
ISBN: 978-0-367-21079-3 (pbk)
ISBN: 978-0-429-26648-5 (ebk)

Typeset in Bembo
by Taylor & Francis Books

DEDICATION

To the memory of Ralph Hummel: colleague, intellectual progenitor, co-author, and best friend.

[Cam]: Ralph and his parents came from Germany to the U.S. in the early 1950s. Ralph's father became a machinist at General Motors in Detroit. Maybe that's how Ralph got interested in how people accomplish their work, especially if they are working with their hands. At some point in their stories, Ralph said, working people will tell you that "there's a little trick to it; you just have to feel it." He spent years as a newspaper reporter in Detroit, New York, and Washington, D.C. before becoming an academic. He was also a philosopher—studying Kant, Husserl, Arendt, and Heidegger (usually in the original German). I think he was drawn to phenomenology because it deals with addressing the world so that it shows itself to you not as pre-conceived but, as he said, "in its own terms." From all accounts Ralph was a fantastic teacher of public administration, even though he had never taken a course in it, and even though he was notoriously unorganized ("What? You want a syllabus?"). Amazingly, students didn't seem to care. They were always telling him he changed their lives. He was also the best listener I have ever known, and an elegant writer. People were always saying things like, "Your book The Bureaucratic Experience? You must have come to my agency!" He loved everything about Maine, especially sailing the Mussel Ridge Channel off Spruce Head Island. The Institute of Applied Phenomenology (appliedphenom.org), which Ralph started up almost forty years ago, lives on.

[David:] Ralph and I spent years talking and arguing about different knowledges competing on the job in public bureaucracies and other organizations that rely on workers. We did eventually come to terms about management ideology. Yes, managers did work, but more importantly, they understood "work" conceptually rather than, as workers did, from direct experience. We called this idea of competing knowledges "the knowledge analytic." This volume carries forward and deepens this fundamental dynamic. It is a kind of physics approach to organization theory. These perspectives are explored in great detail in what follows. I pray that readers will recognize in their own experiences as public servants the perspective Ralph pioneered, upon which we have built. May they imagine what is possible in making organizations more democratic for all those who labor in public service.

CONTENTS

List of illustrations	ix
Acknowledgments	x
Introduction	1

PART I
The Pyramid   9

1 The Failure of Management Reforms: A History   11

2 Knowing in the Public Organization: The Pyramid of Knowledges   34

3 What Workers Know: Felt Sense at the Front Line   47

4 What Managers Know: The Power of the Concept   70

5 What Executives Know: Expertise as "Being Governmental"   89

PART II
The Pyramid in Action   109

6 The VA Case: Knowledge and Power in a Service Bureaucracy   111

    Sequel: Bottom up at the va—the engagement board   128

Attachment: VA Summit Planning Form — 138

Epilogue: The Knowledge Approach to Research — 142

PART III
The Circle — **145**

7 Introduction: From Pyramid to Circle: The Power of Process — 147

8 The Logic of Reasonableness: Experience, Judgment and Dialogue in Administrative Practice — 158

9 The Dialogic Circle in the Bureaucratic Pyramid: Conflict Resolution and Collective Bargaining — 166

10 Circles of Trust in Public Organizations: The Power of Facework — 174

11 Authentic Ethics in the Bureaucracy — 190

12 Competing Knowledges and Public Service Education — 202

Index — *212*

ILLUSTRATIONS

Figures

6.1 Flow chart, appointment process for new patient.
Source: Northern Virginia Technology Council, *Opportunities to Improve the Scheduling of Medical Exams for America's Veterans* (NVTC, 2014)   120

6.2 Engagement Board Community Process.
Source: U.S. Department of Health and Human Services, National Institutes of Health (2011). *Principles of Community Engagement* (2nd ed.). Publication No. 11–7782.   132

9.1 Vectors of Dialogue: Assertiveness and Circularity (by David Carnevale)   168

ACKNOWLEDGMENTS

Many thanks to Veronica Elias for her assiduous and intelligent archival research at Ralph's house in Maine, and to his daughter, Kate Boughton-Hummel, for graciously making the material available.

Thanks to Staci Zavattaro, editor-in-chief of *Administrative Theory & Praxis (ATP)*, for permission to use, in epigraphs that head Chapters 2, 3, 4, and 7, material from Ralph's work that first appeared in *Dialogue*, the newsletter that later became *ATP*'s first volumes.

Thanks to Dvora Yanow for extraordinary critique of a very early draft of Part I.

Thanks to members of the Engagement Board and staff at the Denver VA Hospital.

Thanks to Laura Stearns at Routledge and to reviewers of the draft manuscript for invaluable perspectives and assistance.

Thanks to our families. Thanks also to many colleagues and friends for dialogue and argument and encouragement and support along the way—even those who didn't realize it:

Cam is grateful to fellow members of the Institute of Applied Phenomenology in Science and Technology, especially Nick Zingale, Justin Piccorelli, Bill Denihan, and the late Mary Schmidt; to colleagues at Evergreen and Cleveland State, including Ken Dolbeare, Cheryl King, Jennifer Alexander, the late Larry Terry, Roberta Steinbacher, and David Sweet; and elsewhere: to mentors Matthew Holden, the late David Kirkwood Hart, Charles Goodsell, the late John Rohr; and also to almost-family friends in Maine: the Merchants and the Oakeses, Susan Vollhart, and the Walking Group.

David says thanks to all the people who had good influences on me over time that led to the completion of this project: former colleagues and educational mentors, and others too.

Special thanks to family tech wizard Amanda Beckman whose IT support through thick and thin made this volume possible.

INTRODUCTION

> Old paradigms, like old realities, do not give up without a fight.
> (Carnevale & Hummel, 1994)

Most public administration research is concerned with how to make administrative action predictable and effective, yet the gap between intentions and outcomes persists. It reveals itself in a wide range of government activities, including policing, welfare work, child protective services, border patrol, housing and restaurant inspection, services to veterans, and many others. Decades of management reforms have failed to close the gap. The current focus of reform is *performance*: measurement or management. The watchword is *Results*. Like other management reforms that preceded it ("management by objectives," "re-engineering," "total quality management"), this approach has not yet delivered on its promises. Could it be that the gap requires deeper exploration than it has so far received?

This book offers a fresh way of thinking about the dynamics of public organizations, by calling attention to the existence of disparate knowledges within the bureaucratic pyramid. The deepest roots of our perspective lie in the work of our friend and partner, the late Ralph Hummel,[1] who pioneered a new approach to understanding public organizations almost forty years ago. He focused on the different types of activities in bureaucracies, the different forms of knowledge they entail, and how these knowledges are related to one another. In an early statement, he said:

> The structural analysis of the distribution of the elements of work in the modern organization shows the extent to which the manager is physically removed from the work itself, work and its objects … being mediated by the

worker. At the same time, specific social and cultural aspects of work are structurally removed from the worker.

(Hummel, 1983, p. 2)

Ralph goes on to argue that this structural arrangement insulates managers from direct contact with the tangible work of the organization—in today's terms, from the activities that directly produce whatever counts as results. The manager's world is a world of concepts, whereas the worker's world is one of direct engagement with the material of the organization's objectives, whether these are physical (for example, building a space shuttle, fighting a fire) or interpersonal (helping a client obtain benefits, rescuing a child from an abusive parent).

Ralph's argument, even at this early stage in its development, was that the different experiences of worker and manager, the one in direct contact with the work, the other organizing and supervising it from a distance, result in fundamentally different "life-worlds," to use phenomenologist Alfred Schutz's term. The worker's world evokes an approach to work that Ralph (1983) calls a *logic of reasonableness*, whereas the manager's world is approached through a *logic of rationality*. The relegation of these different logics or knowledges to separated organizational levels results from the division of labor and from hierarchy, which "free" the manager from having to do the organization's work, and "free" the worker from any role in setting organizational objectives (the scare quotes are in Ralph's original).

In this book, we argue that ignoring or failing to recognize the existence and implications of the structural analysis pioneered in Ralph's nearly four decades of work on it is a likely source of repeated management reform failures. The reformers' hope has always been that pyramidal command structures would rationally organize complex tasks and the knowledge and skills necessary to complete them successfully. Yet the pyramid itself—the hierarchy—embodies conceptual rather than experiential knowledge. The extent to which other kinds of knowledge, *though necessary to accomplish organizational goals*, may resist and evade pyramidal rationality has rarely been recognized. Worker resistance to management commands is a frequent, even ubiquitous, topic; the way one knowledge evades control by another is not. Thus, to date, management reform ideas have never gotten to the heart of the problem.

The pyramid assumes that an uninterrupted flow of knowledge is possible between bottom and top. In theory, commands from the top flow down in chains of command through management to become orders issued to frontline workers, and hands-on intelligence flows up through managerial levels to the executive level, where the buck has been famously said to stop. But what if this two-way flow is impeded by discontinuity between the kind of knowledge acquired by direct engagement in the work itself, and the more distanced, objective, scientific knowledge said to be necessary for managerial control and rationalization of work processes? The possibility seems real, or at least worth exploring, that this incompatibility between managerial science and the experience-based knowledge in the hands (literal or figurative) of front-line workers may be more than a result of worker obstinacy; at a more fundamental level, it may be a product of disjunction between forms of knowledge.

We intend to argue that the cognitive gap between the direct, experience-based know-how of front-line workers and the abstract, distanced concepts of management is ignored and/or suppressed by managers and agency executives out of a felt need to control the work. We believe that before complex public organizations can improve their effectiveness, those who care about them must examine fundamental assumptions about what an organization is: in particular, what workers, managers, and executives know, and the extent to which these disparate knowledges and the practices they inform are fundamentally at odds.

As Ralph observed, based on the work of the phenomenologist Edmund Husserl, the ways in which human beings approach/interact with their surroundings, which Husserl called "intentionality," are shaped by their projects at hand and the ways they are encountered. In bureaucracies, there is a cognitive fault line between the individual worker's understanding of the work and that of the rest of the organization. Organizational goals, strategies, and definitions of work are devised at the executive and management levels. Workers, however, because they are in direct contact with the work, understand it and what it requires in a fundamentally different way from the way the organization defines it, and the division of labor and chain of command get in the way of accommodating this difference, or perhaps even being aware of it: "Both management and workers are working with only half a deck" (Hummel, 1982, p. 9).

Our examination encompasses issues of hierarchy, authority, and power, to take into account the fact that, as the great theorist of bureaucracy, Max Weber, said, bureaucracy is domination on the basis of knowledge. We observe that it is no accident that learning from direct experience is central to work at the bottom of the pyramid. At the management level, the responsibility to control hands-on work produces an ideology that privileges conceptual-scientific knowledge. At the top, executive knowledge struggles to extract information and ensure performance from the career civil service, at the same time sizing up and dealing with the political environment. This latter responsibility encompasses the contradictory relationship between rational bureaucratic thinking and the non-rational but reasonable felt sense necessary to political skill.

The bureaucratic pyramid is pervaded with an obsession over control in the service of results. By means of concepts—plans, rules, protocols, and standards—managers try to control workers by shaping what they know from experience. Executives try to control the entire pyramid through a mixture of orders and incentives, all the while responding to external pressures and demands. The struggle for control creates a power relationship in the pyramid organization that is too often corrosive to everyone connected with it: workers as employees, workers as citizens, managers and executives who struggle daily to try to make things run better, and ultimately citizens at large.

We are particularly concerned, however, with the potency of worker knowledge under constant siege by the ideology of management. So-called performance measures proliferate, aiming to translate tacit knowledge and hands-on skills into numerical indicators. Bureaucratic rules restrict workers' ability to make their knowledge count in organizational processes and to resist *irrational* dominance (that is, the kind based on protecting self-interests rather than on what the work requires) by management and the executive in public organizations. In recent decades, hard-won worker rights have been undermined by management strategies to limit employee grievance processes and collective bargaining, all the while spouting commitment to "empowerment schemes," "teamwork," "employee voice" and workers' "expressive" needs. In this battle for control of the worker, the substance of the work itself gets lost so that management authority can prevail.

In its research and teaching, the scholarly field of public administration reinforces the concentration of power at the top of the pyramid, simply by its lopsided focus on management and executive leadership and its neglect of frontline work and public sector unions. Relatively little research has been done on what workers know, how they know it, and in what form it makes its way up the pyramid; instead, when workers are studied at all, the usual focus is on how managers can control workers' exercise of judgment, including in their dealings with citizens.[2]

Granted that this is an important issue of accountability, it is also impossible to deal with reasonably, unless consideration is given to how workers' experience shapes the way they approach situations and what value this knowledge may hold for the achievement of agency mandates. Trendy research into organizational networks obscures the persistence of hierarchy within the boundaries of each organization in the network. Analysis of networks made up of pyramids fails to reach the root of the problem lying at the heart of the worker–management knowledge gap.

And, of course, the very term "public administration" (even more so, public "management") defines the focus of scholarship and education as interaction among executives and managers in the quest to get things done, as if workers only matter as a variable to be manipulated. One effect, among many, is the prevalence of management ideology in our curricula, with little *critical* examination of whether its promises actually can or do pan out. Public administration programs are preparing or upgrading managers, or transforming workers into managers, meanwhile taking for granted or failing to notice the absence of workers and their work as topics of classroom discussions—let alone as members of the class. (Admittedly, Max Weber himself did the same; there were no workers in his bureaucracy.) We examine the underpinnings of these limitations on the field's understanding of itself.

This volume represents our attempt to bring to fruition Ralph's exposé of the managerial bias in modern government organizations and the way we think about them, which limits the development of dedicated people at all levels in public agencies. We believe that what he and we refer to as "worker knowledge" should be better appreciated, accepted, and benefited from within organizations, rather than being ignored, problematized, and suppressed by managers, the executive suite and politicians.

As members of the Institute of Applied Phenomenology in Science and Technology (which Ralph founded around 1980), we subscribe to the philosophy of phenomenology and its application to the understanding of organizations, particularly those where commitment to science and technology prevail, as they do in virtually all public organizations pervaded with the ideology of managerialism (see www.appliedphenom.org).

Phenomenology starts from how things and people show themselves to us *as phenomena*, prior to our converting them to concepts. Phenomenology lays out the way of addressing things and people so that they can show themselves to us in their own terms, that is, as they appear to us in the situation at hand. It is in this ability to show themselves as what they are—in and for themselves—that phenomena appear and appeal to us by way of a silent call. As the great American architect, Louis I. Kahn, once put it: "You say to brick: Brick, what do you want?" (Lesser, 2017). Taking this stance acknowledges the necessity for making sense of things and people, for interpreting situations given their particular aspects, but it insists on preserving that remainder in things and people that eludes conclusive definition. In this sense, we accept that the experience–concept gap can never be fully closed, in that more interpreting can always be done. Improving the way organizations go about what they do entails such acceptance as necessary for human freedom. Still, acceptance does not entail either pretending the gap doesn't exist or failing to address its implications.

Our focus treats workers in public organizations as "first among equals" in the analysis, in that it is they whose knowledge and contribution to agency results have been undervalued—at best, seen as raw material to be transformed for use at higher agency levels. Thus, the parade of management fad after fad, failure after failure, reform after reform, all ending up on the administrative junk heap, while methods dating back to the beginning of the twentieth century still hold sway. We argue that the traditional *managerial philosophy*, on display in models of management, delivers much less than it promises, despite enthusiastic embrace after embrace of conventional thinking, newly decked out, and the repeated dawning of a so-called "new day" for public employees and their organizations.

In what follows, we begin Part I with a review of the decades of management prescriptions intended to control work processes and workers, and offer a diagnosis of the failure of management reforms (Chapter 1). We then lay out the interpretive framework that guides the book, which gives an overview of the different knowledges found in public organizations, how they are distributed within the organization, in what sense they are incommensurable, and how the distribution takes the form of a pyramid of power (Chapter 2). We follow up with detailed descriptions of the knowledges-in-use of workers, managers, and executives (Chapters 3, 4, and 5).

In Part II we present a case study that deploys the framework to interpret an organizational dilemma: the U.S. Department of Veterans Affairs struggle in 2014 and after to improve delivery of health services to veterans. In the process, we illustrate the research framework and approach that makes it possible to interpret public organizations on the basis of their patterns of knowledge.

In Part III we explore whether the organizational pyramid of knowledges is subject to change and suggest possible approaches. Using an alternative image to the pyramid, that is, the circle (a dialectic that also originates with Ralph), we examine the dynamics of interaction among knowledges—the practices, in other words, that mesh or fail to mesh them, and where opportunities may lie for improvement. Can different knowledges be interwoven to produce more effective joint action? We argue that the hierarchy can be tempered, if not displaced, by circular processes and perspectives, which we call "facework." We explore the potential of various ways and means to stimulate more productive dialogue among people with different knowledges and points of view, given that the nature of dialogue (before being warped by hierarchy) is circular. Concluding chapters on broader implications of the circular framework consider issues of building trust among organizational levels; the exercise of discretion and judgment in daily practice; circular ethics; and reshaping education for public service.

Notes

1 Because of our decades-long association with the late Ralph Hummel, we take the liberty in this introduction of referring to him as "Ralph."
2 Valuable research on frontline workers has appeared in recent years, the frequent catalyst being the impact of New Public Management at the front line. We cite contributions to this work in the chapter on worker knowledge and aim to deploy it in the context of our theoretical framework. Behn's (1992) research highlights knowledge differences within the bureaucracy and calls for greater appreciation of the value of worker understandings. Sandfort's (2000, 1999) work is notable for documenting the gaps between front line workers' understandings of their work and those of managers.

References

Behn, Robert D. 1992. Case analysis research and managerial effectiveness: Learning how to lead organizations up sand dunes. Pp. 40–54 in *Public Management: The State of the Art* (ed. B. Bozeman). San Francisco: Jossey-Bass.
Carnevale, David G., and Ralph P. Hummel. 1994. Why management reforms fail: The collision of knowledge and power. Paper delivered at the annual meeting of the Western Social Science Association (April). Albuquerque, N.M.

Hummel, Ralph P. 1982. The nature of work: Philosophy, psychology, and productivity. *Dialogue* 5:1 (Sept.-Oct.), 11–16.

Hummel, Ralph P. 1983. Manager and worker: Phenomenology of time consciousness and rational style. *Dialogue* 6:1 (Fall), 2–12.

Lesser, Wendy. 2017. *You Say to Brick: The Life of Louis Kahn*. New York: Farrar, Straus & Giroux.

Sandfort, Jodi R. 1999. The structural impediments to human service collaboration: Examining welfare reform at the front lines. *Social Service Review* 73:3 (Sept.), 314–339.

Sandfort, Jodi R. 2000. Public management in the welfare system. *Journal of Public Administration Research and Theory* 10:4 (Oct.), 729–756.

PART I
The Pyramid

1

THE FAILURE OF MANAGEMENT REFORMS

A History

> Since for human beings knowledge defines reality, those who have the most invested in a particular reality must protect and defend, with the police if necessary, the system of knowledge on which not only their power but their very existence rests.
>
> *(Carnevale & Hummel, 1994)*

Reflecting on more than a century of management thinking, even a half-awake mind would have to note a certain repetitiveness in the history of management reforms. Early iterations of this book's argument were entitled "Why Management Reforms Fail" (Carnevale & Hummel, 1994, 1996). The authors asked: What is it about modern management that *needs* ever new reforms but is unable to sustain them? Their answer was clear: No reform could prevail if it threatened the dominance of management knowledge. More than two decades later, reforms continue to fall short of promises, because the root of the problem lies at the interface of knowledge and power.

If this argument is going to persuade, it is important to begin by giving a brief account of management thinking over the previous century-plus, in order to make the pattern clear: Why was *management*, the magic formula that would transform industrial corporations and government operations, seen early on as in need of reform? Why has every reform effort eventually failed to live up to its promises? Clearly, the transformative power of reforms has been oversold. The roots of continued failure lie in management's inability, or unwillingness, to go to the heart of the problem: divergent organizational knowledges. Management's use of a science-based ideology to control the actions of workers has denied the legitimacy and indeed the existence of knowledge gained from direct contact with the work itself. In the public sector, this neglect of the link between management knowledge and management power has had political as well as practical consequences.

Scientific Management

Management reforms have repeatedly aimed at tempering the negative effects of the first deliberate scheme: *scientific management*. Frederick Taylor's (1911) vision of transforming operations on the factory floor soon became the rationale for turning the public agency from a sinecure for party loyalists into an expert, neutral system. Taylor created the model—management through standardization—and all subsequent public management reforms have tinkered with aspects of Taylor's plan: striving for the efficiency and control over workers it promised to achieve, while finding ways to soften its side effects.

In scientific management, the worker's craft knowledge, gained through experience, is seen as a hindrance to control from the top because much of it remains in the mind and hands of the worker, and therefore evades systematization and efficiency. A new class, "managers," armed not with craft knowledge but with concepts, would devise the best way to do the work, not by trial-and-error (as workers supposedly did) but by means of controlled experimentation, which would reveal the one best way to do each job. Among government reformers, even though public-sector work consisted more of service delivery than of factory-like physical labor, a consensus developed that scientific management could be the means to de-politicize the ranks of public bureaucracies by substituting science for party loyalty in the selection and training of employees.

Scientific management introduced an alternative to ordinary management, which had regulated work processes through orders given by a gang boss who worked along with the group. Pre-Taylor management recognized that the worker knows something important. In fact, Taylor himself may have been the last management thinker to pay full attention to working knowledge, though because of his negative view of it, he tried to transcend it by turning it into science. Previous management approaches had aimed to regulate work processes through orders, discipline, and incentives—in Taylor's words,

> the management of "initiative" and "incentive," in which those on the management's side deliberately give a very large incentive to their workmen, and in return the workmen respond by working to the very best of their ability at all times in the interest of their employees.
>
> *(Taylor, 1947, p. 39)*

Taylor believed that work organized in this fashion was not adequately controlled because workers still retained their grip on the actual labor process (Braverman, 1974). His move to get workers to accede to the superiority of scientific knowledge over their own experience must be called genius. With science, regulation of the labor process would be in the hands of managers who would "assume ... the burden of gathering together all of the traditional knowledge which in the past has been possessed by the workmen and then of classifying, tabulating, and reducing this knowledge to rules, laws, and formulae" (Taylor, 1911, p. 36).

Taylor's most complete statement of the principles of scientific management opened with a quotation from President Theodore Roosevelt about the importance of "national efficiency." Whereas the President emphasized natural resource conservation as the preeminent goal of national efficiency, in Taylor's eyes the wasted physical effort that rendered human work awkward and inefficient was a more pervasive and important issue. Employers' focus simply on finding the right man (*sic*) for any organizational job was a mistake. Most men could be trained to greater efficiency through the application of proven scientific techniques; therefore, the key to efficient organizational effort was "the true science of management, resting upon clearly defined laws, rules, and principles" (Taylor, 1911, p. iv).

Taylor's entire system was based on the belief that the interests of employers and employees were basically the same rather than at odds. Both were primarily interested in money. Scientific study would reveal the most efficient way to do any job, and this "best way" would be taught to workers. They would work faster and more efficiently, and they would be paid more. Taylor claimed that workers did not have the intelligence necessary to figure out the best way on their own. Employers would pay workers at a carefully calibrated rate that was just enough to motivate them to follow the efficiency scheme. They would work more productively than under the old system, under which workers agreed among themselves to maintain a pace that was brisk but less than the theoretical maximum (a practice known as "soldiering"). Under Taylor's system, as production efficiency increased, the employer's prosperity would rise. It was a win-win situation. Workers wanted higher wages, and owners wanted higher profits. Under scientific management, both would get what they wanted, and control would remain safely at the top, mediated by the cultural authority of science and the structural authority of managers.

The only way to guarantee that the system operated at maximum efficiency, however, was *enforcement* of standardized working moves, of the best implements and working conditions, and of cooperation. Enforcement would be the responsibility of managers, who would show workers the right techniques, and watch and help them until they reached the proper pace. Taylor emphasized that scientific management was a new type of work that employers had never done. Managers, not workers, would develop the scientific approach to each kind of operation, select and train workers, and eliminate (*sic*) any who would not, or could not, learn and practice the proper methods at the most efficient rate. Managers would provide "constant help and watchfulness" throughout the work process. Managers and workers would share the production process equally: the workers doing the work, and the managers coming up with the best ways to do the work, teaching workers how to do it, watching them, and helping as needed (Taylor, 1911, p. 43).

Taylor was emphatic on the point of rendering the labor process independent of the worker's knowledge. "All possible brain work should be removed from the shop and centered in the planning or laying-out department …" (Taylor, 1911, pp. 98–99). In this sense, he did not fully grasp the distinctive nature of experiential knowledge. Yet he clearly saw that he had to convince managers to twist their minds around a paradox: that ultimately the workers still knew more than managers about the work itself.

Taylor argued that analyzing and capturing the working moves of employees would bring an end to the situation in which:

> employers derive their knowledge of how much of a given class of work can be done in a day from either their own experience, which has frequently grown hazy with age, from casual and unsystematic observation, or at best from records which are kept, showing the quickest time in which a job has been done.
>
> *(Taylor, 1911, p. 22)*

In a sense he was right: When the engineers and technicians of scientific management had amassed enough knowledge to produce products in line with their tolerances, working knowledge was simply obscured.

Scientific management caused workers to lose control over the full expression of their work. The philosophy of science was enlisted to separate work into two parts—conception and execution (or idea and action). Through the use of intrusive analytic techniques like time-and-motion studies, the mental aspects of work were separated from its physical manifestations (much as the philosopher Descartes separated "I think" from "I am"). Where once workers enjoyed a broad scope of action over their jobs, they were now deskilled, reduced to carrying out the directives of knowledge elites ensconced above them in the organizational pyramid. For front-line workers, the consequences proved severe. As Braverman (1974, p. 125) notes, "Hand and brain become not just separated, but divided and hostile, and the human unity of hand and brain turns into its opposite, something less than human."

Workers became cogs in the machine—tools in the production process—under scientific management. They were given narrowly specialized jobs to perform under strict supervision. Workers were expected to do less thinking and more doing. Yet even here the terms did not mean what they meant to workers. Doing meant making motions deduced by the efficiency expert and engineer, eliminating even an iota of hands-on working judgment. What was lost in this process of objectifying jobs through science was the circumspection (the "felt sense" [Gendlin, 1981]) so essential to everyday coping and the usefulness of the product (see ensuing chapters). Braverman (1974, p. 136) cites an editorial from the *International Molders Journal* which captures this truth:

> We think of craftsmanship ordinarily as the ability to manipulate skillfully the tools and materials of a craft of trade. But true craftsmanship is much more than this. The really essential element in it is not manual skill and dexterity but something stored up in the mind of the worker. This something is partly the intimate knowledge of the character and uses of the tools, materials and processes of the craft which tradition and experience have given the worker. But beyond this and above this, *it is the knowledge which enables him to understand and overcome the constantly arising difficulties that grow out of the variations not only in the tools and materials, but in the condition under which the work must be done.* [Emphasis added]

Craftsmanship requires felt sense and some measure of independent judgment about how the work needs to be done. It is this freedom of mind and hand that was obliterated by the efficiency expert's stopwatch and slide rule.

Taylor's ideas spread rapidly, not only in private industry but among those who were concerned to systematize the operations of government agencies. For example, U.S. Naval engineering officers were attracted to scientific management, not only because they saw it as a form of human engineering (the American Society of Mechanical Engineering was an early advocate) but because it promised to help engineers gain control of navy yard operations. Unfortunately, line officers perceived that they would lose power under the new system, so ultimately the effort was a failure (Petersen, 1990).

An attempt to institute scientific management at the Watertown Arsenal in Massachusetts also fell short because of resistance by unionized workers, including a brief strike (Aitken, 1985). Widespread efforts to rationalize municipal government agencies had limited success. Reformers claimed to be men of science "cleaving the Gordian knot of politics with one swift blow" by replacing it with scientific disinterestedness and rigor. The scientific public manager would be "the man in control of affairs" (Stivers, 2000, p. 26). Early efforts to systematize government agencies suggest that, despite its objective clothing, when scientific management was introduced into an organization, it was met by existing interests, relationships, and cultural dynamics. Social change, it would seem, may not be as rational a project as scientific management made it out to be. Nevertheless, educated reformers climbed on board.

Why did managers support a production process that deskilled their workers? In private industry, managers and the owner-investors they served were interested mainly in profit that came as a result of producing more at as little cost as possible. In government agencies, reformers succeeded in persuading some legislators and executives that the modern era required government run by experts rather than party loyalists, which appealed to a growing class of professionals. Management, in government as in business, welcomed Taylorism because it increased quantity, raised efficiency, and reduced dependency on skilled (high-priced) labor, and because science seemed to guarantee objectivity. In the public sector, objectivity promised political neutrality. Managers were blindsided, however, by the inevitability that this ruthlessness of numbers would eventually be applied to them as well. In the modern corporation, many a white-collar worker has learned this truth the hard way, downsized out of their careers by the very philosophies they helped to institutionalize in the modern organization. In modern government bureaucracy, "Reinventing Government" and New Public Management had a similar impact, as we will see.

Facts, not Votes

Interest in scientific management was especially keen among the men of the municipal research bureaus, formed in cities in the early 1900s to open government ranks to professionalism (Stivers, 2000). Scientific management seemed to offer an objective rationale for exerting control over public employees in city governments, the majority of whom had gotten their jobs as a reward for political party service. Reformers' talk of municipal inefficiency became more than just talk once there was a system for making all kinds of work scientific. They could present reform as objective improvement, rather than a transfer of power from party loyalists to well-educated experts like themselves. Not only did the reformers exert pressure on mayors (or take steps to get like-minded candidates elected), they invented a new form of municipal government that actually had the word "management" in its name. *City management* not only put an appointed manager rather than elected official in the municipal driver's seat, it also reduced the number of elected representatives to a handful. The closely-related "commission" form even placed particular administrative functions in the hands of commissioners, which had the advantage of taking "a large part of the municipal activity entirely outside the field of the vote ... [making it possible] to still further build up the territory over which facts rather than votes and individual opinion determine action" (Cooke, 1915, p. 489).

Two arguments backed up the reformers' project. First, "the machinery of government is not the object of government" (Cooke, 1915, p. 491). The object is rather to deliver the goods and services, to get results in the form of improving the well-being of the public. This view originated with Alexander Hamilton and continues today in the results rhetoric of contemporary public management: What citizens want is clean water, garbage picked up, and an effective police force, not direct involvement in the mechanics of running the city. Government's task is to deliver the goods, and the means to that end is not a direct public concern, nor should it be, since the best means will be determined scientifically, as Frederick Taylor proposed.

The second argument was that there is basically no significant difference between business and government, since they are both corporations. (Cities, in fact, were corporations.) Frederick Cleveland, the reformer most committed to scientific management, claimed that "the modern democratic state finds its prototype in the modern private business corporation." Since the two are basically alike, "there is nothing inherent in government which stands in the way of highest efficiency." Both can and should be well-managed. Cleveland's theory of the state limited the exercise of the "popular will" to Constitutional amendments, electing and recalling "officers," and initiative/referendum. He saw the Constitution as a trust document and the official "class" as managers of the estate set forth in the deed of trust, that is, the city charter (Cleveland, 1913, pp. 314–317).

In addition to acting as a tool, or weapon, in the fight to rationalize government operations, scientific management fit the theoretical paradigm introduced by Woodrow Wilson (1887) in his well-known essay, "The Study of Administration," and perpetuated for the next fifty years in the writings of public administration thinkers. According to Wilson, there was a clear distinction between politics and administration. Politics was about elections and legislation, therefore about individual and group self-interests, whereas carrying out legislated mandates was non-political administration (indeed, it was a business), much like the management of a private firm. Yet Luther Gulick, an early adopter who became director of the Institute of Public Administration in New York, defined scientific management as "the rational determination of purpose and the intelligent organization and utilization of manpower, technology and things to accomplish that end" (quoted in Van Riper, 1995, p. 7). Few better examples could be found of the expansive tendencies of the scientific reformer. After all, is not purpose—determining what government should do—the point of democratic politics?

In the field of public administration, through most of the first half of the twentieth century, the belief prevailed that efficiency promotes democracy. Administrative mechanics could be left to scientific managers to determine and to get workers to carry out. Managers would get a "mental picture" of each problem situation for which they were responsible as well as the intended results (Cleveland, 1913, p. 315). Here we find the triumph of administration-by-concept in which the power of managers has ever since been rooted.

The first textbook of public administration (White, 1926), maintained that the relevant body of literature for good practice lay not in law but in management. Wallace Sayre later observed that White's text and another that appeared at the same time (Willoughby, 1927) treated organization theory as a design science applying tested principles to practice: hierarchical structure, proper span of control, subdivision of work, scientific job description, employee selection, promotion, and payment. The high noon of this orthodoxy, Sayre famously said, was reached in the work of President Franklin Roosevelt's Committee on Administrative Management (the Brownlow Committee) and its report, published in

1937: "The Report set forth in eloquent language the prescriptions of public administration made orthodox by the texts of 1926–27" (Sayre, 1958, p. 103). The president was the country's chief executive, and as such had to have firmer control over the administrative apparatus.

Reactions to the Brownlow Report were largely negative, perhaps because (in the context of looming threats from European dictatorships) strengthening the chief executive's authority came across as ominous. More than 300,000 telegrams poured in to the White House and Congress, most of them opposing legislation to implement measures for strengthening the President's power to manage his administration. Yet after World War II the first Hoover Commission in 1947 took further structural steps to centralize control and clarify lines of authority, perhaps this time in response to the emerging threat of a "Cold War" (Stivers & Hummel, 2007).

Merkle (1980) characterizes post-war changes in management thinking as the second managerial revolution (after scientific management itself). Like the first, the second revolution, the roots of which we trace to the Hawthorne studies in the 1930s (see below), solidified convictions about the need for more centralized, professionalized, and authoritative management in both private sector and government organizations. Despite its human relations veneer the new wave of reform stressed efficiency, reorganization, close supervision of complex tasks (i.e., of workers), and the necessity of a controlling managerial elite. Thus, the second wave of reform may have been less a revolution than management-as-usual dressed in more attractive, humanist clothing.

The Advent of Human Relations

Unlike its predecessor, the new management thinking focused on the nature of the relationship between managers and workers. After the failure of several efforts to implement scientific management, some of its shortcomings had gradually become visible, especially those rooted in Taylor's limited view of human nature. His focus on workers' economic motivations ignored (perhaps deliberately) the appeal of non-money incentives and the role of groups (notably unions) and group dynamics in the workplace. Labor protests in the private sector had led to industrial relations programs (often known as industrial "welfare work") aimed at making workers feel better and fostering voluntary cooperation—for example, company picnics, Christmas parties, the suggestion box, and so on. But these had never reached the heart of the problem.

Growing concern over the "man problem" and the "human factor" in the workplace triggered social science research into the interpersonal dynamics of work situations. The engineering profession expanded its self-definition from industrial design to techniques for "handling men." Engineering curricula began to include the social aspects of production as well as the technical. Gradually engineering, from which management had first emerged, came to define itself as "the art of organizing and directing human activities" in industry (Noble, 1977, p. 311).

In the public sector, the limits of rationality became visible. The same Brownlow Report that sought to plant the flag of management control more firmly in the presidency was solicited and guided by a supremely political mind, that of President Roosevelt. His aim was to gain control of the more than 100,000 workers hired during the Depression emergency and still subject to patronage. The Report's rational design elements were thoroughly political, and in fact the sense of urgency about the Committee's work came in part from the belief that proper management was not simply a matter of "piling up mechanistic trivia" but the key to democratic effectiveness (Stivers & Hummel, 2007, p. 1011).

Human relations (or personnel management) in the public sector operated within a political (because governmental) framework marked by continuing tension between merit and patronage. Merit represents rationality, lack of bias, system, rules; patronage connotes interests, political dynamics, responsiveness. Management practices in the public sector reflect both elements, which are definitive of the American *political* system, including its administrative aspect. Every scheme to systematize government administration inevitably has political implications. Every rational, unbiased, even-handed management scheme serves some personal or group interests and undermines others. The aim of expanding executive or managerial authority and discretion is as much political goal as administrative "reform." The advent of human relations thinking into the public sector, like every other aspect of governance, was both administrative and political.

Let's look at human relations a bit more closely. The taproot of its development was the research carried out in the 1920s and 1930s at the Western Electric Hawthorne plant in collaboration with Harvard Business School's industrial researchers. What began as conventional Taylorist studies to test the effect on productivity of such factors as the level of lighting in the workplace ended up calling into question fundamental assumptions about worker motivation. Productivity went up even when working conditions were made extremely difficult (for example, when the lights were lowered almost to the level of complete darkness). It turned out that what mattered to the workers was that someone was paying attention to their work and asking them about it. They began to feel that they and what they did were important. Famously, what the Hawthorne studies revealed were the non-rational aspects of the workplace, including the informal relationships among workers and between workers and supervisors. The so-called "informal organization" rapidly became a key element in organizational orthodoxy (see Mayo, 1946; Roethlisberger & Dickson, 1939).

All of a sudden (or so it seemed), the existence of an entire unexplored terrain broke into the overly neat administrative orthodoxy. Motivation appeared to be about more than how much workers were paid; beliefs, emotions, relationships, and even something called the organizational "culture," were revealed as key elements in organizations. In fact, organizations themselves, it now appeared, could be seen not simply as rational structures rather like the buildings they occupied but also as living organisms, brains, cultures, political arenas, even "psychic prisons" (see Morgan, 1997).

The costs of neglecting the psyche of the worker began to seem unacceptably high, and the increasing perception that there was an unfair division of the corporate spoils led to labor unrest that spread and worsened. This dark mood threatened the modern corporation, indeed (it seemed) the welfare of society itself. Awareness that there were limits to human engineering in mass production is reflected in the statement of Clarence Francis, chairman of General Foods, addressing the National Convention of Manufacturers in 1952:

> You can buy a man's time, you can buy a man's physical presence at a given place; you can even buy a measured number of skilled muscular motions per hours or day. But, you cannot buy enthusiasm; you cannot buy initiative; you cannot buy loyalty; you cannot buy the devotion of hearts, minds and souls. You have to earn these things ... It is ironic that Americans—the most advanced people technically, mechanically and industrially—should have waited until a comparatively recent period to inquire into the most promising single source of productivity: namely, the human will to work.
>
> *(www.realgoodwork.com/loyalty-you-have-to-earn/)*

Another business executive said: "We are leading men, not handling robots" (quoted in Bendix, 1974, p. 311).

The effect on management thinking was significant, but one could hardly call it revolutionary. The attitudes and feelings of workers were recognized as important to production, and cooperation of people on the shop floor became an essential objective of management (Barnard, 1966). However, the scientific/rational model was not about to be given up in favor of what workers knew from experience. Within that model, productivity meant designing work organizations and management methods to achieve results with human material of precisely the same kind that the organizing and managing of physical material and motions had produced. Soon the so-called humanizing of the treatment of workers produced such *concepts* as "human resources" and "industrial relations." These were to be treated as tools to organize and control workers, just as material resources and production engineering were controlled. No one in human relations ever asked, or could ask, the question of what it felt like to be treated as a "human resource" or have one's natural social relations converted into "industrial relations." It was on these latter two dimensions that scientific management had failed originally; human relations similarly fell short of real reform. Both ignored what workers knew from doing the work.

Approaching human relations, one could have recognized a profound discontinuity between the defining project of management, to systematize and control for the sake of greater productivity and profit, and the nature of the organization, now revealed by research as only partly rational, deeply emotional and even unconscious. "Handling men" turned out to be much less like flipping switches and pressing buttons to produce calculable behaviors, and much more like family dynamics or political organizing. As an early critic pointed out:

> [T]hese experts have provided little insight into *why* they believe that people should undergo a "mental revolution"; or why *esprit de corps* is necessary if the principles are to succeed. The only hints usually found are that resistance to scientific management occurs because human beings are what they are, or "because it's human nature." But, *why* does "human nature" resist formal organizational principles? Perhaps there is something inherent in the principles which causes human resistance.
>
> (Argyris, 1957, p. 57)

The human relations lens encourages greater employee participation in organizations. Employee motivation and commitment are secured through a broad set of inducements: so-called extrinsic and intrinsic factors like pay and the opportunity to do interesting and meaningful work. But *both* are extrinsic: never is the worker allowed to define the intrinsic meaning of the work itself. Humanistic work organization claims to be integrating social and technical aspects of work, employing enriched job design, and involving work teams in production. Because of the limits of the top-down knowledge structure in modern organizations, however, it occurred to no one to probe how employees understood, that is, *knew* their jobs.

On the surface, the main difference between scientific management and human relations is their focus. Scientific management concentrates primarily on leveraging the body's physical movements while human relations concentrates on influencing the human personality; *both, however, operate on the work from the outside in and labor in the service of the instrumental interests of the organization. The locus of power in organizations is not altered in any significant way by the introduction of organizational humanism.* Neither is the relationship between science and management. Human relations theory is mostly silent on the issue of power. It sees conflict as misunderstanding. What is misunderstood? The purportedly superior knowledge of management. Refusal to comply is attributed to a lack of good communications between people with essentially the same interests. Conflict is a problem of attitude. At the end of this kind of thinking looms the "personality conflict." This enables the organization to blame the individual for what he or she knows best: how instructions and job design actually work in practice.

Being scientific, the core knowledge underpinning human relations rested in the social sciences. Industrial psychology was enlisted, not just to recruit and select the one best worker for each job, but to reveal the conditions under which workers would cooperate and give their full effort in performing tasks designed by the industrial engineer. Scientific management had set the conditions for the rise of industrial psychology and sociology and also influenced the direction, scope, and nature of its research agenda. Now, there was growing faith in the social sciences. Managers may have felt that they were making use of social science out of an enhanced sense of social responsibility, but the facts of low job satisfaction, poor morale, raised costs, and reduced profits also drove their interest in humanizing the workplace. Science would help solve the human problems of production and, in doing so, become the servant of modernity and its preference for ideas over material practices (cf. Baritz, 1960).

Instead of working a sea change, the human relations movement produced a new kind of professional: the management consultant, whose role became rather like a family therapist or encounter group facilitator. More humane, even democratic, management turned out to be a matter of psychotherapeutic technique in the service of control (Scott, 1969). The buttons and switches were less obvious but the approach was similar: to help managers and executives induce workers (and one another) to perform at a higher level, but this time by "satisfying" their unmet and sometimes unconscious emotional and/or existential needs. Humanistic schemes and organizational development projects were devised to change the attitudes and actions of people who take orders instead of giving them. "They supply management with a human technology entirely consistent with the values of [the governing elite] .... Industrial humanism supplies mechanisms to 'deal' with nonrational behavior so that effective managerial teams are formed and maintained." Despite their interpersonal trappings, therefore, "[h]umanist techniques are ... rational, technical methods for the management of conflict" (Scott, 1969, p. 48).

Human relations drew management's attention to the experiential aspects of organizational life. But it also aided organizational authorities in their ongoing struggle against unions and helped to improve productivity. Thanks to insights from social science research, organizations were encouraged to treat workers like adults, not children (Argyris, 1957), to satisfy their needs (Maslow, 1962; Herzberg, 1966), to involve them in decisions about how managerially-defined work was done (Likert, 1961), to better integrate the technological and social systems in the workplace (Trist & Bamforth, 1951), and to provide employees with more interesting, challenging, and meaningful work (Hackman & Oldham, 1980). Yet workers' ability to define the work on the basis of their direct involvement in doing it was not recognized.

What continued to be ignored in the second managerial revolution was what workers actually know about the work from being in direct contact with it, with their hands (and minds and feelings and perceptions) on it. A crucial question went unexamined: To what extent can workers' felt sense of the work, and the accumulated skills they draw upon in their daily activities, actually be systematized and controlled? We argue that the second managerial revolution, like the first, failed because both missed the possibility that the keys to greater productivity and quality lie primarily, if not totally, in the experienced hands and minds of the people who do the work. If this is so, then in a fundamental sense controlling workers and work is possible only to a very limited degree.

Humanizing Public Administration

For several decades after World War II, public administration explored various approaches to humanizing work dynamics in public agencies. An early article put the effort in managerial terms: The question was "how to achieve desired goals through the actions of others." Public managers "are interested in better human relations management because they have seen that it can contribute to organization effectiveness" (Platt, 1947, p. 194).

Over the next several decades the theory and practice of what became known as "organizational development" abounded in the public sector. "Interpersonal skills" became widely accepted as a key requirement for good management, to foster "productive staff meetings," "more effective ... relationships with employees and other individuals," "creating an organizational climate [for] self-improvement," "developing a communications network," helping employees "feel they have an investment in the organization," and "increasing the ability to talk about and consider trouble spots" (McGill, 1974, p. 101 [quoting a statement developed by Neely Gardner for the California State Personnel Board in 1954]). Techniques such as T-groups, TQM (total quality management), and other team-building exercises became part of public administration curricula and agency improvement campaigns.

In both public and private sectors, new interest grew up around the organizational "culture," the elusive web of beliefs, practices, and symbols that provided the interpersonal glue. Management thinking viewed culture, as it had viewed its cousin, the informal organization, as a strategic variable—of interest as a potential fulcrum from which to achieve control, with little recognition that culture actually may be one of the most difficult organizational variables to manipulate, since so much of it is not consciously designed or enacted.

The emphasis, despite humanism, remained on greater worker (and sometimes manager) productivity. The guiding assumptions continued: Productivity depends on ever more sophisticated technologies, including human relations techniques to discipline the workforce; the function of management is to bring about maximum productivity through the application of necessary technologies and techniques (Pollitt, 1990).

The Expansion of Managerialism

In the late 1970s and early 1980s, when American corporations faced declining market share and profits, it became evident that competitiveness could no longer be achieved through established norms of quantity production, i.e., cutting costs, squeezing labor costs, routinizing work, and top-down control of every aspect of manufacturing. According to Abernathy and Wayne (1974, p. 118), the fundamental problem with mass production is that "conditions stimulating innovation are different from those favoring efficient, high-volume, established operations." Creativity and innovation introduce costly variation intolerable in mass production systems. In fact, the more successful a company is in producing high volumes of standardized goods and services, the more likely it is to have trouble competing in a market based on quality, diversity, and rapidly changing customer preferences. It becomes the victim of its own success: trapped in a quantity knowledge system that is inadequate in a world where quality and variety are the dominant performance criteria.

As a result, in the 1980s, thinking about management shifted yet again. American management enthusiastically embraced three approaches that combined over time into the Lean Production approach: general excellence programs (e.g., Peters & Waterman, 1982); Japanese management techniques (e.g., Ouchi, 1981); and Total Quality Management (TQM) programs (e.g., Deming, 1986; Juran, 1988). There is no single Lean Production formula, although there are core assumptions. A typical lean production system includes (1) customer or client satisfaction; (2) human capital development; (3) continuous improvement.

(1) Customer or client satisfaction as the primary goal of the organization. A "customer" includes those internal to the organization, such as employees in other departments, and those external to the organization, such as taxpayers, contractors, regulators, and suppliers. Lean organizations are "customer driven." Satisfying customers is perhaps the single most important goal in all forms of Lean Production, but it is not a radically new notion. Although customers were not central in scientific management, for example, their interests were hardly ignored. Taylor, for example, saw them in ways familiar to contemporary quality enthusiasts when he drew attention to:

> the third great party, the whole people,—the consumers, who buy the product of the first two and who ultimately pay both the wages of the workmen and the profits to the employers ... And this third great party should be given its proper share of any gain.
>
> *(Taylor & Copley, 1919, p. 136)*

The issue of the "customer" in government continues both popular and problematic, although the typical view embraces the idea of taxpayers as customers whether or not they are the direct beneficiaries of the goods and services produced by government. Because they pay the bills, like the private investor, taxpayers expect a fair return on investment and expect quality, even though in government the investor and the consumer of public goods and services are often not the same people.

(2) Human capital development throughout the organization. In Lean Production, there is strong commitment to the notion that everyone in the organization must be provided the tools and training needed to satisfy customer requirements. The rhetoric has a contemporary feel, but the idea of human capital is not that far from Taylorism. Both share a view of employees as corporate resources, in somewhat the same way machines and buildings are. The difference, if there is one, may lie in the idea that contemporary organizations are seen as open systems, therefore with increased need for new learning, adaptability, and critical thinking (e.g. Senge, 1990; Carnevale & Carnevale, 1993). From our perspective the concept of human capital falls short of acknowledging the distinctive contribution workers' experiential knowledge brings to the organization. Human capital objectifies "work" as a variable that can be measured and "caused" to expand according to management concepts. There is also the question of whether any human being, including the government worker, is adequately understood in purely economic terms.

(3) Continuous improvement. In most forms of Lean Production, work processes are continuously improved as quality is "built in" rather than "inspected in." As *re-engineering*, work processes are totally redesigned from the bottom up by work teams. "Continuous improvement" in this form means starting all over "with a blank sheet of paper" to reconstitute work processes. Therefore, re-engineering is more advanced than "continuous improvement" implies, for example, under a typical total quality management (TQM) program. In the words of Hammer and Champy in their popular book, *Reengineering the Corporation*:

> Quality programs work within the framework of a company's existing processes and seek to enhance them by means of what the Japanese call *kaizen*, or continuous incremental improvement. The aim is to do what we already do, only to do it better. Quality improvement seeks steady incremental improvement to process performance. Reengineering, as we have seen, seeks breakthroughs, not by enhancing existing processes, but by discarding them and replacing them with entirely new ones. Reengineering involves, as well, a different approach to change management from that needed by quality programs.
>
> *(Hammer & Champy, 1993, p. 49)*

The key word here is "process." If the process that constitutes the sequence of working operations ends up in quantitative and objective terms that leave no room for detecting the ongoing emergence of work reality, then reengineering is not accidentally so labeled. It is an offspring of rationalistic and scientific knowledge and its standardized new technologies of organizing work are as immune to moment-to-moment circumspection and coping in work as whatever system it replaced.

There is a strong commitment to employee involvement, teamwork, and a climate of mutual trust throughout the organization in all of the Lean Production models, including Excellence strategies, Theory Z programs, TQM methods, and reengineering designs. The real question, however, is not whether people *get along* in their work but whether that getting-along is shaped out of a recognition of individual and collective insight into working reality or instead because of social concerns put to the service of corporate interests. The latter can make working life easier without making it more realistic, or less instrumental.

The high-water mark of new management thinking in the 1990s was the Reinvention movement (Gore, 1993), which aimed to make government more entrepreneurial (Osborne & Gaebler, 1992) by cutting red tape, putting customers first, empowering employees to get results, and getting back to basics (reminiscent of Peter's and Waterman's [1982] advice to "stick to the knitting"). Here all the usual suspects are rounded up. Reinvention can mean many things. Its fate within the halls of the federal government is particularly instructive.

The Triumph of Public Managerialism

Human relations and organizational humanism in public bureaucracies began to seem rather a luxury or indulgence in the 1980s, the era of Ronald Reagan and Margaret Thatcher. The two heads of state shared and stoked a new wave of negative judgments about government in general and bureaucracy in particular. As government came to be seen not as the answer to societal problems but a problem itself, two goals dominated. One was to get rid of as much government as possible, and the second was to turn what remained into something much more like a business than a state. The first aim was both legislative and administrative: elect anti-government representatives and divest the state of as much responsibility as possible by cutting budgets and turning functions over to the private sector. The second was specifically administrative, or, as the ideology had it, purely a matter of *management*.

Public agencies were no longer to be administered, a term that embraced a definitive element of service ("ministering") or concern for the public good; now they would be managed—with a vengeance. Taylorism came out again from underneath the humanistic draperies in which it had been cloaked and Hamilton woke up from his slumbers. Once again, it was claimed that what citizens want from government is not a voice but results. And how to ensure those results? First, let managers manage, that is, give them enough flexibility to work their magic. That means getting rid of crusty entanglements of "red tape," put there in the dark ages to foster procedural fairness and even-handedness. Due process was on its way to being an outmoded concept, the concern of sentimentalists. What was wanted was maximum productivity at minimum cost. Second, in contrast to *managerial* flexibility, *workers* were going to be disciplined. Their "performance" was going to be "measured." And they were going to have to adhere to newly draconian rules for doing their jobs. In particular, no more indulging the whims of their clients! The bureaucratic frontline was going to have to get tough.

A number of proponents (besides Reagan and Thatcher) were responsible for making the case for management on steroids. Strategically, the answer to public managerialism's prayers was *Reinventing Government*, the how-to and what-for manual that rapidly became famous among public administrators (now to be thought of as public managers) for its recommendation of entrepreneurialism applied to the public sector. Within a year of publication (Osborne & Gaebler, 1992), the "reinventing" notion was institutionalized in President Bill Clinton's report *From Red Tape to Results: Creating a Government That Works Better and Costs Less* (Gore, 1993) and in a federal government-wide change effort labeled as the National Performance Review (NPR) and led by Vice-President Al Gore.

As noted in the fifth edition of *Classics of Public Administration* (Shafritz, Hyde, & Parkes 2004), Clinton's NPR saw the same problems and offered similar reforms as previous assessments in 1910, 1937, 1949, 1972, and 1982: Government, especially the federal government, was fragmented, disorganized, and poorly performing. According to the NPR's "new" version, the situation is one of good people trapped in bad systems. Government fails to deliver because of excessive red tape and "unfunded mandates" passed down to state and local governments. The answer is—what else? Free up managers so they can get results out of workers. Plus, serve the "customers" (citizens, in a previous reality). Produce and measure the results. This was to be the newly entrepreneurial form of governance.

Clearly, however, it was not a plan that lacked political implications. Many of the budget and procurement reforms promoted by NPR failed to get through Congress. The biggest tangible result seems to have been the disappearance of several hundred thousand federal jobs. NPR as such disappeared with the election of President George W. Bush. Yet the veritable fetish for measurement of results seems to be a lasting effect, at least for the time being.

From NPR to NPM

The "reinventing" impulse was solidified and institutionalized in the notion of *new public management* (NPM). The advent of NPM in the 1990s took place on an ideological foundation that had been laid at least two decades earlier. In the United States, the seed was planted when the expansion of government responsibilities in the War on Poverty came into question (see Aberbach & Rockman, 1997). An anti-tax revolt started in California, when a ballot proposition was approved by the electorate that disconnected government budget levels (therefore tax rates) from levels of public need. A generalized austerity rhetoric reflected and hastened loss of trust and confidence in government among the general public. Anti-government sentiment expanded, along with calls for "downsizing" public agencies and their budgets. Advocacy of less government led to the proliferation of market alternatives to publicly provided services, for example, outsourcing, public-private partnerships, and privatization (see King, Stivers, & Collaborators, 1998). By the early 1990s, unsurprisingly, frank calls to run government like a business came from many quarters, inspired by *Reinventing Government* (Osborne & Gaebler, 1992). Something called "New Public Management" (NPM) emerged (Pollitt, 1990; Dunsire, 1995; Barzelay, 2001; Gruening, 2001).

The point of NPM is to instil business values and practices in the public sector; this means importing private sector understandings of the issue of worker control over to the public sector. In other words, to standardize working moves along Tayloristic lines, but this time, because public sector workers' moves are largely situational/experiential, control consists of reducing the content of worker authority, giving them a narrower range of things to do (contracting out the rest) and less discretion (stricter rules and measurement of performance).

Standardization takes the form of imposing numerical benchmarks on skillful work of a sort (we argue) that—because it consists of interpersonal interaction and judgment—is by its nature subject to mathematical calculation only to a limited extent. Sample benchmarks might be the use of standardized test scores to rate student learning and thus the quality of education in different schools, or developing a numerical scale to rate teachers' classroom performance. The first example assumes that numerical test scores are a valid measure of something called "learning." The second assumes that the interactive process among teachers and students can be quantified. Both are examples of what has been called "the triumph of numbers" (Hummel, 2006)—a victory that can only be won by failing or refusing to examine basic epistemological assumptions.

NPM is known for this transfer of private corporate management practices to the public sector, through:

- Stress on *disciplining* workers by demanding rigid adherence to rules
- More *visible* managerial control as contrasted with former management practices
- Imposition of quantitative performance *measurement* as a replacement for trust in employees' craft skill and professional standards.

The result has been a redefinition of public sector "management reforms" away from decades of emphasis on empowering workers, teamwork, total quality management, etc., toward reducing worker discretion and greatly increasing surveillance, standardization, and disciplining. The current hostility to public unions that goes along with such disciplinary strategies is a faithful copy of what happened in the private sector. Notably, the "reinventing" emphasis on customer service, which by its nature requires sensitivity to individual clients, has almost disappeared with the onslaught of numerical disciplining from the top. Although the difficulty of quantitatively measuring the results of public agency efforts has been acknowledged, the experiential knowledge that workers acquire and rely on has been almost totally ignored and devalued, as has the discontinuity between experiential knowledge and the conceptual knowledge said to be in the possession of managers.

As we have seen, and Christopher Hood's (1991) widely-cited summary explains, new public management was (and is) not really new. Its themes include the freedom to manage, performance and results measurement, decentralization, competition, doing more with less, and the belief that government should and can operate like a business. Yet NPM has grown rather firm roots; the idea of business-like public management is now widely accepted, though objections have not died out. Contracting-out and privatization are orthodox, often preferred, practices, and the list of inherently governmental functions has shortened considerably. The proliferation of government contracts with nonprofit and profit-making entities has added network management to managerial responsibilities and raised the profile of "collaboration" and "coordination" on the list of desired managerial skills. Strangely, however, *in-house* collaboration between managers and frontline workers is rarely discussed; rather, collaboration occurs among designated managerial and executive representatives in a network of multi-organizational hierarchies. The necessity of empowered managers continues virtually unchallenged, as does the need to discipline workers to higher performance and better results.

The Concrete Particulars

David Rosenbloom (1993) once cautioned, "Have an administrative Rx? Don't forget the politics!" The concerted push to strengthen the hands of managers has nearly always been characterized (by the pushers) as non-political. Frederick Taylor insisted that he had only the best interests of workers at heart, and indeed that their interests were the same as those of owners. The workplace was not the site of a power struggle, but neutral terrain shared by those with common interests. The Progressive municipal reformers presented their Tayloristic proposals as simple cost-saving and systematizing measures, which they held were actually democratic since effective government (i.e., results) were what citizens wanted. (Curiously, the possibility that among the things citizens really wanted were government jobs or a voice in the process seems to have escaped their notice.) When it became clear that stringent disciplinary supervision of workers had negative effects, the human relations movement appeared: not as humanism for its own sake but as a means to cost-effectiveness. Finally, some thirty or so years ago, managerialism acquired renewed legitimacy, trendy versions of which have only further strengthened it.

Throughout this history, two patterns stand out. First, Rosenbloom's advice has been widely, if not entirely ignored. In an update (Rosenbloom, 2010), he observes that managerial values still have to compete with political values like responsiveness, with legal values such as due process, with the balance of administrative authority between legislative and executive, and with court decisions. Greater awareness of this need for balance among competing values—one we argue is constitutive of the American government—is sorely needed in what we continue to call *administrative* (rather than management) theory and practice.

Second is the virtually complete absence of serious attention in management reform to the workers themselves, other than as the targets of relentless control efforts. Yet workers are the ones that get the results, if there are any. Their hands are the ones that pick up the garbage and clean the streets. They counsel clients in need of help, put out fires, maintain order, guide airplanes, guard borders, take care of national forests and parks, watch over public health, and teach our children. During all these activities, they acquire detailed, close-at-hand *felt* knowledge that is the core of their effectiveness. Not that they always do everything the way citizens like, nor are they always permitted to follow their felt sense of the work, but when things do go right, the experiential skill of those in direct contact with situations in which government has a role to play is arguably the key resource that makes it so. We say "arguably" because the need for closer examination of the role of worker knowledge is great, and with a few honorable exceptions (e.g. Mastracci, et al., 2012) it continues to be ignored.

As Carnevale and Hummel (1994) argued, management's resistance to taking worker knowledge seriously can be traced to the fundamental difference between the quantity of work and its quality. By quality, they mean not simply whether the work is excellent or poor, but whether its *substance* is taken into consideration: "Judgments of quality can be made only from *within* the working situation; they cannot be forced from without. ... We must know *what* we are doing before we can say *how much*, *where*, and *when*. Quantity *follows* quality" (p. 7; emphases in original). Putting quality first is a fundamental threat to management's dominance over the work process. This is why management reforms continue to fail.

In an eloquent essay on "Administering and the law," the critic Jacques Barzun observed:

> It is curious that the modern world under the sway of science and technology, which pride themselves on exact performance, is so contemptuous of small detail in what affects everybody in private and social life. ... All true professionals, except the leaders of our social and political institutions, know that nothing is too small for their expert attention.
>
> But in institutional life and in the public mind, it is considered trivial and below one's dignity to bother with details. ... Everybody is for efficiency; nobody is against evenhanded justice, given out promptly and cheaply. In other words, policy is soon stated and hardly needs argument. ... The trouble comes over the means, the arrangements ... It is at the level of the concrete particular that the law touches and affects the citizen.
>
> *(Barzun, 2002 [1976], p. 492)*

So-called management reforms have advanced the need for managers to see the big picture and make sure that it is achieved. Could it be that, without the knowledge and judgment of those in direct contact with "concrete particulars," reforms will only continue to fail?

References

Aberbach, Joel D., and Bert A. Rockman. 1997. Back to the future? Senior federal executives in the United States. *Governance* 10:4 (Oct.), 323–349.

Abernathy, William J., & Kenneth Wayne. 1974. Limits of the learning curve. *Harvard Business Review* 5 (Sept.), 109–119.

Aitken, Hugh J. 1985. *Scientific Management in Action: Taylorism at Watertown Arsenal*. Princeton, N.J.: Princeton University Press.

Argyris, Chris. 1957. *Personality and Organization*. New York: Harper's.

Baritz, Loren. 1960. *Servants of Power: A History of the Use of Social Science in American Industry*. Middletown, Conn.: Wesleyan University Press.

Barnard, Chester I. 1966. *The Functions of the Executive*. Cambridge, Mass. and London: Harvard University Press. Originally published 1938.

Barzelay, Michael. 2001. *The New Public Management: Improving Research and Policy Dialogue*. Berkeley, Calif.: University of California Press.

Barzun, Jacques. 2002. Administering and the law. Pp. 488–491 in *A Jacques Barzun Reader* (ed. M. Murray). New York: HarperCollins.

Bendix, Reinhard. 1974. *Work and Authority in Industry*. Berkeley & London: University of California Press.

Braverman, Harry. 1974. *Labor and Monopoly Capital: The Degradation of Work in the Twentieth Century*. New York: Monthly Review Press.

Carnevale, David G., and Anthony Carnevale. 1993. Public administration and the evolving world of work. *Public Productivity & Management Review* 17:1 (Autumn), 1–14.

Carnevale, David G., and Ralph P. Hummel. 1994. Why management reforms fail: The collision of knowledge and power. Paper delivered at the annual meeting of the Western Social Science Association (April). Albuquerque, N. M.

Carnevale, David G., and Ralph P. Hummel. 1996. Why management reforms fail. Paper delivered at the annual meeting of the Oklahoma Political Science Association (November). Tulsa, Oklahoma.

Cleveland, Frederick A. 1913. *Organized Democracy*. New York: Longmans, Green.

Cooke, Morris. 1915. Scientific management of the public business. *American Political Science Review* 10:3 (Aug.), 488–495.

Deming, W. Edwards. 1986. *Out of Crisis*. Cambridge, Mass.: MIT Press.

Dunsire, Andrew. 1995. Administrative theory in the 1980s: A viewpoint. *Public Administration* 73:1, 17–40.

Gendlin, Eugene. 1981. *Focusing*. New York: Bantam.

Gore, Al. 1993. *From Red Tape to Results: Creating a Government That Works Better and Costs Less*. Washington, D.C.: National Performance Review.

Gruening, Gernod. 2001. Origin and theoretical basis of new public management. *International Public Management Journal* 4, 1–25.

Hackman, J.R., and G.R. Oldham. 1980. *Work Redesign*. Reading, Mass.: Addison-Wesley.

Hammer, M. & J. Champy. 1993. *Reengineering the Corporation: A Manifesto for Business Revolution.* New York: Harper Business.

Herzberg, Frederick. 1966. *Work and the Nature of Man.* Cleveland, Ohio: World Publishing.

Hood, Christopher. 1991. A public management for all seasons? *Public Administration* 69 (Spring), 3–19.

Hummel, Ralph P. 2006. The triumph of numbers: Knowledges and the mismeasure of management. *Administration & Society* 38:1 (March), 58–78.

Juran, J. M. 1988. *Planning for Quality.* New York: Free Press.

King, Cheryl Simrell, Camilla Stivers, and Collaborators. 1998. *Government Is Us: Public Administration in an Anti-government Era.* Thousand Oaks, Calif.: Sage Publications.

Likert, Rensis. 1961. *New Patterns of Management.* New York: McGraw-Hill.

Mastracci, Sharon H., Mary E. Guy, and Meredith A. Newman. 2012. *Emotional Labor and Crisis Response: Working on the Razor's Edge.* Armonk, N.Y.: M. E. Sharpe.

Maslow, Abraham. 1962. *Toward a Psychology of Being.* Princeton, N.J.: Van Nostrand.

Mayo, Elton. 1946. *The Human Problems of an Industrial Civilization.* Boston: Harvard University Press.

McGill, Michael E. 1974. The evolution of organization development 1947–1960. *Public Administration Review* 34:2 (Mar.-Apr.), 98–105.

Merkle, Judith A. 1980. *Management and Ideology: The Legacy of the Scientific Management Movement.* Berkeley, Calif.: University of California Press.

Morgan, Gareth. 1997. *Images of Organization.* (2nd ed.). Thousand Oaks, Calif.: Sage Publications.

Noble, David F. 1977. *America by Design: Science, Technology, and the Rise of Corporate Capitalism.* Oxford, UK: Oxford University Press.

Osborne, David & Ted Gaebler. 1992. *Reinventing Government: How the Entrepreneurial Spirit Is Transforming the Public Sector.* Reading, Mass.: Addison-Wesley.

Ouchi, William G. 1981. *Theory Z: How American Business Can Meet the Japanese Challenge.* Reading, Mass.: Addison-Wesley.

Peters, Thomas J. & R. Waterman. 1982. *In Search of Excellence: Lessons from America's Best Run Companies.* New York: Harper & Row.

Petersen, P. B. 1990. Fighting for a better Navy: An attempt at scientific management (1905–1912). *Journal of Management* 16:1, 151–166.

Platt, C. Spencer. 1947. Humanizing public administration. *Public Administration Review* 7:3 (Summer), 193–199.

Pollitt, Christopher. 1990. *Managerialism and the Public Services: The Anglo-American Experience.* Oxford, U.K.: Basil-Blackwell.

Roethlisberger, J. and W. Dickson. 1939. *Management and the Worker.* Cambridge, Mass.: Harvard University Press.

Rosenbloom, David H. 1993. Editorial: Have an administrative Rx? Don't forget the politics! *Public Administration Review* 58:6 (Nov.-Dec.), 503–507.

Rosenbloom, David H. 2010. Public sector human resource management in 2020. *Public Administration Review* 70: Supp., S175–S176.

Sayre, Wallace. 1958. Premises of public administration: Past and emerging. *Public Administration Review* 18:2, 102–105.

Scott, William G. 1969. Organization government: The prospects for a truly participative system. *Public Administration Review* 29:1 (Jan.-Feb.), 43–53.

Senge, Peter. 1990. *The Art and Practice of the Learning Organization*. New York: Doubleday.
Shafritz, Jay, Albert C. Hyde, and Sandra J. Parkes. 2004. *Classics of Public Administration* (5th ed.). Belmont, Calif.: Wadsworth.
Stivers, Camilla. 2000. *Bureau Men, Settlement Women: Constructing Public Administration in the Progressive Era*. Lawrence, Kans.: University Press of Kansas.
Stivers, Camilla, and Ralph P. Hummel. 2007. The Personnel Report: Politics, administration and the passion for anonymity. *Public Administration Review* 67:6, 1010–1017.
Taylor, Frederick W. 1911. *Principles of Scientific Management*. New York: HarperCollins.
Taylor, Frederick W. & Frank Barkley Copley. 1919. *Two Papers on Scientific Management: A Piece-Rate System and Notes on Belting*. London: G. Routledge & Sons.
Taylor, Frederick W. 1947. Testimony before the Special House Committee to Investigate the Taylor and Other Systems of Shop Management. Reprinted in *Scientific Management*. New York: Harper.
Trist, Eric & K. W. Bamforth. 1951. Some social and psychological consequences of the longwall method of coal-getting. *Human Relations* 4:1, 3–8.
Van Riper, Paul P. 1995. Luther Gulick on Frederick Taylor and scientific management. *Journal of Management History* 1:2, 6–7.
White, Leonard D. 1926. *Introduction to the Study of Public Administration*. New York: Macmillan.
Willoughby, William F. 1927. *Principles of Public Administration with Special Reference to the National and State Governments of the United States*. Baltimore: The Johns Hopkins University Press.
Wilson, Woodrow. 1887. The study of administration. *Political Science Quarterly* 2 (June), 197–222.

2

KNOWING IN THE PUBLIC ORGANIZATION

The Pyramid of Knowledges

> In the helping professions, there are two kinds of care: standing in for others and so helping others that they can stand in for themselves.
>
> *Hummel (1979, p. 11)*

Modern organizations have been understood in many different ways. One writer has called these ways "images of organization" (Morgan, 1997). Morgan's inventory of organizational images demonstrates that how you look at (or think about) an organization makes a difference. If your attention is drawn to structure, moving parts, and production technologies, you are seeing the organization as a kind of machine. If you focus on survival needs and the environmental interface, you are thinking of the organization as an organism. Such images are not mutually exclusive. One can interpret the same organization in different ways, at different times and on different grounds.

People in organizations often sense that the organization is just not working as well as it should. In order to figure out what the difficulty is so it can be fixed, they try to draw back from day-to-day activities, diagnose the problem and decide how to solve it. What they see when they do this is shaped by the image of the organization they carry around with them (and may not even be aware of). If what jumps out at them is the need to reorganize, they are assuming that the organization is basically a machine with its parts out of whack. If the need seems to be additional resources or interaction in the environment, they are seeing the organization as an organism. If what appears most urgent is the ways the organization processes information and makes decisions, they are seeing the organization as a kind of brain that analyzes data and makes rational choices.

People in organizations often fail to realize that they have already interpreted the organization *as* something, even before a problem arises. The result is that they remain blind to the wider implications of their unnoticed perspective. For example, if without being aware of it you assume that the way organizations process information is their most important feature—that organizations are brains, in other words—you have tacitly committed yourself to certain implications that you might question if you were aware of the image you were taking for granted. There might be other ways of looking at the organization, ways your chosen image does not disclose. For example, a focus on information processing foregrounds cognition and rational analysis, leaving employee feelings and power dynamics neglected. Or, a focus on the structure of the organization—its machine-like qualities—tends to highlight aspects like the chain of command, ignoring the environmental interface. A key part of becoming skilled at understanding organizations is having more than one possible way of interpreting them.

The image examined in this book is the organization as a pyramid of knowledges. Like other images it focuses on certain aspects of the organization, in our case the *public* organization, and leaves others out of the analysis, though we hope to remain alert to as many wider implications as possible. Our image combines two distinct elements: it foregrounds different *knowledges* and it sees these knowledges as forming a *pyramid*. This book is essentially an argument for the importance of adding the pyramid of knowledges to the repertoire of organizational images, and for considering how circular processes enable and challenge these pyramidal dynamics.

In order to understand what such a pyramid entails, we begin by laying out a theory of knowing—in other words, if there are *different* kinds of knowing rather than just one, in what respect are they different, and what is it that they have in common? In the modern world, we tend to see knowledge as of one kind only, and most modern organizations run based on that assumption. We will claim that this kind of knowledge is not the only kind.

After supporting this assertion, we move to consider why it is useful to see a public organization as a pyramid of knowledges, on what basis this way of seeing makes sense, and what this way of seeing discloses. Because our argument is critical of many widely-accepted assumptions about what a modern organization *is*, the discussion heads ultimately toward the suggestion that the pyramid organization (i.e. the bureaucracy) depends to a significant extent on the existence of circular processes within it. Underneath the linear chain of command lie circular interactions, abilities, and understandings: work teams, intra-organizational networks, reflective practitioners, emotional labor, collaboration, dialogue, participation, and judgment. Unlike most other treatments of these circular elements (e.g. the informal organization), we see them not as alternatives that inevitably reduce the organization's linear rationality (by costing money, for example, or falling short of the Truth), but rather as constructive: they weave the social fabric on which the deployment of rationality relies. Although we lack the temerity to argue that somehow these circular processes could replace the pyramid, still we believe that recognizing how deeply pyramids rely on good circular working relationships might in time lead to organizations less committed to an ideology of linear rationality, therefore more likely to avoid or reduce bureaupathology. As Ralph Hummel suggested:

> In that [circular] spirit, human beings again find themselves as human beings. There is a reassertion of human values, social relations are again between people and not between roles, work again becomes meaningful and not alienating, ethics is again given content and integrated into organizations and society, and politics is restored to its supreme place in the progress of human populations.
>
> (Hummel, 1990, p. 202)

Knowing is Being

The typical way of understanding the term *knowledge* is to see it as ideas inside a person's head, in other words a possession. This understanding can be traced to the 16th-century philosopher Descartes and his struggle to pin down how one can know anything. Descartes saw a gulf between the individual perceiving-thinking mind, and everything outside the mind, including the individual body: a gulf between mind and matter. His assertion—"I think, therefore I am"—was his way of saying that the only thing one can be sure of is one's own mind, because it is right now thinking this thought. Everything else—the material world, the minds of others—is subject to doubt.

This version of knowledge sees it as a matching up process between the so-called real (external) world and ideas or concepts in the mind—for example, between the *concept* "motivation" and the observable *actions* of organizational employees. We observe what we can perceive (actions) and take it as a valid indicator of what we can't (concepts). The corollary to this model is the claim that the scientific method is the only one you can trust to produce knowledge of the world. Anything else that calls itself knowledge is basically untrustworthy.

When Ralph Hummel (1982) started to think about modern public organizations and the nature of the work within them, he began with Edmund Husserl's concept of "intentionality," which Husserl had offered as a specific alternative to the Cartesian theory of knowledge. Husserl traced what he called the "crisis of European sciences" to the "extravagant elevation" of Cartesian epistemology as an all-encompassing theoretical system intended to "rationally [order the] progress of inquiry." Questioning what constitutes knowledge, that is, metaphysical inquiry, would be eliminated from philosophy. The resulting understanding of "science," Husserl predicted, would ultimately transform human existence in its entirety. Instead of culture evolving out of intentionality, i.e., human beings' immersion in direct experience and tradition, society would turn to science for guidance. The "relative truths that arise in human life," the "situational truths" produced by intentionality, would be supplanted by "the general idea of truth-in-itself" (Husserl, 1970 [1954], pp. 8, 287). By terming it a "crisis," Husserl signaled his apprehension about the future of modern society.

As Hummel (1982) argues, following Husserl, the way people work is shaped by intentionality, i.e. the myriad and often tacit ways in which they approach the task based on the accumulated understandings they draw upon to guide it. Like Husserl, he warned that interposing "management" in between the worker and the intentional feel he or she has for the work was headed for a "never-never land of numbers" detached from a tangible reality for which the worker has a felt sense of appropriate action (Hummel, 1990).

Philosopher Martin Heidegger, who studied with Husserl, took his teacher's insights in his own direction, arguing that the Cartesian starting point should be reversed to "I am, therefore I think." In other words, philosophy should begin with the question of existence—what does it mean for something or someone to *be*—and only from that foundation consider the question of knowledge. He began not with an isolated subject equipped with concepts and seeking to know objects, but with what he called Being-in-the-world (*Dasein*). All of us are always already existing, he argued, not abstractly but in particular situations with particular understandings of them (Dreyfus, 1991, p. 11).

Each different way we go about ordinary activities reveals something we *know* how to do, a way of approaching what we do. *A way of knowing, then, is also a way of being*, and vice versa. Knowing in this sense is *a certain understanding* of the situation and the objects and/or people in it. Our stance, our comportment toward the situation, our very being, thus has what Heidegger called an *as*-structure. We always understand situations *as* something or other, whether we understand them as repairing a car, making dinner, conducting an interview with a client, or pursuing a scientific study. The implication: There is not just one knowledge, or way of understanding, but many.

In this respect, Heidegger departs completely from prior definitions of knowing as *connecting* a subject (the knower) and an object (the known), whether the connection is practical, as in using a hammer to drive home a nail, or theoretical, as in conceptualizing the structure of an organization as a chain of command, or conceiving of worker action as driven by some mysterious phenomenon called "motivation." Rather than making a subject-object connection, human knowing and acting consist of "directing-oneself toward, of being directed-toward" (Dreyfus, 1991, p. 51).

Everyday action takes the form of coping. We need to write something down, so we grab a pen or pencil. We need to run an errand, so we jump in the car. Ordinarily, our engagement with equipment like this goes unexamined. We know how to write with a pen, we know how to start and drive the car. Mostly we remain unaware of this engagement: we find the right way to hold the pen, we find the starter pedal and press it, without reflection. Only if the pen refuses to write, or the car refuses to start, must we stop, recognize the existence of a problem, and start figuring out what to do. In other words, theorize.

This background of absorbed coping in the world is fundamental, according to Heidegger. It reveals to us what it is to "be." The crucial point is that everyday activity is not *primarily* in our minds, but in the skillful ways we are accustomed to dealing with things and other beings. Mental content (rules, analyses, and beliefs) is useful but derivative: "considering" how to diagnose an equipment breakdown— or an organizational malfunction—always takes place within the background of the ongoing everyday world and the *as* structure we understand at the moment (Dreyfus, 1991, pp. 74–5). Thus, contrary to philosophical tradition (e.g. Descartes' "I think therefore I am"), *pure mental states (thoughts) are not basic*. We are absorbed in coping with daily life without experiencing this activity as grounded in ideas and concepts. When there is a temporary breakdown, the object in question reveals itself not as a separate substance but by its failure to "show up" as expected.

The everyday coping of an experienced worker, as we will see, is grounded in this kind of hands-on, skillful activity—in experience—rather than in the ideas and concepts couched in management theories. There is a fundamental difference between what you know about the organization's work by being directly involved in carrying it out, and what you know about it from thinking at a distance about how it might be done differently. This is not a matter of more or less knowledge, but about different *kinds* of knowledge. The phenomenologist Maurice Merleau-Ponty said that "the relations between the organism and its milieu"—between the worker and the work— "are not relations of linear causality but of *circular causality*" (quoted in Dreyfus, 2014, p. 234, italics added). This suggests that prevailing views of how to achieve organizational "results" may, at a minimum, need an upgrade.

As Hummel observed, to have a feel for the work, you yourself have to do it. Workers develop "an unquantifiable feel for things, to tune into what can and cannot be done. The manager wants to be in touch, but he [sic] is standing outside the work. Look at the words he uses, they've got nothing of touching in them. They are 'eye' words, not 'feel' words" (Hummel, 1987, p. 75ff.). Hummel cites Heidegger's image of blueprints to clarify the difference: Numbers pinpoint aspects of reality; on a blueprint or in a model, things show themselves as and only as ideas have pre-formed them. For managers, reality has to correspond to the blueprint; it literally has to measure up.

As George Steiner points out, "Appropriate use, performance, manual action possess their own kind of sight." Theory, on the other hand, looks at things not in terms of their usefulness in the particular circumstance, but abstractly. A stonemason or sculptor looks at stone quite differently from the way a geologist looks at it (Steiner, 1987, p. 90). Working with a material has a different as-structure from studying it.

Coping with People

In organizational everyday situations, we cope with equipment, such as the computer or the copying machine, and we also cope with people, whether they are clients requesting services, citizens wanting information, co-workers with whom we are collaborating, people we supervise, or people who supervise us. In being-in-the-world, we encounter not only entities that are "equipment," but entities whose mode of being is the same as our own. That is, they are also being-in-the-world.

Being-with other humans like ourselves does not depend on actually being face-to-face with them. Others are there in the world whether or not we are directly sharing the same situation. They are tacitly there in the web of shared understandings that each of us takes into account as we act and speak. Further, according to Heidegger (1962), others are never encountered abstractly, but in context, including at work: people engaged, as we are, in everyday coping. I can be *with* other people in the way I cannot be with objects, such as chairs or copying machines. Other people understand the world we share, as do I, though we may understand it differently. This has implications for coping with them. As Hummel (1979) noted drawing on Heidegger, in the helping professions, including public service, there are two ways to approach situations, two kinds of *care*: standing in for others versus helping them in a way that they can stand for themselves. We can treat them like objects or we can facilitate their ability to become who they want to be.

We have now laid some fundamental groundwork for our critical theory of modern bureaucracies. The key points are these:

1. Existence is not split between subject and object. We are all always already in the world.
2. The everyday world of ordinary activity is the ground of everything, because it is there that being-in-the-world shows itself most clearly.
3. Being is knowing and knowing is being—that is, every mode of existence shows itself as something in particular rather than abstractly. Knowledge is not *first* a stock of concepts accumulated in the individual mind but a set of practices in the world, which reveal our understanding of what it means to be.
4. Therefore, there is not just one kind of knowledge, but many, depending on the situations in which we find ourselves.

The Organization as a Knowledge Structure

How do *patterns* of knowing-being come to be shared, to persist and be perpetuated in organizational form? How do these patterns become something we call "reality"?

The notion that people's understandings of their situations constitute a reality is captured in the phenomenological term, "Life-world," which refers to "the province of reality which the wide-awake and normal adult simply takes for granted in the attitude of common sense" (Schutz & Luckmann, 1973, p. 3). In this everyday mode of existence, I take it for granted that I am in the world with others and that they are essentially similar to me, that is, they experience the world much as I do, and vice versa. There are things "everyone knows" about how to go on with daily routines. These take the form of "typifications": shared common-sense understandings of elements in the shared reality, or life-world.

People who come into an organization for the first time encounter an existing web of familiar and unfamiliar typifications, widely shared and taken for granted. The distribution of typifications—such as understandings of what an "employee" is, what a "boss" is, what it means to "supervise" someone, and so on—may be familiar, but their particular connotations for this organization probably are not, at least to a new entrant. The web of typifications persists over time as elements in a meaningful shared understanding of what an organization is. Each organization is made up of the understandings its members have about it, which often take the form of "how we do things around here," how "normal" problems are solved in the course of work activities, and so on. A significant part of life-world activities consists of everyday coping, getting things taken care of without giving it much thought, or perhaps any at all, unless something goes awry. Assumptions about how to cope on a day-to-day basis are the ground on which organizational dynamics unfold.

A key feature of this shared reality, however, is that not all aspects of it are equally available to everyone. There are things I know that some of my co-workers don't, and vice versa. Organization members have varying prior experiences, educations, even cultures. Their placements, responsibilities, and activities within the organization are also diverse. The distribution of different stocks of knowledge takes on a particular pattern because of these disparities, especially ones based on various kinds of expertise—some in the form of hands-on knowledge gained from experience, some in more abstract, conceptual form. And, of course, these disparities perpetuate themselves, since I interact differently with co-workers with whom I share expertise than I do with those whose expertise is not accessible to me, or is unfamiliar.

This *division of labor*, which defines all modern organizations beyond the very smallest, produces differentiated roles (typifications about who does what), each of which has its own stock of accumulated knowledge as well as problems specific to it. Heidegger believed that the sort of knowledge gained in immersion in work activities, without routine resort to conceptual analysis, is bedrock—that is, it constitutes the basic "being-in-the-world" structure of reality. If so, the key difference among role-specific knowledges is the extent to which the activities assigned to a particular role require or involve direct contact with the "material" (things or people) being worked on. The sort of understanding characteristic of skilled coping with daily activities makes all other modes of comportment possible. Unreflective everyday activity is the ground on which deliberation and propositional assertions about work can stand. Management has no role in the organization without the existence of people who do the work that seems (to managers) to need managing. The outcome of executive strategies ultimately depends on the work at the frontline. Different roles, then, entail different proportions of unreflective coping, practical deliberation, and theorizing (Dreyfus, 1991).

Clusters of people with different sorts of expertise can, however, interact productively when they share "higher order" typifications about organizations in general that seem to explain the existence of differences: "The institutional world develops a canopy of legitimation, stretching over it a protective cover of both cognitive and normative interpretation" (Berger & Luckmann, 1966, p. 60). Organizational members weave a network of organizational logic that reassures them that things are going as they should, or at least, going in a way that is comprehensible even if it is objectionable to certain members. You, the worker, may not like having to take orders from a boss, but you very likely accept that it is normal in the work setting to have a boss.

This book's theory is based on the following notion: that activity in direct contact with the work itself, such as frontline or street-level employees perform in public organizations, produces a characteristic form of knowledge, which we'll call, somewhat metaphorically, "hands-on." In contrast, employees—typically "managers"—whose responsibilities to plan, organize, and control the work are fulfilled at a distance, whether great or small, from direct contact with the work itself, accumulate a different form of knowledge, one that is necessarily more conceptual or abstract.

In line with Heidegger's thinking, frontline knowledge is particular to the situation in which members are immersed; management knowledge, which is removed from the hands-on actions in the organization, is made up of objectified interpretations of sets of everyday situations, which are their raw material. Executive knowledge necessarily entails strategic action with outside forces, based on managerial interpretations of hands-on work, but also on an experiential sense of political dynamics. Each province of knowledge develops its own practice logic and methods. Clearly, frontline workers do have a stock of conceptual knowledge in addition to their hands-on skill: sometimes, to solve problems they have to step back and "think." Managers do rely on daily experience as well as on concepts and abstract analysis. Executives engage in daily coping and problem-solving as well as macro-visioning. But workers, managers and executives have distinctive kinds of jobs to do, and as we will see, this makes a difference in the way their *characteristic* knowledges (those that define their roles) interact—or don't.

The upshot of different knowledges is that in the organizational reality it is no longer sensible to assume, as we do in the unexamined life-world we all share, that everyone has the same stock of knowledge, or approaches problem-solving in the same or similar ways. Although a general stock of knowledge remains, the various provinces of role-specific knowledge become distanced from general knowledge and increasingly specialized. It is no longer safe to assume that everything a given individual knows is accessible to "everyone."

Berger and Luckmann's image of the organization as a shared network of meanings created and maintained by its members within a cultural context meshes with Heidegger's view of reality in several ways. Key for our purposes is that organizational order is rooted in the stocks of everyday knowledge its members have of it—the typifications to which they subscribe as relevant to their activities, and the knowledge they develop during their day-to-day work. They note:

> It follows that the analysis of such "knowledge" will be essential for an analysis of the institutional order in question. ... The primary knowledge about the institutional order is knowledge on the pretheoretical level. It is the sum total of "what everybody knows" ... maxims, morals, nuggets of wisdom, values and beliefs ... On the pretheoretical level ... every institution has a body of transmitted recipe knowledge ... that supplies institutional rules of conduct.
>
> (Berger & Luckmann, 1966, p. 65)

The knowledge of organizational members gets objectified by means of language and language-based cognitive processes (whether *all* such knowledge can be expressed in words remains a debated question). In objectified form, it can then be re-internalized as objective truth, and therefore used as a means of control, of processes and/or people. We suggest that the more readily expertise can be expressed in language and formulated as concepts, the more it is likely to take on the mantle of organizational truth. This puts the experiential, hands-on knowledge at the frontline at a disadvantage. The reason for this is that *science tells people in modern organizations that knowledge itself consists of ideas that can be turned into testable propositions and studied objectively. Testable propositions ignore the differences among observations in favor of the similarities. Working knowledge, in contrast, is gained directly in situations, every one of which is different from the others. It is the power of scientific knowledge, rather than the power of working knowledge, on which the power structure of the organizational pyramid rests.*

The Organizational Pyramid

Given that there are different forms of knowledge, which constitute different stances toward the world, the question becomes: Why is it that the introduction of the division of labor based on these differences leads to a structure in the shape of a pyramid, that is, with a great many people at the bottom and very few at the top? What, in other words, is the basis for certain forms of knowledge to come to dominate others?

Schutz and Luckmann (1973) argue that there is no possibility of translating the knowledge in one sub-universe—one province of meaning—to that of another. The transfer from one to another is a "leap" from one form of comportment to another. The example they offer is a scientist shifting from dinner-table talk into the theoretical attitude. Anyone can, in the course of a day, travel through many such provinces, during which one's stance toward the world also shifts, or perhaps it would be more accurate to say that one's stance can shift if one is attuned to the need for it. The immediacy of the face-to-face encounter with someone else enables me to share his or her conscious life, in a way that reflecting back on the encounter does not: "The more I give myself over to reflection, the less I live in the common experience and the more [the other] whom I experienced immediately becomes the Object of my thought" (pp. 61–64). Role-specific knowledge tends to perpetuate itself by being passed on to people *within* the role, thus institutionally isolating itself. Separations then occur: between everyday knowledge and various forms of specialized knowledge. For the worker, the manager becomes an Other, and vice versa.

The fact of these separate knowledge spheres is largely taken for granted or even goes unnoticed. When it is noticed, it tends to be explained in idiosyncratic rather than structural terms: My supervisor "doesn't understand my situation" not because she is interpreting it in terms that are foreign to mine, but because she refuses to listen. For the manager, workers can seem unreasonably uncooperative: "They just don't want to work hard."

We have, then, in an organization, knowledge that "everyone knows," that is, general everyday knowledge, which is distributed throughout the organization, and specialized role-specific knowledge, which is not. The division of labor and the resulting growth of different forms of expertise reduce the likelihood that, in any particular situation, people who occupy different roles see the "same" problems. As Schutz and Luckmann (1973, p. 313) note: "what occurs here is that similar 'biographies' (i.e. similar categories of subjective experience) develop." Practical experience in a particular role, together with whatever specialized training the role requires, produces different ways of seeing situations. Even the general everyday knowledge shared by "everyone" in the organization takes on socially differentiated versions: "It is just this 'inequality' which is one of the most important characteristics of the complex social distribution of knowledge" (p. 314). In fact, with the division of labor, specialized knowledge (in the comprehensive form possessed by experts in the role) is not accessible to everyone, and is not meant to be.

As a result, the sheer fact that specialized, autonomous knowledges exist in the organization becomes part of the general stock of knowledge. "Everyone" takes for granted that there are provinces of meaning that not everyone shares: "Knowledge can become more and more of a power factor ... Groups of experts form one of the institutional catalysts of power concentration" (Schutz & Luckmann, 1973, p. 315). The division of labor based on specialized expertise (the kind that can be called "scientific") generates a division of power. In particular, "The task conceptions held by any given set of administrators can be expected ... to differ from the conceptions held by those who carry out the tasks" (Jehenson,

1979, p. 124). If one knew nothing about modern organizations, one might reason that the people who have their hands on the work, and therefore know directly about how it should go, would amass power as a result. But the opposite is actually the case.

The Power of Conceptual Knowledge

In modern society, the high value assigned to rational-technical knowledge has led to privileging it over hands-on knowledge gained from dealing directly with specific work situations. Max Weber's (1964) theory of bureaucracy (see Gerth & Wright Mills, 1978) is premised on exactly this recognition of the value accorded by modern society to specialized professional-technical training, through which conceptual-scientific knowledge is acquired: knowledge possessed only by those who have received the training. He defined bureaucracy, in fact, as domination through knowledge—that is, professional-scientific knowledge, which is the restricted province of those who occupy the administrative-managerial ranks of an organization. Domination, in Weber's theory, is defined as the claim of legitimate authority to issue commands and have them obeyed: in the case of modern bureaucracy, legitimate domination is grounded not in intimate, hands-on contact with the work itself, but in abstract knowledge.

According to Dandeker (1990), modern industrial (and post-industrial) society has taken hierarchical bureaucracy as a necessary, rational, and indeed inevitable response to increasing technical complexity of social as well as manufacturing processes. Bureaucratic (rule-governed) processes promise to exert control over societal dynamics and, through disciplinary ordering and monitoring, over the personnel who make up the bureaucracy as well as the objects and people who are the targets of bureaucratic effort. Theories of modern society have generally viewed hierarchical authority relations as functional to the accomplishment of organizational goals, and, particularly in the case of government bureaucracies, have argued their legitimacy in terms of their ability to promote fairness and the achievement of common interests. As a group, the early theorists of public administration, such as Frederick Cleveland (1913) and Woodrow Wilson (1887), rationalized the pyramidal chain of command in government agencies as the most efficient and effective means of delivering the goods to a public supposedly more concerned about results than about participation in governing processes. Dandeker notes:

> Bureaucratization [in Max Weber's view] involved a "funneling up" of knowledge in organizations and a routinization of action through the imposition of bureaucratic rules and administrative systems for the monitoring of organizational behavior. The divorce between conception and execution and the organization of the work of the majority in terms of a detailed division of labor ... was, then, a generalized tendency of modern industrial societies;

knowledge was subordinated to discipline and both were expressions of rationalization.

(Dandeker, 1990, p. 206)

Theories of modern organization all assume this link between knowledge and discipline, but their understandings of the relationship vary. In other words, they start with the basic rationality of the chain of command. In our view, the distinctiveness of hands-on, direct knowledge gained from contact with the work, a form of knowledge that has been characterized as "practical" or "tacit" to signal that it is at best only partially subject to formalization, *calls into question the entire project of managerial control over the dynamics of work as it is currently conceived.* We argue that the nature of worker knowledge implies that attempts to conceptualize it, as the prerequisite to shaping, guiding, controlling, measuring, and evaluating it, are bound to fall short. Full management control of the worker is the core of an ideology, not a goal that can be attained, or one that should be desired.

As we will explain (see Chapter 4), the benefit gained from attaching a concept to a phenomenon in the world is efficiency; the cost is that no concept ever perfectly matches any particular example of it. Thus, the attachment of the concept to the phenomenon requires the exercise of judgment—that is, it requires seeing the particular example *as* fitting the general concept. The upshot is that the notion so widespread in modern theories of organization and management, of "funneling up" or "translating" hands-on, tacit knowledge into management terms, as well as the opposite dynamic—imposing a management template onto work situations and expecting the subsequent actions to conform to it—need, at a minimum, re-examination. Yet most theories of organization take it for granted that craft knowledge is not only inferior to conceptual knowledge but that an uninterrupted flow or translation from one to the other is possible and desirable.

The history of management reforms reviewed in the previous chapter is a story of repeated failures to achieve the sort of control over work processes that the entire enterprise of management has promised since its inception. In the ensuing three chapters, we examine three bureaucratic life-worlds and the stocks of knowledge associated with each: going progressively up the pyramid, the worlds of front-line workers, of managers, and of political (appointed) executives. In the frontline world, we present material that, based on workers' own descriptions, shows their knowledge to be experiential and situational, gleaned from direct contact with the material and people who are the targets of policy. It is a world in which direct knowledge struggles to hold its own and maintain its integrity in the face of managerial efforts to reinterpret experience or discount it entirely. In the world of managers, the mandate to exert control over the work from a distance is paramount. Managers' knowledge of the work takes the form of conceptual assertions and generalizations, which are the basis on which managers struggle to gain abstract understanding and conceptual control over the work process and the people directly engaged in it. At the top, the world of political executives, the power of concepts (especially numbers) is brought to bear in a political struggle to account to elected officials and the public for bureaucratic performance (particularly for its frequent failure to meet expectations), as well as to mobilize the strategic and political capital necessary to keep the entire game in play.

References

Berger, Peter L., and Thomas Luckmann. 1966. *The Social Construction of Reality*. New York: Doubleday.

Cleveland, Frederick A. 1913. *Organized Democracy*. New York: Longmans, Green.

Dandeker, Christopher. 1990. *Surveillance, Power and Modernity: Bureaucracy and Discipline from 1700 to the Present Day*. Cambridge, U.K.: Polity Press.

Dreyfus, Hubert L. 1991. *Being-in-the-world: A Commentary on Heidegger's* Being and Time, Division I. Cambridge, MA: MIT Press.

Dreyfus, Hubert L. 2014. *Skillful Coping: Essays on the Phenomenology of Everyday Perception and Action* (ed. M. W. Wrathall). Oxford, U.K.: Oxford University Press.

Gerth, H. H. and C. Wright Mills (Eds.). 1978. *From Max Weber: Essays in Sociology*. New York: Oxford University Press. Originally published 1946.

Heidegger, Martin. 1962. *Being and Time* (eds. J. Macquarrie and E. Robinson). New York: Harper Perennial.

Hummel, Ralph P. 1979. On the human condition: Being in the company of others and satisfying human needs. *Dialogue* 2:1 (Sept.-Oct.), 11–16.

Hummel, Ralph P. 1982. The nature of work: Philosophy, psychology, and productivity. *Dialogue* 5:1 (Fall), 2–12.

Hummel, Ralph P. 1987. Behind quality management: What workers and a few philosophers have always known and how it adds up to excellence in production. *Organizational Dynamics* 16:1 (Summer), 71–78.

Hummel, Ralph P. 1990. Circle managers and pyramid managers: Icons for the postmodern public administrator. Pp. 202–218 in Henry D. Kass & Bayard Catron (Eds.), *Images and Identities in Public Administration: Discourses on Governance*. Newbury Park, Calif.: Sage Publications.

Husserl, Edmund. 1970. *The Crisis of European Sciences and Transcendental Phenomenology*. Evanston, Ill.: Northwestern University Press. Originally published 1954.

Jehenson, Roger. 1979. The social distribution of knowledge in formal organizations. *Human Studies* 2:2 (April), 111–129.

Morgan, Gareth. 1997. *Images of Organization* (2nd ed.). Thousand Oaks, Calif.: Sage Publications.

Schutz, Alfred, and Thomas Luckmann. 1973. *The Structures of the Life-World*. Evanston, Ill.: Northwestern University Press.

Steiner, George. 1987. *Martin Heidegger*. Chicago: University of Chicago Press.

Weber, Max. 1964. *The Theory of Social and Economic Organization* (trans. A. M. Henderson & T. Parsons, ed. T. Parsons). New York: Free Press. Originally published 1947.

Wilson, W. 1887. The study of administration. *Political Science Quarterly* 2 (June), 197–222.

3

WHAT WORKERS KNOW
Felt Sense at the Front Line

> Why and how does work escape from the control of the manager?
> *(Hummel, 1983, p. 3)*

To explore worker knowledge, let's begin by listening to workers' voices:

> It's hard to explain why I did that and why it worked. I've been here a long time, and I've learned what makes these people tick. They know me, too. I know that's no answer, but if you watch a pizza baker throw dough in the air and asked him what he did to make it come down in a circle all the time, he probably couldn't tell you either. It's just something you learn over time, is all.
> *(Police officer; Toch & Grant, 2005, p. 64)*

> The hardest part is not getting excited before you get there ... If I'm calm, everyone stays calm. I control my facial expressions ... It all depends on the situation ... I've had experience in it to where it is who I am ... I'm as nervous as the guys are, but I don't believe that they see it.
> *(Firefighter; Mastracci, et al., 2012, pp. 31–32)*

> I feel so deskilled because there are so many restrictions over what I can do. Yes, I go out and do assessments, draw up care plans, but then we aren't allowed to do anything. I can't even go and organize meals on wheels for somebody without completing a load of paperwork, submitting a report to a

load of people who would then make the decision ... I just wonder why I'm doing this. It's not social work.

(Social worker; Jones, 2001, p. 554)

Do workers know something management doesn't? In modern organizations, we prefer not to think so. A popular cartoon once captured the lurking fear: A manager tears his hair out in anguish, exclaiming to an unseen worker: "Oh, no! You did it exactly like I told you!"

Evidently, to a degree the manager is at the mercy of the worker, and he knows it. He can't do his job if the worker doesn't do hers. But even managers are aware that despite their directives to workers, following orders in rote fashion will not produce good results and could even lead to disaster. So, what *is* the worker's job? Who in a public organization are the "workers" and what kind of work do they do? We need answers to such questions before we can get a grip on why the cartoon manager is so upset.

Practically everyone in an organization of any kind, including a public bureaucracy, would stoutly maintain that they "work." So, differentiating workers from managers in terms of what they do and what they know requires clarification. Is there something distinctive about what workers do? We maintain that there is.

Workers' distinctiveness begins with their organizational location. Workers, as we use the term in this book, are people in public organizations who are at the interface between the organization and the environment. They are often referred to as street-level or frontline employees, which implies service delivery to human clients, but many are technicians who work primarily with non-human material. Barley (1996, p. 418) calls this sort of work "managing the empirical interface." In the first category are social workers, probation officers, nurses, border patrol personnel, counselors, police officers, emergency responders, and many others. The second category includes sanitarians, restaurant inspectors, computer repair personnel, water quality testers, public works engineers, medical technicians, and more. Both categories are defined by their direct contact with the external physical world. As such, despite being at or near the bottom of the bureaucratic pyramid, they fill the crucial gap between policy and the targets of policy, human and otherwise (Watkins-Hays, 2009). They are the link between administrators and clients, between the material world and what can be said and done about it, between the law and its application on the street. As such, they act as "translators" (Yanow, 2004), who turn policy ideas into actions as they decide the meaning of an agency rule or a test result, and express their take on it in bureaucratic language.

Workers are organizational border-crossers. They are the only ones in the bureaucracy who have access both to knowledge of internal rules and procedures *and* to direct, face-to-face knowledge gained from experience of the world outside (Prottas, 1978), whether this be a social worker's feel for the lives of clients, or the way the material of an earthen dam feels to a construction worker (Schmidt, 1988). This strategic position at the outside-inside boundary is a source of the considerable power workers possess. Their work is the organization's work; its project is their project. Without them, there is no "performance," there are no "results." Bureaucracies cannot routinize this work beyond a modest degree without paying a high price (Prottas, 1978), as the cartoon manager's exclamation signifies. At least this is the case in any but the most placid environment—and few bureaucratic environments are placid.

Because of their location in the bureaucracy, the primary knowledge they acquire and practice is of a distinctive kind. It is experiential knowledge—knowledge learned from doing. Again, practically everyone in an organization will maintain that they learn on the job. If this is the case, then what is distinctive about the learning that goes on where the work that defines the organization gets done? It has been characterized as local knowledge, hands-on know-how, situational knowledge, contextual understanding, knowing in practice. Yanow (2004) has made the important point that worker knowledge qualifies as "expertise" fully as much as the manager's conceptual and scientific approach. It is experiential expertise.

The above terms (local, situational, etc.) convey an initial sense for what worker knowledge is. We have a sense of it from our own lives. Can you learn to knit or ride a bike by reading instructions? Can you know a person just from reading a case file?

The Philosophy of Experience Knowledge

As we suggested in Chapter 2, this hands-on work takes two forms: *everyday coping*, in other words, dealing directly with material, and *solicitude*, dealing with people close-at-hand (Heidegger, 1962). In coping and solicitude, the actions a person takes are guided by his or her project in the moment (what they are up to) and by the way things and people show themselves in that context, far more than by any abstract set of rules. We do greater justice to the work-situation at hand the more we are attuned to it and let ourselves by guided by it, with abstract rules receding into the background. Coping and solicitude are not mechanisms but modes of awareness, forms of experience opening onto the world and the things and people in it. "We find ourselves in a situation and are interwoven with it, encompassed by it, indeed just 'absorbed' into it" (Gurwitch, 1979, quoted in Dreyfus 1991, p. 67). We can call this "taking a stance toward the work": giving primary attention to the unique circumstances facing us, sensing what they require in the way of effective action.

From our perspective, a central problem with public bureaucracies is that direct experience and the knowledge and skills it produces and relies on to achieve results have been demoted to the bottom of the pecking order, or even ruled out of order entirely. Everyday coping and solicitude require attuning yourself to the situation as it shows itself to you—that is, as you *experience* it and address it. All human beings attune themselves to their situations in daily life, without much thinking about it. But the work of frontline workers requires attunement in order to do it. Workers learn from direct experience with material and people, and the more experience they have, the more skilled they are likely to become at attuning themselves to situations and sensing what they require (Dreyfus and Dreyfus, 2000). But in modern organizations, workers' direct experience is no longer trusted as a source of knowledge; the bureaucratic project has become one of exerting distanced control over the work performed at the organizational boundary—in essence, concepts rather than direct experience control the work, ideas control actions. Fatally, the concepts and the ideas are separated from the work and the actions. The organizational watchword has become "We (managers) think and you (workers) do." Yet this control project has widely failed: Managers may be able to control *workers*, but by this means can they control *the work itself*? Our answer is, no.

This fatal flaw in organizations is the centerpiece of our argument. Not to get ahead of ourselves, however, more needs to be said about the nature of frontline work.

The Worker's World

When we work, we *find ourselves* involved in a project, in something of the same way we sometimes find ourselves humming a tune with a certain feel to it. We already have at least some of the *know-how* to be able to *tell* what the situation requires. In the flow of work with which we are familiar, we are *attuned* to the situation at hand, we *understand* what the work calls for, and we pay attention to the back-talk that comes from something we do or say before we make a next move. Not one of these experiences requires that we first make a concept for ourselves of what's going on. We may have relied on concepts when we first began to learn the skill, but the more we practice it and the better we get, the less we need consciously to call on them. "Attunement" need not be notated; "understanding" can be implicit (it does not require "values" pasted onto it); "telling" aspects of the situation speak to us, often silently; "back-talk" need not be a mode of speech, although what is going on between the worker and the work can be thought of as a discourse.

We can be out of tune with our work. This may be due to a change of mood, or some problem that stops the flow of the situation. At that point we sense that we don't have a feel any longer for what the work calls for. Then we have to stop, deliberate, think in terms of concepts. But ordinarily, in the flow of working, we understand ourselves as capable of dealing with what comes up, and we listen to the back-talk coming from the situation so that we can tell what move to make next (see Hummel, 1982, 1995).

Whether they work on physical material or with human clients, workers are bridges or translators between the physical world and what it means. They employ some sort of "technology" to gather information about the situation facing them. It may be a medical test, collection and analysis of a river water sample, or simply asking questions of the client across the desk. That probing of the world triggers some sort of response ("data"), which the worker interprets and responds to. Frontline workers gather information from the world, transform it through interpretation into something meaningful, and then may act to change the situation in some way in light of the new understanding (see Barley, 1996).

Time for some examples. We start with work on physical things.

The Grouters at Teton Dam

In 1975, as the U.S. Bureau of Reclamation was filling the reservoir behind the newly constructed Teton Dam in Idaho, the new dam suddenly collapsed. The resulting instant and massive flood killed eleven people, damaged 3,000 homes, drowned sixteen thousand head of cattle and inundated 100,000 acres of newly planted farmland. Subsequent investigations chalked up the failure to inadequate design and to the Bureau's overconfidence, both of which led managers to ignore or underestimate a number of safety factors. The site was far from ideal, since the bedrock was full of cracks and peppered with holes. The project engineer had concluded that filling the holes with grout (a mix of cement and water) would take care of the problem. But even the Bureau's own grouting expert commented during a Congressional post-mortem that grouting is not an exact science but more like an art, requiring a certain feel for the work.

On the Teton project, the grouters were working at the bottom of a steep-walled canyon. Their job was to pump grout under pressure into holes closely spaced across the dam, extending three hundred feet down into bedrock. This underground wall of grout was supposed to prevent water from trickling down inside and running out from underneath the dam, thus undermining it. The rock beneath the dam was so full of holes, however, that the water pumped in to measure the size of them often disappeared as if into a bottomless pit. Because of the site's complex geology, the Bureau hadn't been able to develop a formula for the proportions of sand, salt and water, so the grouters were given the freedom to adjust the mix of sand and salt in the grout if they suspected large holes. In other words, the decision was left up to the workers, who had a feel for just how big the holes were and therefore the particular mix required at each location. This was a mode of everyday coping, based on their experience. Unfortunately, far above them, managers and designers were making decisions abstracted from the qualities of the site situation, issuing orders to rush certain aspects of construction and to fill the reservoir more rapidly than normal.

Mary Schmidt (1993, 1988), who studied the event and its aftermath, has posited that three kinds of knowledge were at work at Teton. First, the workers had hands-on knowledge of grouting, a feel acquired over many different situations—knowledge that could not be fully verbalized. Second, collective knowledge was needed among everyone involved in the project about the situation as a whole. Schmidt argues that the growth of shared knowledge was blocked by the division of labor in the formal organization, with designers at the top, project supervisors in the middle, workers at the bottom—in this case, physically as well as organizationally, and by working conditions, such as three shifts of workers who never talked with one another. Thus, nobody had a view of the whole, so to speak, which would have involved *weaving together conceptual designs with the felt characteristics of the land and the material*. Third, there was a kind of passive knowledge that marked the workers' reactions to orders from above. When they received an order that clashed with their hands-on feel of the situation, they would try to make sense of it: "Well, they must know what they're doing up there ..." Thus, a key factor in the dam's collapse was the gap between ideas and actions traceable to the separation (in this case physical as well as cognitive distance) between designers at the top, managers/supervisors in the middle, and workers at the bottom, elbow-deep in the building material.

What if designers and engineering supervisors had encouraged workers to convey their feel for the situation as best they could before managers changed plans? Perhaps people literally handling the material, sensing directly how the material reacted from move to move, could have voiced their doubts about the way designers and engineers understood the situation. Perhaps the workers' doubts might have given pause to the accelerated working pace and shaken the confidence designers and engineers had that the work was on the right track and that they had solved all the problems—a hubris rooted in the firm belief among designers that they could build a dam anywhere (Schmidt, 1993).

Or perhaps not. Sometimes even when workers do voice their doubts, nobody listens, at least nobody in a position to stop the inexorable forward motion of a project. The Teton Dam story conveys a sense of how workers' knowledge of the situation can be ignored, especially when the pressure is on—whatever the source of that pressure is.

Firefighters' Everyday Coping

In the 1980s, a study of the District of Columbia fire department documented the way firefighters go about their work. Robert McCarl (1985) spent months riding on fire trucks as they sped to fires, and hanging out in the firehouse between alarms, interviewing firefighters and absorbing aspects of their daily lives. Their comments revealed some of what they saw as key aspects of their know-how.

One firefighter described a fire in a bowling alley, where the fire was located deep in the building, behind a maze of little offices. The firefighters got about two-thirds of the distance to the fire and realized the fire hose was too short. They were about to go back and lengthen the hose:

> So we start back but we hadn't gotten fifty feet back and here comes the wagon driver dragging two bags of stand-pipe hose. And *he'd anticipated*. *Nobody told him*, but he had anticipated that this was a large deep building and there may be a need ... It looked like something we had drilled for; the most important part was that he had anticipated. So many times after that, I would remember that, and *if it fit the situation*, grab one of those bags and take it in so that it was there if they needed it.
>
> (McCarl, 1985, p. 69; emphasis added)

Here concerned coping (know-how) means using past experiences to look ahead to what's liable to be coming at you. Because it was a narrow, deep building, the wagon driver doesn't need an expert or a theory to tell him he'd better bring an extra-long hose as back-up. The one telling the story learns the importance of anticipation, and thereafter if the situation calls for it, he too grabs an extra-long hose.

An experienced pumper man offers this:

> When a run comes in, I hear the address. And then on my way to the fire I'm thinking what side of the street is it on ... *I'm saying to myself* that's a narrow street or whatever. And then I have to make sure I let the truck get in there ... So I *tell myself*, hey, I'm going to pull up tight on this side and let the truck come on around. And then I'm *thinking about how* I'm going to get this daggone hydrant open, because on a lot of the hydrants the caps are hard to move. ... It doesn't happen often, but it does happen, and it's just *something you have to watch*.
>
> (McCarl, 1985, p. 77; emphasis added)

Another form of anticipation shows itself, again based on prior experience. The pumper man is visualizing the street where the fire is (the situation is showing him what it needs), and even which side of the street the building stands on, so the pumper truck can park so as to make room for the truck with the hoses to get in close. Then the pumper man is targeting his next move, to get the hydrant open, because sometimes the caps are tricky. Although he doesn't verbalize it, one can imagine that he's running through in his mind his experience with different types of hydrant caps and how he managed to get them open in the past.

In the next excerpt, a firefighter tells what he learned from an old hand:

> I learned a lot from this old truck driver ... He would take you aside and *tell you* everything he knew. ... one of the things he taught me was about going up on the roof, especially at night. ... He told me you should always test the roof with one foot while you keep ahold of the ladder, because if you go through you don't stand a chance. Just a couple of months ago ... I went to take the hatch off. And it was spongy and I just stuck one foot on the roof to

> lift that hatch off and the fire come up through it. ... you could have punched your toe right through it. So *those little things* come through for you now and then.
>
> (McCarl, 1985, p. 83; emphasis added)

Sometimes firefighters learn from the experience of others, from stories told by an old hand to a relative beginner. The beginner then cements the story in his own stock of know-how later on, when he remembers to test another roof with his own toe, and saves himself from being engulfed in flames. Reference to "those little things" (sometimes "little tricks") reveals the expertise of experience.

Another example of clues that help size up the situation:

> *I always gauge*, in a high rise or an office building, the intensity of the fire by how many people are coming out. If it's three o'clock in the morning and there's not a sucker at the door, you know it's food on the stove, or a trash chute. But if you come up the street and everybody is flying out of the place, you know you got something, even if there's nothing showing.
>
> (McCarl, 1985, p. 87; emphasis added)

Sizing up the situation, experience has taught this firefighter what to look for, whether there are a lot of people coming out or none. Later in the interview, this same firefighter referred to how he could often tell what kind of fire it was from the way it smelled.

Another part of the firefighter's learning is "practice makes perfect":

> ... we got off on the third floor and went to the fourth where the fire was and the door was locked. And *it's a panic thing* with me—a fear to be stuck in the smoke chamber or the hallway and not be able to get in. ... banging on this metal clad door and everybody is behind me. So *I always make it a conscious effort* when I'm walking through a door to play with it, to see if I can break this lock.
>
> (McCarl, 1985, p. 87; emphasis added)

Even off duty, this firefighter is practicing how to fiddle with locks so he can break them if he needs to, in order to avoid being trapped in a hallway outside the fire, one that is filling with smoke and with other firefighters coming up behind him blocking his way out unless he can get that locked door open. The reference to "the panic thing" signals how the *mood* of anxiety primes him to deal in practice with such things as locks *before* his life is on the line.

Notice how in all these narratives, the firefighter's coping is concrete and hands on, rather than following an abstract rulebook in the head. The expertise of experience is carried partly in the head, it is true, in the form of pictures, scenarios (the way the street looks, the depth of a bowling alley, imagining oneself stuck in a smoky hallway with no way out). But it is also expertise carried in the body: in the hands that know how to haul the hoses, pry the cap off a hydrant, or break a lock. Firefighters attune themselves to situations by bringing to bear the lessons of experience; their feeling (both mental and physical) for the situation taps into what happened to them in previous similar situations; they let the particular fire, the particular building, the particular street tell them what the situation requires—what fits; their mood helps attune them to what is required. Perhaps the key theme marking the coping of firefighters is anticipation: knowing from experience that the hose may be too short, the roof may give way, the street may be too narrow, the door to the fire may be locked—and coping *ahead* of the event rising up to meet you, by means of remembered events and their lessons, as well as tools that may be necessary if the worst happens.

In a recent study of crisis responders (Mastracci, et al., 2012), the captain of a fire-rescue unit sums up experiential skill: "I've always thought that the best firemen are not the smartest firemen, not the most intelligent, but the firemen who have the greatest sense of common sense." He goes on to explain what this means: "the ability to size up a situation quickly, to determine how to resolve it while keeping everyone safe, and to put the plan in motion, all the while maintaining control over their emotions" (p. 34).

Being-with Clients: Solicitude

The second category of frontline work includes a wide range of activities to take direct care of other people. The presence of others is an aspect of the basic structure of reality. Others are part of my world even if I am home alone, or on a desert island, or the only person left alive on the planet. My world is a world with others.

Solicitude is Heidegger's term for this basic with-ness. It doesn't have the same positive overtones for him that it tends to in its English version. He uses it to signify *being-with*, whether positive or negative. In daily life we can get along with one another or be on the outs or be completely indifferent. Whatever the particular situation, being-with is an aspect of being human.

According to Dallmayr (1981), "others are first of all encountered in conjunction with work." Even in working on objects, others are part of the situation since the work may be intended for them, or only possible because others have designed the tools or taught the worker something about how to use them. As Heidegger (1962, p. 160) says, "Others ... emerge in the ready-to-hand life context."

In other words, we don't *encounter* others in the abstract, but more or less face to face in the course of our everyday work. In the public agency, for example, we encounter others as co-workers, supervisors, clients, and so on. When our particular work is *directed* toward another, such as a client, it can take on the authentic mode of empathy, or it can fall into inauthenticity, that is, fall under the sway of what everybody says, what the boss demands, what the experts recommend, what the rules say. Interestingly, Heidegger specifically mentions "*managerial solicitude*," which is manipulative and commonly marked by overt or covert domination (Dallmayr, 1981, p. 242; see also Bernstein, 1985). In managerial solicitude the other's freedom is taken away from them in the moment. The manager leaps in and takes over whatever the other is engaged with, rendering the other passive (recall the grouters at the Teton Dam site, who passively concluded that the guys at the top "must know what they're doing"). In contrast, the liberating form of solicitude frees the other to approach the situation authentically, in the way that seems likely to fit. This solicitude "helps the other to become transparent to himself in his care and become *free* for it" (Heidegger, 1962, p. 158).

The relevance of solicitude in its authentic and inauthentic modes seems clear for public service, particularly since a great deal of frontline public-sector work is work with people—clients, citizens, and so on. We can think of caseworkers, police, probation officers, nursing home staff—the list is long. Thus, in articulating the nature of frontline work, we must keep in mind Heidegger's implicit warning: that such work can be inauthentic or authentic. It can dominate others and render them passive (or worse), or it can free them to find their own modes of being-in-the-world.

"Being-with" at the Nursing Home

Work in nursing homes is a good place to begin, because it is a visible blend of the authentic and the inauthentic (Diamond, 1992). The researcher in this case worked as an aide for some months at several different nursing homes, having gone to school for six months in order to get the necessary certification. As he learned on the job how to do the work, through trial-and-error and watching and listening to more experienced co-workers, he acquired both physical skills, such as how to change the bed of an incontinent patient (in two minutes, and with the patient remaining in the bed), and what he came to call the work of caring.

A striking feature of Diamond's account is the contrast between the formal specifications of the working rules and the part that was not only never written down but went largely unacknowledged by the organization. The organizational rule was, "If it's not charted, it didn't happen." Although intended to ensure documentation, this guideline ruled out much of what the assistants actually did during a shift, lumping a complex assortment of actions under an abstract heading in the job description, "assist as needed," which largely shaped the patients' quality of life.

Feeding patients, for example, required not only patience, persistence, and technical agility but person-to-person acuity. An old hand told Diamond: "Try doing just like we do everything else with Alice," whose mouth was still tightly closed. "Try a song." Diamond began to sing "When Irish Eyes Are Smiling," and Alice eventually opened her mouth. Another experienced aide advised: "Keep looking in their eyes, especially the ones who don't talk" (Diamond, 1992, p. 133). Another patient, ninety-eight years old, was supposed to be fed mashed food squeezed through a feeding tube. When Diamond tried it, the patient screamed, kicked, choked. A more experienced co-worker made it look smooth and easy; the patient smiled. The aide said to Diamond: "Sorry, but this isn't as easy as it looks. There's more to this work than they teach you in that school" (p. 135). As Diamond noted, the same box got checked on the chart, no matter who fed this patient, but the experience could be completely different, both for her and for the one feeding her.

Through experience, the aides learn to *attune* themselves to the needs of each patient in particular, to *listen to the "talk"* coming from each of them (even when they are silent), and try to respond in a way that *fits*. They learn to be "close but not too close," friendly but not overly familiar. They learn that putting lotion directly on the fragile skin of a ninety-year-old could actually hurt, that it would go on better if they squeezed the lotion into their own hands first to warm it. When some particularly difficult or onerous task confronted them, they learned, as one said, to "pretend he's your father" (p. 164). They learned how to sense in advance who needed water, or lotion, or a change of clothing or bedding: "Arthur needs changing," an experienced worker told Diamond from across the room. "How do you know?" asked Diamond, standing next to the patient. "Oh, I don't know," she replied. "I guess it's just a *sixth sense* you get in this work" (p. 145).

The know-how that accumulates from experience, the sixth sense, the anticipation of needs, the use of the imagination to bridge the gulf between patient and care-giver ("but don't ever tell these people you know how they feel" [p. 146])—these are the forms of solicitude that get written out of the records and made invisible. Many little actions are never acknowledged: the quick wipe-down given a surface that's dusty or soiled, the re-positioning, as you pass by, of a patient who has slid down in her chair, the pause to answer a patient's question or offer reassurance, being around when visitors leave to try and fill the gap made by their departure.

Not all the work of care is caring, in the conventional sense. Aides get impatient, they sometimes bark orders or fail to listen. But they learn that raw power often fails to work. They aren't saints, but the daily round of tasks and interactions among patients who are there day after day seems to favor the practice of attunement: learning to get along with them, to coax rather than order.

Diamond observes that higher-ups "often did not know the work. Even if they knew the skills, they did not know the relationships" (p. 156). He linked the work of caring to mothering, perhaps a reasonable interpretation since virtually all the workers except him were women. He comments:

> I was fast enough at picking up on the power to lord it over my charges and efficient in deploying the drilled technologies. The learning that came later,

and slowly, was how to think, listen, see, feed, touch, change, clean, and talk ... the knowledge most of the women brought to the job from their skills as mothers, wives, daughters ... I had none of these skills ... *It was not a lack of emotion or concern* ... What came so slowly were the *actual skills of performance*. It became clear there was a base of skill behind that which was named, stemming from experience in unnamed domains, that was simply presupposed and written into the job. That is, written *out* of the job ... the invisible skills of caretaking ...

(Diamond, 1992, p. 156; italics added)

As the researcher concluded, the managerial mandate that "if it isn't in the chart, it isn't real" shines a direct spotlight on the chasm that yawns between experiential knowledge and what goes into the records. Managers seldom learn what workers know, because they don't do the work and therefore tend not to trust what workers know from doing it; and the records never include the invisible skills, the solicitude, that can't be quantified or written down. The unwritten has been ruled out of reality; this seems to us to qualify as a working definition of inauthenticity.

Other sites of frontline work, ones where getting the work done requires cultivating relationships with clients or patients, present similar contradictions between experience-based caring and the requirements of organizational rationality. Workers deal with these contradictions in different ways, with varying results.

Casework as Solicitude

Frontline social work is a prime example of solicitude: it requires dealing directly, whether authentically or not, with clients, practically all of whom are sitting across the desk from you, the caseworker, because they are in desperate straits of one kind or another. Over the last twenty years or so, the context of this care work has changed dramatically with efforts to toughen up the system, save money, reduce client dependency, and get measurable results—a way of thinking often summed up as New Public Management (NPM). A stream of research has documented how, in the context of this trend, caseworkers describe their work and how it is changing. Sandfort's groundbreaking work documented the sense-making process at the front line, unrecognized either by managers or by academic researchers, through which "staff generate collective schema that help them to understand their work and efficiently utilize organizational resources" (Sandfort, 2000, p. 731). As Yanow observed, their "local" knowledge—of the situation, the context—is both mundane and expert: because it is situational, that "does not mean that it necessarily lacks specialized expertise. It is the character of expertise that is different"—i.e. "experiential-contextual" rather than "scholarly-academic" (Yanow, 2004, p. S12).

In social work over the last two decades, as the following comments illustrate, caseworkers have had their work redefined by policy makers and managers, a change they experience as loss of their ability to do "real" social work as they struggle to impose new rules on their clients:

> Being a care manager [*sic*] is very different from being a social worker as I had always thought of it. Care management ... is all about budgets and paperwork and the financial implications for the authority, whereas social work is *about people*. That's the crucial difference.
>
> (Jones, 2001, p. 553)

> The contact with the client is more fleeting, more regulated and governed by the *demands of the forms*...
>
> (Ibid.)

> [Welfare reform] is inherently discouraging of creativity that is at the heart of *compassion* in social work. Instead we have created a series of complex bureaucratic responses to human need that deny the essential humanity of both those who wish to care and those who need care.
>
> (p. 556)

> I can't see how you can do social work unless you've got some *sensitivity and awareness about the impact of life events on people*. I find it amazing that this agency which is supposed to be highly *attuned* to this and highly aware cannot actually recognize the needs of its staff.
>
> (p. 559; italics added)

Social workers define their work as being about people rather than budgets and paperwork; about compassionate contact rather than what goes on the forms (remember the nursing homes?); sensitivity to the conditions of people's lives—to sum up, social work is about listening to what the situation tells you. It is a form of caring that facilitates the client's freedom to shape her own life rather than imposing ever more rigid rules. Social workers seem to resist the notion that *care* can be *managed*.

Granted, frontline social work is a more equivocal practice than the above comments might lead one to believe. They are responses to a dramatic change in the substance of a practice as well as an overall speed-up and toughening of working conditions. Dealing with the impact of NPM is a story about what happens to hands-on work when "They" redefine it from above. Jones (2001, p. 551) reported considerable stress among social workers, who spoke of seeing colleagues in tears, walking away from their desks in disgust, frequently calling in sick, and being "completely 'wrung out'" at the end of the week.

What caseworkers had to say must be heard in the context of changes triggered by NPM. Nevertheless, they illustrate, in our judgment, an underlying structural contradiction, not one that is new, between how workers define their work, based on experience and direct contact with clients, and how policy makers and managers define it. Consider this comment from 1974:

> Our agency had a rule that the parents could come and visit the children every other Sunday. I remember feeling frustrated over this, as I felt it was hardly enough contact. I remember asking my supervisor how this decision was arrived at and being told by my supervisor that he didn't know: It had always been that way.
>
> *(Hummel, 2008, p. 27)*

Policy changes such as welfare reform are useful for spotlighting the dynamics of work in public organizations. They turn up the volume on background noise (the polyphony of laws, regulations, agency rules, and management demands) that had been there all the time but at a more or less tolerable level. At lower intensity, most workers learn to work as voices in the musical texture; but radical new rules make old skills seem irrelevant and new ones (filling out more and more forms, imposing new demands on clients, forgoing actions that used to be encouraged) foreign to their understanding of their practice.

Considered in light of the stream of research on the discretion exercised by "street-level bureaucrats" (Lipsky, 1980; Prottas, 1978; Sandfort, 1999; Sandfort, 2000; Maynard-Moody and Musheno, 2003; Brodkin & Majmundar, 2010), one could interpret worker response to welfare reform, NPM, and similar policy shifts as a sign of how central to their identity is the freedom to use their knowledge to make decisions. To quote one British police officer:

> I think what they want is an android ... somebody who is not really human, just somebody who is totally correct, mechanical, follows every policy document, every strategic vision to the letter, with no disaffection, no criticism and totally loyal to the head of the organization, and a bit boring, really.
>
> *(Thomas & Davies, 2005, p. 694)*

As Lipsky (1980) expressed it, street-level bureaucrats don't just carry out policy, they make it: first, by exercising wide discretion, and second, by practicing according to different perspectives, knowledge, and values than higher-ups, giving them practical, if not formal, authority. This body of research on what we call frontline workers concentrates on the *power* they have, but whatever power they do have stems largely from what they *know* from doing the work. As Sandfort (2000, p. 743) explains, welfare bureaucracy frontline staff "engage in a social process that has structural characteristics—it provides framework for interpreting events, justifying daily actions, and rationalizing inaction ..." This social process is missed by the NPM approach.

If, at least practically, workers used to have greater freedom to size up situations and exercise their discretion as to the proper way of responding, then their reaction to the NPM-induced tightening up of rules and protocols for dealing with clients is not surprising. Their knowledge, which is contextual-situational, has been ruled largely irrelevant. Moreover, the part of their knowledge they find difficult or impossible to put into words (the "feel") has now been adjudged unreal. If it's not in the charts, if it can't be expressed numerically, it didn't happen.

Frontline workers' reactions to these trends are no doubt a blend of objections, some self-interested, to reductions in the scope of their discretion, with genuine concern for the effects of increasing bureaucratization on clients in need. One social worker declares:

> If you are going to make up a rule, you need to make it be where there is no supervisor discretion. That way, ... we can both refer to the book and get the same answer ... as opposed to now, where the book states the rule and ... the supervisor can make the decision. I think that's unfair ...
> (DeHart-Davis, 2017, p. 71)

Yet, as one study of worker resistance to managerialism notes, in practice, all the reform talk of empowerment and strategic problem-solving at the front line is contradicted by the overriding emphasis on codifying practice into numerical terms and routinizing everyday tasks. As one teacher noted, "Every head teacher knows that in the end unless they manage to move the exam result along they're regarded as a poor head teacher" (Thomas & Davies, 2005, p. 698).

Cop-work as Care-work

Policing was one of the earliest frontline government practices to be investigated by researchers. In those days (the 1960s and 1970s), investigations often described in detail what police officers know—what they have learned from experience. One notable study focused on policing on skid row (Bittner, 1967). The study found that the foot patrolman had extensive, fine-grained knowledge of his beat:

> He is likely to know every person who manages or works in the local bars, hotels, shops, stores, and missions. ... he probably knows every public and private place inside and out ... he ordinarily remembers countless events ... which he can recount by citing names, dates and places with remarkable precision. Though there are always some threads missing in the fabric of information, it is continuously being woven and mended even as it is being used. New facts, however, are added to the texture, not in terms of

structured categories but in terms of adjoining known realities. In other words, the content and organization of the patrolman's knowledge is primarily ideographic [first-hand, situational] and only vestigially, if at all, nomothetic [scientific].

(Bittner, 1967, p. 707)

The beat cop draws on this detailed acquaintance with the fabric of the neighborhood to achieve his primary objective, which is to maintain operational control, to keep the situation from getting out of hand, to prevent his authority from being challenged. One patrolman said it this way:

If I want to be in control of my work and keep the street relatively peaceful, I have to know the people. To know them I must gain their trust, which means that I have to be involved in their lives. But I can't be soft like a social worker because unlike him I cannot call the cops when things go wrong. I am the cops!

(Bittner, 1967, p. 709)

As Bittner comments, skid row patrolmen adjusted their responses to situations by balancing the law with their sense of the people involved and the dynamics of neighborhood interaction. They maintained that when they stretched the letter of the law in the direction of violating civil liberties, it was simply in tune with how people in the neighborhood treat each other. Thus, they were more aggressively direct in their treatment of skid-row residents than they might be in another neighborhood. Sometimes this directness takes a helping form, such as finding someone a source of food or a place to sleep. Other times, their judgment took a form the law would not recognize as valid. As one patrolman said:

There is always the risk that the man is testing you and you must let him know what is what. The best among us can usually keep the upper hand in such situations without making arrests. But when it comes down to the wire, then you can't let them get away with it.

(Bittner, 1967, p. 711)

Bittner sums up police behavior on skid row in this era as follows: The best use the law to help people keep from sinking even deeper into their misery; the worse use it for personal gain. In both cases, however, police work is an *attuned* practice that relies on *listening* closely to the *back-talk* of the situation and developing a direct *feel* for its details. Best or worst case, police officers "claim to have knowledge of such a degree of certainty as would normally be sufficient for virtually any kind of action except legal proceedings" (Bittner, 1967, p. 711). They use their knowledge to handle situations so as not to lose control of them; in fact, maintaining control *is* their job. On the other hand, police craftsmanship dictates judicious exercise of their authority, such as avoiding an arrest for a minor offence if there's another way to handle the situation.

In recent years especially, there have been enough questionable (to say the least) incidents of police violence against unarmed people, especially African-American men, that the issue of police exercise of discretion cries out for attention. Within the boundaries of this book, it signals at a minimum the need for better understanding of how police officers decide whom to single out for their attention. A recent study of investigatory stops, aimed at people who in the officer's judgment look suspicious, concluded that institutionalizing this practice as a policy has had only modest benefits and substantial, mostly unrecognized, costs. The people pulled over are disproportionately minority group members, and most are innocent. Research has shown that "officers unintentionally exaggerate how often they find drugs or guns. In truth, it is extremely rare" (Epps, et al., 2014, p. 153). In our view, the current controversy over police shootings and "stop and frisk" moves directed at people of color reflects the impact of opinions and stereotypes in the surrounding environment, an element Heidegger and other philosophers consider both impossible to get rid of and necessary to resist taking for granted or ignoring.

Mastracci, et al. (2012) conclude, based on a wide range of interviews, that crisis responders "rely on professional norms more than on agency rules. This is due in large part to the powerful influence of their professional socialization … [T]o a person, crisis responders identified principally with their profession and their team rather than their jurisdiction" (p. 124). The unresolved problem, then, is how to retain the positive aspects of professionalism—as one of their respondents put it, "be good at what we do and try to put our heart in it" (p. 103)—and gradually get rid of the negative cultural aspects, such as race and gender bias.

Recent "street-level bureaucrat" research has emphasized discretionary power over knowledge, but the two are actually inextricable: "Standing … orders and … operating procedures standardize processes, but the actual behaviors can never be totally scripted. Exigencies of the moment rule" (Mastracci, et al., 2012, p. 22). Workers can only make good on their judgment if they have some freedom to take steps they judge to be in line with it; in other words, organizations can only get work done if workers are given a certain modicum of freedom to size up situations in which they find themselves. This freedom, for both good and ill, is the root of whatever power they have. On the other hand, workers' power is only actionable based on what they know about situations, about where flexibility is possible and warranted, and where it is not. The recent emphasis (in research findings as well as in the press) on workers' use of stereotypes such as those based on race or gender, on their reliance upon their personal values to judge clients as worthy or unworthy regardless of regulations, has brought about an important shift in our understanding of frontline work. In this book, we see worker reliance on stereotypes as inevitable to a limited extent. First, it signals the force of "the They," the background stock of accepted understandings (sometimes including racial and other stereotypes) against which every human being-in-the-world acts, and second, because no rule or regulation can be written so clearly that there is no "wiggle room" when it comes to applying it. On the other hand, going by what "They" say is not inevitable. We see one challenge raised by street-level research as pointing to the need for deeper understanding of worker knowledge and its implications for the manner in which organizations function.

As Epps and his coauthors state with respect to policing:

> The immediate task is to change institutionalized practices that have become the take-for-granted definition of professionalism of what it means to do good police work. ... Changing practice means confronting the norms and ideas that undergird the prominence of investigatory stops.
>
> *(Epps, et al., 2014, p. 160)*

The authors look to proactive leadership in changing norms of what constitutes "good work," to the adoption of new internal guidelines, and the reinforcement of "probable cause" standards. They note that such steps can have positive effects: "Forty years ago the police shot black people at dramatically higher rates than whites" (p. 162). A key factor in this disparity was the "fleeing felon" rule. When it was replaced by "defense of life," racial disparities in shootings declined. We would add that the project of re-shaping norms requires the inclusion of members of the rank and file from the get-go in order to understand and enlist street-level knowledge—as well, of course, as members of the public.

Being-with as Regulation

There is a great deal of frontline work in the public sector that involves various forms of regulation. Some of it, such as work in border patrol, immigration, worksite inspection, probation, and parole, is akin to police work, but each has its own context and therefore its own form of local knowledge and expertise. Like frontline work in general, however, the regulatory kind is a form of solicitude, of being-with: "It all comes with *experience*. You've just got to *feel* it, nothing more. Be sure that they're telling the truth first of all. Then you can go about determining if he's admissible" (immigration inspector; Gregorio, 1978, p. 237).

Here, an inspector stationed at an entry point between Canada and the U.S. describes how he knows when an entrant facing him is telling the truth and when not. There are things he can look for. For example, there's the phenomenon of the "overdocumented alien"—someone who has too much information to support his claim of legality: police clearances, diplomas, letters of reference. Too little information may mean the person's case is weak, in the inspector's eyes, but too much may also raise suspicions. Hence, the inspector relies on experience: each case gets judged in the context of countless other encounters, from which the inspector has developed a "feel" for who's telling the truth. One person's wad of cash may be his life savings; another's may signal a criminal background. Being an effective inspector means attuning oneself to the details of each instance on the basis of past experience.

Or take the example of a mine inspector:

> There's basically your *large companies* that are often cold to you, but you know they're going to do what you tell them. And you also know they're going to contest every violation you write them. ... Whether they have a dog's chance or not, they'll still try. And then you've got your *small operators* that are real nice to you and bend over backwards. And as far as their image goes, they'll promise you the moon and never do anything. These are the worst of all.
> *(Lynxweiler, et al., 1983, p. 431)*

This inspector, who visits mines to discover violations of worksite regulations, describes his feel for the situation. In this instance, his feel is demonstrably more rooted in stereotypes than in complex details. From the quote alone, it's difficult to tell to what extent the generalization about large versus small companies is based on his personal experience and how much is a form of "what everyone knows." As the researcher noted, inspectors are told "Goddamn, you're a cop. Get your ass out there and enforce the law" (p. 429). Inspectors have quotas—numbers of violations they are expected to find, which must surely influence the way they exercise their judgment. On the other hand, finding a company in violation is an interpersonal hassle, leading inspectors sometimes to overlook minor violations. On the whole, this research concluded that inspectors place high value on a company's willingness to cooperate. Large companies "work the problem out in a rational manner," while some small operators are "frothing at the mouth" (p. 432). Knowing how hard to come down is a delicate balancing act between upholding the law in a rigid way (being a cop, meeting the quotas) and employing "gaming strategies" to induce compliance (p. 430).

The same seems to be the case with building inspectors. Here one talks about a former colleague who became an agency enforcement tool:

> One guy several years ago thought of the whole code as black and white. It drove him nuts. ... [H]is mentality was that there was right or wrong and no in-between. He was wound tighter than a tick. So we used him. ... He was a loose cannon and we'd point him wherever we could. ... He had a big ticket book he'd love to keep writing in. ... He later committed suicide.
> *(DeHart-Davis, 2017, p. 75)*

Here's another example of a gaming strategy, this one from a parole officer:

> You have to handle things off the record. If the cops catch one of my men shooting up, I go through the motions of requesting a warrant. But if I catch one of my men shooting up, I handle it my own way. My way accomplishes the same thing and only takes one-tenth the time. I've got my own style. If I went by the book, they'd have me down here six days a week writing reports.
>
> (McCleary, 1977, p. 578)

In this instance, the officer avoids writing up a violation, thus saving time and effort. His explanation is that the official way is bureaucratic ("writing reports"), but one can't help noticing that the official way also makes extra work for him, or the fact that when the parolee is caught out by police, the parole officer "goes through the motions of requesting a warrant." As the researcher notes, this comment has to be understood in light of the fact that, at the time of the research, most parole officers were part-time employees. Thus, having to get a warrant cuts into the officer's "free" time, and reduces his freedom to do it "his way." Yet the officer seems rather proud of having his own way of doing things, and justifies his way as a form of saving time and resources.

Here is a border agent's feel for his situation:

> The Immigration Service has a good mission; aliens are far more dangerous than drugs, because they come in such numbers. But I feel sympathy for Mexico, especially the Mexican peons who come to work. If I catch one in the morning, we might be out all day, so I'll share my lunch. I know Mexican villages, if you're a peasant in Mexico, that's a hard row to hoe.
>
> (Heyman, 2000, p. 640)

One striking aspect of this agent's comment is the contrast between his empathy for the people he catches and the stereotypes with which he sums them up. He can envision being a peasant in Mexico, and may even share his lunch with one. But at the same moment he sees them not as individuals but as a horde ("they come in such numbers" and are "more dangerous than drugs"). Another (Anglo-American) agent commented, "if the role was reversed, I'd be more difficult than most to be arrested." An agent of second-generation Mexican ancestry said, "If I was in Mexico and starving, the Border Patrol would have hell catching me." At least in the case of these three agents, imagining yourself in the shoes of the migrants is part of the skill you acquire in your work; yet you also acquire a stock of knowledge based in stereotypes about those you are trying to apprehend: they are impoverished, semi-feudal (peons), and worse than drugs (p. 641).

As the border researcher notes, "*The sympathetic position is couched in face-to-face terms, the exclusionist policy in faceless numbers*" (Heyman, 2000, pp. 641–2; italics added). This observation crystallizes the middleness of the frontline worker. Direct contact with the people they are serving and/or regulating immerses them in information about life situations and knowledge of the uniqueness of each situation and each person, and develops a variety of skills relevant to working with them. This contact carries with it at least the opportunity for authenticity. On the other hand, their stock of knowledge includes the formal policies and the pressure from above to translate experience into numbers, which lead inevitably in the direction of inauthenticity—of treating people as cases, as stereotypes, as elements in a statistical summary. These are two modes of being-with, one could say, at war within the heart of one being-in-the-world. As DeHart-Davis observes, rules can be thought of as meaningless apart from their application, or as software programs that trigger prespecified actions. They are two-sided: "This is why rules cannot be understood as either-or propositions. Rules are … top-down and bottom-up all at once" (DeHart-Davis, 2017, p. 64).

Conclusion

To sum up working:

- Working is being tuned in to the work's own logic and feel; working is being attuned to the concrete situation; working is knowing your way around; working is being able to tell what fits; working is being authentic, and doing what the work itself requires (Hummel, 1982).
- Working is spanning the gap between the material world and human action. It is probing the world to see what it says, and then making that response meaningful in human terms. It is acting to take care of humans-and-(in)-the world, based on the sense you have made of what it has said.
- Working is the activity out of which experiential knowledge emerges.

Time now to turn to the source of the pressure from above: management.

References

Barley, Stephen R. 1996. Technicians in the work place: Ethnographic evidence for bringing work into organizational studies. *Administrative Science Quarterly* 41:3 (September), 404–441.

Bernstein, Richard J. 1985. *Philosophical Profiles: Essays in a Pragmatic Mode*. Philadelphia: University of Pennsylvania Press.

Bittner, E. 1967. The police on skid row: A study of peace keeping. *American Sociological Review* 32, 699–717.

Brodkin, Evelyn Z. and M. Majmundar. 2010. Administrative exclusion: Organizations and the hidden costs of welfare claiming. *Journal of Public Administration Research and Theory* 20:4, 827–848.

Dallmayr, Fred. 1981. *The Twilight of Subjectivity*. Amherst, Mass.: University of Massachusetts Press.

Diamond, Timothy. 1992. *Making Gray Gold: Narratives of Nursing Home Care*. Chicago and London: University of Chicago Press.

DeHart-Davis, Leisha. 2017. *Creating Effective Rules in Public Sector Organizations*. Washington, D.C.: Georgetown University Press.

Dreyfus, Hubert L. 1991. *Being-in-the-world: A Commentary on Heidegger's* Being and Time, Division I. Cambridge, Mass.: M.I.T. Press.

Dreyfus, Hubert L. & Stuart E. Dreyfus. 2000. *Mind over Machine*. New York: Simon & Schuster.

Epps, Charles E., Steven Maynard-Moody, and Donald Haider-Markel. 2014. *Pulled Over: How Police Stops Define Race and Citizenship*. Chicago: University of Chicago Press.

Gregorio, D. J. 1978. Enforcement is the name of the game: An essay on the immigration inspector at work. *Sociological Focus* 11:3, 235–246.

Gurwitch, Aron. 1979. *Human Encounters in the Social World*. Pittsburgh: Duquesne University Press.

Heidegger, Martin. 1962. *Being and Time* (trans. J. Macquarrie & E. Robinson). New York: Harper Perennial.

Heyman, Josiah McC. 2000. Respect for outsiders? Respect for the law? The moral evaluation of high-scale issues by U.S. immigration officers. *The Journal of the Royal Anthropological Institute* 6:4, 635–652.

Hummel, Ralph P. 1982. The nature of work: Philosophy, psychology, and productivity. *Dialogue* 5:1 (Fall), 2–12.

Hummel, Ralph P. 1983. Manager and worker: Phenomenology of time consciousness and rational style. *Dialogue* 6:1 (Fall), 2–12.

Hummel, Ralph P. 1995. Why work and the study of work won't mesh: Toward standards for practical knowledge and research. *Administrative Theory & Praxis* 17:2, pp. 1–14.

Hummel, Ralph P. 2008. *The Bureaucratic Experience: The Post-Modern Challenge* (5th ed.). Armonk, N.Y.: M. E. Sharpe.

Jones, Chris. 2001. Voices from the front line: State social workers and new labour. *British Journal of Social Work* 31, 547–562.

Lipsky, Michael. 1980. *Street-Level Bureaucracy: Dilemmas of the Individual in Public Service*. New York: Sage.

Lynxweiler, John, Neal Shover & Donald A. Clelland. 1983. The organization and impact of inspector discretion in a regulatory bureaucracy. *Social Problems* 30:4 (Apr.), 425–436.

Mastracci, Sharon H., Mary E. Guy, and Meredith A. Newman. 2012. *Emotional Labor and Crisis Response: Working on the Razor's Edge*. Armonk, N.Y.: M. E. Sharpe.

Maynard-Moody, S., & M. Musheno. 2003. *Cops, Teachers, Counselors: Stories from the Front Line of Public Service*. Ann Arbor: University of Michigan Press.

McCarl, Robert. 1985. *The District of Columbia Firefighters Project: A Case Study in Occupational Folklife*. Washington, D.C.: Smithsonian Institution Press.

McCleary, Richard. 1977. How parole officers use records. *Social Problems* 24:5 (June), 576–589.

Prottas, Jeffrey. 1978. The power of the street-level bureaucrat in public service bureaucracies. *Urban Affairs Quarterly* 13:3 (March), 285–312.

Sandfort, Jodi R. 1999. The structural impediments to human service collaboration: Examining welfare offices at the front line. *Social Service Review* 73:3 (September), 314–339.

Sandfort, Jodi R. 2000. Public management in the welfare system. *Journal of Public Administration Research and Theory* 10:4 (October), 729–756.

Schmidt, Mary R. 1988. Planning for the Management of Technological Risk. Ph.D. diss., Department of Urban Studies & Planning, Massachusetts Institute of Technology.

Schmidt, Mary R. 1993. Grout: Alternative kinds of knowledge and why they are ignored. *Public Administration Review* 53:6 (November/December), 525–530.

Thomas, Robyn & Annette Davies. 2005. Theorizing the micro-politics of resistance: New public management and managerial identities in the U.K. public services. *Organization Studies* 26:5, 683–706.

Toch, Hans & J. Douglas Grant. 2005. *Police as Problem Solvers: How Frontline Workers Can Promote Organizational and Community Change*. Washington, D.C.: American Psychological Association.

Watkins-Hays, Celeste. 2009. Race-ing the bootstrap climb: Black and Latino bureaucrats in post-reform welfare offices. *Social Problems* 56:2 (May), 285–310.

Yanow, Dvora. 2004. Translating local knowledge at the organizational peripheries. *British Journal of Management* 15, s9–s15.

4

WHAT MANAGERS KNOW

The Power of the Concept

> The manager's world is ... insulated from the direct impact of the physical; in that sense it is a world of ideas, his logic always an ideology.
>
> (Hummel, 1983, p. 2)

In the previous chapter, we saw that workers, who occupy the front lines of bureaucracy, acquire their characteristic knowledge from doing their work—from direct experience. As they span the boundary between the agency and its environment, where services are delivered and results attained, they develop experiential know-how that enables them to act according to what each situation requires.

Management is different, or so it has been suggested for more than a century. For one thing, management is not usually given the label *work*. Perhaps this is because historically, as we will see, the role of manager has been defended on the basis of the need for someone, or a class of someones, to control *workers*. Since Aristotle, "work" has generally signified exertion directed at producing something. The philosopher Hannah Arendt (1958) defined it as fabrication—the making of things. The sociologist Peter L. Berger (1964, 211–212) says: "To be human and to work appear as inextricably intertwined notions. To work means to modify the world as it is found. ... to build a world." Work is an activity that has some tangible product or result, whether it be nuts and bolts, or service to a client. Management's product, if it has one, is not tangible, at least not in the same way.

On what basis did *management* become prominent in the conventional picture of public *administration*—of how public organizations conduct the activity of governing? At first, administration and management seem to be synonyms. But digging deeper, *administration* is derived from the Latin *ad-ministrare*, to minister.

One who ministers serves, furnishes something necessary or helpful, dispenses justice, guides or directs, executes the duties of an office. Management derives from the Italian *maneggio*, meaning the training or handling of horses. In the late nineteenth century, American efforts to reform government used *administration* to signify activities of governing: establishing organizational purposes and policies. The tools or skills for organizing collective effort to accomplish said purposes became known as *management* (Person, 1926a, Sheldon, 1923). In these early days, administration was in charge of accomplishing ends, with management in charge of mobilizing the means in accord with established policies.

Over time, however, the relative positions of the two have shifted. Public management's growing popularity as a model for *governing* lies in its powerful self-image as scientific and grounded in hard facts, whereas public administration has struggled to balance political values with technical ones. Early management thinkers foresaw management's expansion, predicting that exact knowledge would "transform some of the things which are now chiefly matters of policy into matters of execution" (Person, 1926b, p. 219). Facts would establish the principles on which policies would be based, making most policy debate unnecessary. What remained would be "only" execution—that is, management, positioned to eliminate the need for deliberation, discretion, and judgment.

Max Weber (1947; see also Gerth & Mills, 1978), saw the career civil service (he meant those we now call "managers") as a threat to politics for exactly the trend just described. Modern bureaucracies, he believed, existed to rationalize government operations, that is, to enable them to achieve maximum efficiency in the achievement of goals. *The defining feature of bureaucracy, in his view, was the exercise of control on the basis of scientific-technical knowledge.* Scientific knowledge was the source of legitimate power in modern society; the link between the two was definitive. The authority of bureaucrats was justified by the rational neutrality of its exercise. Elected or appointed officials, those at the top of the organizational pyramid or completely outside it, were at a disadvantage when it came to controlling, influencing, or steering it, because their expertise was largely political rather than scientific. The contemporary expansion of New Public Management at the expense of administration, which retains a political dimension, provides visible support for this theory. Probing it is a central element in our analysis.

The Advent of Management

The invention of management in the latter part of the nineteenth century introduced a new role and class into modern organizations. The Industrial Revolution had greatly increased the complexity of manufacturing processes and had led to the splintering of work tasks (the *division of labor*) into smaller and smaller fragments. At first, factory production was organized into "gangs" of workers, each gang headed by a foreman (who was also a hands-on worker). Control over the work process was exercised in direct contact with it, by someone who shared the same working knowledge as the gang. In these early days, control by "management" took the form of literal super-vision, that is vision from above—surveillance, typically by the factory owner, often physically from a walkway or office that looked out over the shop floor (Clegg & Palmer, 1996).

As assembly line production spread, the complexity of the production process and owners' dependence on workers' willingness to contribute their skills to the process led to a fundamental change. Direct management was replaced by management not only at a physical distance but an intellectual distance as well. The leading edge of this change was the introduction of scientific management.

Its architect, Frederick Taylor (1911), maintained that scientific management was less a set of specific tools than "a complete mental revolution on the part of the workingmen ... and equally complete mental revolution on the part of those on the management's side" (Bendix, 1974, p. 276). His vision was that both management and workers would take their eyes off the division of the profits and turn their attention to making the work process so efficient that profits would increase, both sides would be amply (though not equally) rewarded, and friction between them would cease. Taylor presented scientific management as a neutral approach through which the best way to do the work would be objectively identified and formulated as laws. The end result: no more wrangling between owners and workers, since the supposed facts would speak for themselves, and thus no further need for unions. The managers' job would be to extract from the heads and hands of the workers:

> all the great mass of traditional knowledge ... acquired through years of experience, which in the past has been in the heads of the workmen, and in the physical skill and knack of the workman, which he has acquired through years of experience
>
> *(Bendix, 1974, p. 278)*

and, through careful study of working moves, to identify and codify all the most efficient methods to work. Managers would then match each job to the best person to do it, through testing and placement.

The structure of industrial capitalism necessitated two forces: "the introduction of machinery into the production process [and] the transformation of human labor into an abstracted means of commodity production and capital accumulation" (Noble, 1977, p. 259). The best machinery would not produce maximum results unless the labor force were organized so that its energies were rationalized to the highest degree. The transfer of skills from worker to manager, as Taylor advocated, was also the transfer of authority over the work process. The task of the new managerial class was to gain "cooperation" from "human resources" (workers) in the face of resistance and the increasing complexity of production processes. As Bendix (1974) has argued, authority shifted away from its traditional basis in the personal qualities of the corporate leader. The exercise of authority over workers became a task assigned to managers, rendered legitimate (it was hoped) by the guise of neutrality imparted by science.

Scientific management did indeed produce a mental revolution, though not exactly the one Taylor foresaw or advocated. Most owners agreed with his view of human nature, especially his belief that workers would try to get away with as little work as possible (known as "soldiering"), but owners disliked being asked to substitute scientific analysis for their personal judgment, and they weren't particularly eager to cooperate with workers. On the workers' side, it didn't take long to see that their part of the revolution would consist of losing all the things that made their work worth doing: pride in individual craftsmanship, significant group control over the work process, and remuneration tied to their productivity (known as "piecework"). It was this expropriation of their skill and their authority over the work process that led to what management thinking dubbed "the man problem," or worker resistance of various kinds.

Scientific management's real revolution consisted of a vast increase in the number of managers and in the perceived significance of management within organizations. An ideology developed around the figure of the manager and his expertise: the "man of brains" needed to organize the work process and ensure its execution according to plan. The function of this ideology, according to Bendix (1974, p. ix), was to "justify the subordination of large masses of men to the discipline of factory work and to the authority of employers." As complex production processes led to bureaucratization (further division of labor and a lengthening chain of command), control over the work force became a distinct task requiring specific skills, especially conceptual capacities necessary to organize and sustain workforce cooperation. The manager, someone whose job consisted to a large degree in the "skillful handling of others," replaced the old-fashioned leader, often a self-made man, who stood out because of personal characteristics like fairness and honesty (pp. 297, 301).

According to Jacques (1996), the advent of management transformed the American understanding of social control, from raw power backed up by punishment, to control by means of inducements and objective rules. The bureaucratization of work actually served democracy's demand for political equality, depersonalizing authority by lodging it in the neutral truths of science (Gerth & Mills, 1978). *The triumph of management was this ideology, which justified the manager's exercise of power on the basis of objective truth.* Workers' loss of direct control over their work could be seen as necessary because the point of the work was maximum productivity, which required maximum efficiency, and maximum efficiency was a question to which science could give the right answer.

Management's knowledge, then, took on two forms: a conceptual model of the "one best way" to get maximum working results, and a conceptual model of how to handle workers ("motivate" them) so that their efforts conformed to the managerial conception of the work. Managerial competence lay in making the best use of resources, both material and human. A gulf was introduced, dividing what managers know from what workers know (Hummel, 1982; Hummel, 1983). Workers' hands-on knowledge was gained through individual experience and shared in part among the working group (Sandfort, 1999). It was situational and difficult to generalize beyond the immediacy of the work team; on this basis it was demoted to a lesser form, and patronized as "know-how" that required systematizing. Managers' conceptual knowledge, grouping heterogeneous experience under abstract ideas, greatly increased the organization's big-picture ability through such operations as central planning, monitoring, and measurement of results.

The ideology that grew up around this model held that management could and should control the means of production (i.e., the work). Its concerns should be efficiency and predictability of work processes. This ideology has expanded beyond public and private organizations into modern society at large (Ingersoll & Adams, 1986). Its values legitimate the manager's social role, claiming that managers are integral to the accomplishment of organizational goals, that they are devoted and trustworthy, and that management is the source of organizational innovation and progress (Scott, 1985).

This chapter explores this ideology of management, which lies at the heart of what managers are said to know. It describes the cognitive skills managers are said to have, and considers from a philosophical viewpoint the strength of these skills, which lies in the power of the concept as a tool for organizing experience. Next to this management model, the discussion will juxtapose a summary of research into what managers actually do, a stream of work pioneered by Henry Mintzberg. This research suggestively documents a gap between the management ideology, by means of which managerial authority is justified, and the managerial reality. Because this is a book about public bureaucracy, this chapter will describe what the literature of "public management" has to say about what is implied when a person is advised, as a Challenger space shuttle project engineer was, to "take off your engineering hat and put on your management hat" (Bergin, 2007).

First, however, a few words about *ideology*. In one sense, ideology refers simply to the symbol system of a society. In this sense, it is impossible to have a society without ideologies. Shared ideas consolidate and pattern society, "making firm the human order that could be shattered by external or internal disturbances" (Ricoeur, 1991, p. 318). Ideology grounds and sustains human society. "Democracy" is an ideology in this sense, in that many social actions, plans, and institutions are justified on the basis that they are "democratic," even in the face of differing or even contradictory definitions of it.

In another, more critical sense, ideology refers to ideas advanced by a particular group or class within a society to justify its exercise of authority over others outside the class. Here the term is skeptical; the idea-system is thought to be "a disguise of the real nature of a situation, the true recognition of which would not be in accord with [the] interests" of the group (Mannheim, 1936, p. 55). This use of the term implies the existence of distortion; the symbol system in question not only conveys meaning, it also justifies domination. For example, "free market" ideas justify capitalism, obscuring or downplaying the fact that owners and investors benefit much more from the system than do workers. The belief that nearly all Americans are middle-class is an example of capitalist ideology since it covers over material differences between rich and poor.

It is difficult to draw a hard line between these two kinds of ideology. As ideology makes social action meaningful, it sometimes also has the effect of making it legitimate, and that always opens the way to the possibility of domination. The line between legitimate authority and domination is at the forefront of any discussion of management, including this one.

What Do Managers Know?

The idea of management came from industrial engineers, charged with advancing factory technology by rationalizing the efforts of the human beings making up the production process. According to David F. Noble (1977), engineers regarded the human aspects of production in much the same way as the material aspects: as a technology. Engineers quantified and systematized operations, devising administrative procedures that defined lines of authority and divided the work. In the 1880s, the work of men like Henry Towne and Henry Metcalfe advanced a view of management as the development and application of technical solutions to the so-called man problem, such as the size of wage incentives and the "engineering" of worker activity. Taylor ultimately became the most prominent spokesman of the idea and may have been unique in that he was not a professional engineer but someone who, though he had middle-class origins, started out on the shop floor (see Kanigel, 2005). In a way, Taylor simply doubled down on the engineering vision that people could be controlled just as machines could. The man problem, i.e., motivation, was a technical cause-and-effect puzzle that had a correct, scientific answer.

By the 1920s, scientific management had taken hold among management thinkers. According to Roy Jacques (1996), by this time management rhetoric already sounded much the same as it would by the end of the twentieth century. It had two broad themes: first, how to make work processes mechanically more efficient in order to increase profits, and second, how to get workers to go along with these so-called improvements. The persistence of this two-pronged emphasis through an entire century (and into the twenty-first) provides a clue as to what managers are said (and expected) to know. Their knowledge has been summed up in various ways. Examples follow, but it is important to keep in mind as we discuss management knowledge that we are talking about an ideology, a justifying narrative, for the moment setting aside the question of the extent to which it matches reality.

Management Has Principles

Henri Fayol's (1997/1916) *General Principles of Management*, was the first text to set forth general principles (he was also a practicing manager). As Pugh's (1997) anthology of organization theory notes, Fayol's analysis has stood the test of time and his principles are still prominent in the mainstream literature of management: for example, division of the work, unity of command, discipline, centralization, and lines of authority.

The emphasis on rationalizing and systematizing the work process is evident. Fayol's argument is notable, however, for his insistence that managers must use the principles flexibly and adapt them to different situations, which is "a difficult art requiring intelligence, experience, decision and proportion" (Pugh, 1997, p. 253). This theme of management as an art set in motion a debate that has persisted in the management literature ever since. "Is management an art? A science? Maybe it's both!" But can it be both? One issue never adequately dealt with is the fact that "art" refers to capacities that are not rational in the sense that the management ideology promotes. Yet these are among the very capacities that are said to set management apart from "work." Fayol's list does not include "art" itself but rather treats it as necessary to skillful application of the principles. Today, we might call this art *judgment*.

By the 1960s, the typology of management skills had changed little. Peter Drucker, perhaps the best-known mid-century management writer, described management as "the organ of society specifically charged with making resources productive, that is, with the responsibility for organized economic advance" and therefore in harmony with "the basic spirit of the modern age" (quoted in Scott & Hart, 1991, p. 45). Organizing for maximum productivity requires several kinds of skills, but all of them serve the overriding purpose of productivity, whether profit, as in the private sector, or best possible use of available resources, as in the public. March (2006) noted that in the service of productivity, managers favor the use of rational approaches, such as causal analysis of situations, quantitative data gathering, ranking of available options, and in general, organizational processes purposefully shaped toward the achievement of pre-selected outcomes. Management knowledge can be organized, sorted, and drawn upon, its validity demonstrated by means of empirical evidence. This form of knowledge amounts to "proposed control over events realized through measurement, planning and review." Management knowledge is propositional, "hard-edged, visible, ... acting as a dominant logic ... based on facts" (Chia & Holt, 2008, pp. 142–143).

The upshot: after about a century, it seems that the more things change, the more they remain the same. A 1980s literature review of "what managers do" (Hales, 1986, p. 95) found the following common threads running through management studies:

1. Acting as figurehead and leader
2. Acting as liaison with other organizations or units

3. Monitoring and disseminating information
4. Allocating resources
5. Handling disturbances and maintaining work flows
6. Negotiating
7. Innovating
8. Planning
9. Controlling and directing subordinates.

The characteristic activities of managers differ in at least one significant respect from what workers do. According to the management literature, managers rely on *concepts* about the organization's work rather than engaging directly in the work itself. Conceptual knowledge sets managers apart from, and over, workers. Before we get into whether this model (itself a concept, of course) actually matches management in practice, it seems important to clarify what a concept is and the role it is said to play in management.

The Power of Management Concepts

Modern management claims the right to control what workers do; this claim takes the form of asserting a monopoly over organizational knowledge. It is taken for granted among managers that knowledge itself is conceptual. Managers' unique conceptual expertise largely deals with controlling the application of workers' expertise, which consists of know-how rather than knowledge. What managers are said to *know* is how to control what workers *do*. We learned from Frederick Taylor that what workers "know" is raw material that needs science to convert it into concepts. Somehow, thereafter, the reality that management knowledge—the science of management—is an abstraction and refinement of its source, what workers know from doing the work, disappears in a blizzard of rhetoric about managers' two kinds of expertise, science and art.

Management at its thinking best does have a significant form of knowledge. It is rooted in the power of the concept. Out of a multitude of experiences, a concept can make one idea; from that idea can be derived a few rules for knowing and acting whenever that idea comes into play. The concept is always more efficient in mental operation than simply repeating actions one after another, associating a current observation with a similar one in the past without distilling possible patterns. Managers have the ability borrowed from science to decide how an object of work is defined, how it should be approached and worked on, and what shall count as success. Conceptualizing means to make yourself mental pictures: of the worker, of working processes, and of work's objects. It means generalizing (abstracting) from many real-life examples, focusing on their similarities and neglecting or ignoring their particularities.

Concepts act as shortcuts over and above matching a present problem with a past event and its solution. Conceptual word pictures enable the mind to capture corresponding objects in reality, but at a higher level of abstraction (not just this chair, but "chairs"; not just this client, but "clients"). Science calls this, without a sense of irony, objective knowledge. Management knowledge claims to be objective knowledge, which is reality reflected in the mind.

The modern idea of the concept owes its origins to Galileo (see Carnevale & Hummel, 2007). He asked what would happen if an object were hurled into a space where it would encounter no obstacles. The answer, which Newton later formulated as the first law of motion, is that the object would continue on its course forever. But here it is not the answer that interests us, but the form of the question. *I conceive*, said Galileo, of an object that, nothing intervening, will move on into infinity. "I conceive in my mind ..." Here is the beginning of the modern use of the concept. Once it has been tested, it can become a law. We no longer have to throw things over the parapet and wait to see what happens, as Galileo did. We have formed (and tested) a concept of what will happen when we do. Just so does science-based management operate with a concept in someone's mind. The concept is both a method, a way of mentally conceiving, and a product. In both forms it forces us to pay attention only to those things in nature that can be conceived in the mind, observed, tested and turned into laws, or at least into rules for the time being. Knowledge comes from observing repeatable events, which can be counted and analyzed, rather than from hands-on experience, which does not lend itself to being measured and conceptualized.

To *think*, according to science and management, is therefore to combine a collection of varied things or events into one idea. The similarities get swept in, and the differences drop out. To think is also to take ideas apart—to analyze them, to break them down into component parts and perhaps recombine these parts into different new ideas. Thus, thinking can calculate causal and mathematical relations and adjust for greater economy, efficiency, productivity. This is a lot cheaper and easier than moving actual things or people.

But the mind has no hands; it needs real "hands" to accomplish work. The danger in giving priority or exclusivity to the scientific form of knowledge is that managers, combining and taking apart concepts, lose touch with the variety in actual things or actual people. Workers, in dealing with these, lend a hand. Real things, real bodies in space and time, real people—these tend to wear out or get tired, to resist or show a mind of their own. Ignoring this reality, management thinking is tempted to deal with concepts as if we lived and worked in a timeless, frictionless reality in which the same working moves, once developed, can be used again and again because work tasks eternally repeat themselves. Managers will fall into thinking that there is no difference between moving concepts around and dealing with actual people or objects. They will conceive of *thinking as work*. The next step is to devalue work itself, direct fabrication and service, in favor of ideas.

The irony is that this type of mistake was recognized early in the history of management by the pioneer we encountered above—Henri Fayol:

There is nothing rigid or absolute in management affairs, it is all a question of proportion. Seldom do we have to apply the same principle twice in identical conditions; allowance must be made for different changing circumstances, for men just as different and changing and for many other variable elements.

(Fayol, 1997, p. 253)

Fayol's notion that management is as much art as science keeps a firm grasp on the difference between work and ideas of work. Yet, as we will see, management's grasp on the actualities of work slipped as its theory was elaborated.

The Model versus the Practice

All in all, the management models we have described so far strike similar themes—that is, they deploy the same concepts of what management is and what managers do: formalize, rationalize, organize, evaluate, control. Another stream of research, however, has tackled empirically the question of what managers actually do. By following managers around on the job, reading the memos that cross their desks, and interviewing them, this research has revealed a gap between theories of management and actual practices. The pioneer is Henry Mintzberg. His groundbreaking book, *The Nature of Managerial Work* (Mintzberg, 1973), was the result of what he called "structural observation," over an extended period, of five American chief executive officers (CEOs) from a variety of private and public organizations. Summarizing what he had learned from his research, Mintzberg noted that if asked what they do, managers will likely *say* that they plan, organize, coordinate and control—in other words, they present an image of their work that largely conforms to the management model. Yet observation reveals a discontinuity. Giving new weight to empirical evidence of managers' actual activities, Mintzberg described four persistent myths reflected in managers' self-image as well as management theories:

Myth #1: Managers are systematic planners.
Reality: Managerial activity is fragmentary, fast-paced, and largely non-reflective.
Myth #2: Managers don't have much regular work to perform themselves; they mostly delegate.
Reality: Managers have a lot of regular duties, including presiding on ritual occasions, negotiating, and processing information from the environment.
Myth #3: Managers need aggregated information, like the intelligence produced by management information systems.
Reality: Managers rely heavily on telephone calls and meetings for information gathering. [Note: Clearly, web-based intelligence such as from emails and web-based networks is today playing an expanded role here.]
Myth #4: Management is fast becoming a science and a profession.

Reality: Managers' expertise remains largely a matter of judgment and intuition, therefore only formalizable and transferrable to a limited extent.

Mintzberg observes that, rather than being a rational calculator and organizer, as the image portrays, the manager is a figurehead, a leader, a negotiator, a resource allocator, an entrepreneur, and a liaison who cultivates and relies on an informal, personal, external information system. None of these roles relies *solely* on rational calculation; all require as well as develop and hone experience-based human relationships, wisdom and judgment. The biggest challenges for practicing managers, Mintzberg maintains, have less to do with becoming scientific, systematic, and calculating, and much more with finding ways to share crucial experiential information with subordinates, step back from the daily flux to discern the bigger picture, and make time for general reflection and contemplation.

During an interview in 2000, Mintzberg (who is Canadian) observed: "I have said in the past, jokingly, that God invented Americans to test theories, but she never realized that there would be so many Americans and so few theories worth testing" (McCarthy, 2000, p. 32).

Despite Mintzberg's work, the long-standing rational model persists in the minds of managers. A recent ethnography of an Australian government agency provides an illustration. Asked to describe her work, Beryl, the manager, emphasizes rational, objective techniques needed to maintain order and control: attaining "'project definition', developing 'business plans', undertaking 'analysis' and defining 'measurables'" so that the work can be verified. She rejects the researcher's suggestion that managers can be "learners," noting that "the learner [is] a novice ... : 'I wouldn't present myself as a learner because that would suggest that you didn't know what you were doing'". She characterizes managers as "the knowers" and people at the lower levels of the organization as "the learners." She remarks: "We call ourselves the intelligentsia of the organization, the brain trust of the organization." The lower levels are where the problems lie, "clouded and overlaid with stories" in contrast to the "objective advice" of the senior managers. Although Beryl's characterization of her role strives to maintain the image of rationality, she acknowledges from time to time that senior public managers also need to be skilled politicians, navigating over "shifting ground ... driven by external factors ... complexity in the job ..." (Harman, 2011, pp. 280–284). Beryl's contrast between managers (the brain trust) and workers (storytellers) is noteworthy.

Another study describes how managers see themselves as people who practice "getting things done through people." The managers in this study talked of:

> making sure the people who work for me are doing their utmost to reach [the] target [by] moulding people ... driving or guiding—no, not driving—people down a path within certain boundaries. ... [T]he people out there need me to give them the confidence to make decisions.

Another says: "Essentially a manager is there to get the best out of people so that their contribution to the company's objectives can be best placed" (Watson, 1994, pp. 36–45). This theme harks back to the origins of management as "handling people."

The people aspect of management is often expressed conceptually, as this comment from a human resources manager illustrates: "I start with a model that has two basic processes: disclosure and feedback. ... I believe in peer review 100 per cent as a knowledge device, as vital to a learning—a self-learning—organization" (McKinlay & Taylor, 1998, p. 183).

The crux of management is expressed numerically:

> The difference between well-managed companies and not-so-well managed companies is the degree of attention they pay to numbers, the temperature chart of their business. ... How much variation is tolerated between budget forecasts and actual results? How deep does management dig for answers?
> *(Hopper & Macintosh, 1998, p. 131).*

Numbers and concepts shape not only the management model of an organization but the individual manager's self-understanding:

> Once the image of how a superior-performing manager should think and act has been developed through the first two stages [of our model], people can determine where they stand on each competency through use of the self-assessment ... specifically chosen to measure the competency. ... It is through the realization of personal discrepancies between the ideal and the real ... that people can perceive and feel a need for change.
> *(Townley, 1998, pp. 202–203)*

These quotes from management studies show how the management ideology serves not only as a justifying framework in organizational and societal settings but as a disciplinary force shaping the individual manager's sense of identity. This numerical, conceptual way of understanding management theory and practice has become ubiquitous, indeed, taken-for-granted. People improve their performance by spotting a discrepancy between the ideal and the real; they improve not by learning from direct experience but by filtering their occupational sense of themselves through a grid of abstractions.

The Ideology of *Public* Management

In the public sector, the ideology of management has long been a central element in defending the legitimacy of the administrative state. The power of bureaucrats in a representative democracy needs justification, given that they are not elected and (after a probationary period) are exceedingly difficult to fire. Thus, the basis on which they fit in a political system held to be rooted in The People is a perennially contested question. In this contest, the need for management of governing processes is a key justification. Granting authority (power) to unelected, tenured bureaucrats is defended on exactly the bases that comprise the management ideology. This has been the case at least since Woodrow Wilson (1887) penned his famous essay, "The study of administration." Wilson argued that the field of administration was a field of business; that administration lay outside the boundaries of politics; that there were best principles for fixing responsibility and authority in the administrative sphere; and that there was no danger in administrative power as long as it was exercised responsibly. In other words, management power was justified in government on the basis that management didn't count as politics; it was simply execution, or as it later came to be called, "implementation." Management ideology entered the halls of government, where it donned the mask of objectivity and political neutrality. No one needed to worry about administrative power, because it wasn't really the kind of power citizens needed to worry about; it was merely detailed execution of legislative orders.

Frederick Cleveland (1913), the chief early proponent of scientific management in government, upped Wilson's ante by arguing that there was nothing about government that stood in the way of efficiency. The problem was not government itself but the attitude of the people towards the government. He maintained that the government was analogous to a corporation and citizens to its stockholders. The people, like stockholders, express general principles and exercise oversight, the legislators they elect decide on policies, and the administration executes those policies using precise methods. Cleveland went so far as to suggest that public managers should formulate most policies, which could then receive what is today called an "up or down vote" in legislatures.

Two decades later came one of public administration's signature theories: Luther Gulick's POSDCORB. Gulick's (1937) pioneering work sought to draw attention away from distinguishing administration from management, a favorite conceptual debate at the time, to the question of what managers actually do; his answer was entirely conceptual—POSDCORB: planning, organizing, staffing, directing, coordinating, reporting, and budgeting. Amplified in organizational terms, the manager (1) works out what needs to be done and how to do it; (2) establishes formal authority structures and the division of labor; (3) arranges for finding and training workers; (4) makes decisions and gives orders; (5) interrelates diverse aspects of the work; (6) maintains records and is accountable to those to whom he [sic] is responsible; and (7) conducts fiscal planning, accounting and control. The notion of "Principles" signaled that there were eternal verities that, if clearly stated, could guide managers regardless of the contexts in which they found themselves. It seems fair to say that Gulick tended to blur the distinction between what managers do and what he thought they should do.

Dwight Waldo (1948), a critic of the management movement, summed up the managerial argument for government legitimacy in this way: Governmental power is justified by replacing political controls such as the separation of powers and checks and balances with administrative controls like division of functions that were intended to enable power rather than tame it. In other words, *administration was sold as a rational basis for public power*. Its rationality tempered it by neutralizing it. Further, centralizing power in the executive branch became a key accountability mechanism, making power responsible by making it clear where the buck stops, so citizens at least know whom to blame if things go off the rails.

The upshot of this managerial public philosophy was the notion that what citizens really care about is *end* results rather than wanting to be directly involved; therefore, there is nothing dangerous about turning over the *means* to managers. What makes this point of view ideological, in the second sense noted above, is that it goes beyond simply serving as a guiding mesh of broadly held values to setting in motion and supporting troubling power disparities between citizens and the administrative (managerial) state. The managerial ideology promulgates a notion of governing power based on rationality, that is, specialized (law-like) knowledge that is exclusively the possession of a particular class equipped with scientific expertise. Weber saw the danger of rationality as a justification for power; he could not have foreseen the extent of its expansion. It is up to us not to look away from it today.

Recent research like the examples above is beginning to document how managers enact, or have difficulty enacting, the managerial ideology in the course of their activities. The catalyst has been the advent of New Public Management (NPM), which has sharply increased the force of managerialism in public service. Advocating a private sector-oriented model of public management as entrepreneurial, strategic, market-oriented, and measurably performance-based, NPM called upon, even pressured, public sector managers to redefine their responsibilities, and indeed their professional identities, in ways that many of them see as at odds with public and professional values, particularly those (such as stewardship, care, duty, and service) that clash with the tough-minded, bottom-line, results-driven NPM model (Thomas & Davies, 2005; Exworthy & Halford, 1999). Professionals like those in social service agencies are expected to adopt strategic approaches and performance measures, to codify the delivery of care in terms of standardized compliance. As one manager said:

> If every box was ticked they'd be very happy but if then you said to them, "Now what about the quality of care?" ... [T]he culture that we're in now is about making sure that you can show that you've followed the procedures so that if something goes wrong you won't be criticized.
>
> *(Thomas & Davies, 2005, p. 696)*

This same manager remains committed to strategic thinking and quantitative targets, even as he expresses a measure of cynicism about them. Professional social workers, teachers, and police managers in the same study are loath to give up their identities as professionals in public service, yet at the same time they are drawn to the managerial ideology and the organizational power it carries with it. The researchers sum up another study participant, a head teacher, as (in her own eyes) "someone in control but not overly controlling, someone who cares but is also efficient, someone who is businesslike but not at the expense of professional quality and pedagogy" (Thomas & Davies, 2005, p. 698). The paradoxes and contradictions in this vision—trying to care, but not too much—remain in place.

The above study and others like it are important because they suggest that it is not only frontline workers who are being controlled and disciplined by public-sector managerialism. Managers themselves feel the force of the renewed and expanded campaign to define governance as control for the sake of the numbers and the bottom line. This discontent could be an expression of the difficulty of switching gears between incommensurable forms of knowledge. History suggests that the balancing act between care and control cannot be maintained indefinitely, at least not if it remains unexamined.

Management's Hat Trick

When someone who spans the organizational boundary between hands-on work and management is told to "take off your engineering hat and put on your management hat," what are they actually being told to do? In the run-up to the Challenger disaster, the project manager told his engineer subordinate to change hats. What does this mean? Various answers have been given to why the project team failed to prevent the Challenger space shuttle from exploding shortly after take-off. For our purposes, the change of hats reveals something that usually goes unnoticed: the *discontinuity* between two kinds of knowledge in an organization—between hands-on, experiential knowledge gained where the work of the organization is done (here, the "engineering hat") and the management "hat" that operates at a conceptual remove from the work itself. In the Challenger example, the engineer-manager, who was unusual in that his job required him to *mesh* both kinds of knowledge, was being asked to *change* ways of knowing, to shift perspectives on the issue at hand: from what he knew from having his hands on the shuttle mechanisms to what he knew from understanding the shuttle project in terms of management concepts.[1]

The entire management enterprise assumes that the gap between two kinds of knowledge can be bridged. In terms of the Challenger case, bridging the gap exemplifies management's "hat trick." Frederick Taylor argued that it was the manager's job to extract the working knowledge—the rules of thumb—inside the heads (or hands) of workers and transform it into scientific principles, the "one best method" for each task. Taylor (1911) saw this as the responsibility of management rather than of workers because he believed that the worker was incapable of fully understanding the science of the work. In his view, the transformation of working knowledge into laws or principles would come about as the result of careful experimentation that would bring to light the most efficient ("best") way of performing each task. Yet in the case of the Challenger engineer, what he is asked to do, in effect, is not to import worker knowledge into the bigger picture but instead to *discount* what he has learned in direct contact with the work, and go with management concepts. In other words, to change hats, leaving the gap between them in place, rather than figure out how or whether the two could be brought into some kind of harmony or mutual adjustment.

Implications

All previous management reforms aimed to temper the negativities of scientific management. Our aim here is to clarify the difficulty, indeed the danger, of importing into a public agency what Frederick Taylor did to the factory floor. Taylor established the model, and all subsequent "reforms" have tried to mollify aspects of scientific management without losing the efficiency it promised to achieve (see Chapter 1).

In Taylor's eyes, the worker's craft knowledge hindered efficiency because the knowledge each worker gains from doing the work cannot be standardized. Management was invented to control work through science. But the disparity between conceptual and experiential knowledges was never taken seriously. A century after Taylor, two implications of the gap between knowledges are clear. One is that manager knowledge and worker knowledge are mutually irreducible: Each has its distinctive assumptions and procedures, none of which can be transformed in totality or imported into any of the others. There is no alchemy that will *convert* worker knowledge from direct experience into manager conceptual knowledge, or replace what workers know with what managers know. If, as we argue, crucial ingredients of worker expertise are impossible to translate *fully* into management concepts, managers must acknowledge the uniqueness and legitimacy of worker expertise. Rather than greater control over workers, what public organizations need is better ways for managers and workers to join their efforts to make the work go well. The word "collaborate" has been largely appropriated by NPM to serve control purposes, but so far nobody seems to have taken seriously Mary Follett's notion of taking orders from the situation, everyone involved developing a shared understanding of what will fit the circumstances and then acting on that basis (Fox & Urwick, 1973). We discuss this possibility in Part III.

A second implication is that, with management knowledge revealed as more ideology than actuality, worker knowledge and manager knowledge may not in practice be as different as the ideology insists they are. Workers sometimes sum up and reflect conceptually on their experiences, especially when the "material" (human or physical) "talks back." Managers learn from direct experience as well as from concepts, especially by means of face to face interactions with workers. *Maintaining the distinction between the two serves to justify the power of management by encouraging us to see it as rational rather than self-serving and unnecessary to the work itself*. If so, reasoned argument will never be enough to destabilize it. We will argue that these two interpretations can co-exist: The two knowledges are indeed fundamentally different, but both workers and managers can and do use both kinds of knowledge. This stance makes it possible to envision new ways of understanding knowledge-related organizational dynamics that do not keep management ideology in place as a justification of management power. As Chia and Holt (2008) suggest, research into managerial knowledge should investigate how managers use the word "knowledge" in various kinds of situations and what sorts of clarity or confusion ensue.

Note

1 "After the decision was made by those wearing management hats to overrule the concerns of the engineers, [team leader] Lund put his engineering hat back on and the decision was conveyed to the NASA managers as if it were an engineering decision. ... The managers attempted to justify accepting high levels of risk by ... representing to others their managerial judgment as engineering judgment" (Herkert, 1991, p. 618).

References

Arendt, Hannah. 1958. *The Human Condition*. Chicago & London: University of Chicago Press.

Bendix, Reinhardt. 1974. *Work and Authority in Industry*. Berkeley & London: University of California Press.

Berger, Peter L. 1964. Some general observations on the problems of work. Pp. 211–241 in P. L. Berger (ed.), *The Human Shape of Work: Studies in the Sociology of Occupations*. New York: Macmillan.

Bergin, Chris. 2007. Remembering the mistakes of Challenger. https://nasaspaceflight.com/2007/1/remembering-the-mistakes-of-challenger/ Downloaded 12/11/2017.

Carnevale, David G., and Ralph P. Hummel. 2007. The innovation and discovery in factory and bureaucracy: Theory, art and method of the knowledge analytic. *Public Voices* 10:1, 5–22.

Chia, Robert, & Robin Holt. 2008. On managerial knowledge. *Management Learning* 39:2, 141–158.

Clegg, Stewart R., & Gill Palmer (eds.). 1996. *The Politics of Management Knowledge*. London: Sage Publications.

Cleveland, Frederick. 1913. *Organized Democracy*. New York: Longmans.

Exworthy, M., & S. Halford (eds.). 1999. *Professions and the New Managerialism in the Public Sector*. Buckingham, U.K.: Open University Press.

Fayol, Henri. 1997. General principles of management (trans. C. Storrs). Pp. 253–274 in *Organization Theory: Selected Readings* (4th ed., ed. D. S. Pugh). London: Penguin Books. Original work published 1916.

Fox, Elliott M., & Lyndall Urwick (eds.). 1973. *Dynamic Administration: The Collected Papers of Mark Parker Follett*. New York: Hippocrene Books.

Gerth, H. H., & C. Wright Mills (eds.). 1978. *From Max Weber: Essays in Sociology*. New York: Oxford University Press. Originally published 1946.

Gulick, Luther L. 1937. Notes on the theory of organization. Pp. 3–13 in *Papers on the Science of Administration* (eds. L. Gulick & L. Urwick). New York: Institute of Public Administration.

Hales, Colin P. 1986. What do managers do? A critical review of the evidence. *Journal of Management Studies* 23:1, 88–115.

Harman, Kerry. 2011. Everyday learning in a public sector workplace: The embodiment of managerial discourses. *Management Learning* 43:3, 275–289.

Herkert, Joseph R. 1991. Management's hat trick: Misuse of 'engineering judgment' in the Challenger incident. *Journal of Business Ethics* 10, 617–620.

Hopper, Trevor, & Norman Macintosh. 1998. Management accounting numbers: Freedom or Prison—Geneen versus Foucault. Pp. 126–150 in *Foucault, Management and Organization Theory* (eds. A. McKinlay and K. Starkey). London: Sage Publications.

Hummel, Ralph P. 1982. The nature of work: Philosophy, psychology, and productivity. *Dialogue* 5:1 (Fall), 2–12.

Hummel, Ralph P. 1983. Manager and worker: Phenomenology of time consciousness and rational style. *Dialogue* 6:1 (Fall), 2–12.

Ingersoll, Virginia, & Guy B. Adams. 1986. Beyond organizational boundaries: Exploring the management myth. *Administration & Society* 18:3, 360–381.

Jacques, Roy. 1996. *Manufacturing the Employee: Management Knowledge from the 19th to 21st Centuries*. London: Sage Publications.

Kanigel, Robert. 2005. *The One Best Way: Frederick Winslow Taylor and the Enigma of Efficiency*. Cambridge, Mass.: M.I.T. Press.

Mannheim, Karl. 1936. *An Introduction to the Sociology of Knowledge*. London: Routledge & Kegan Paul.

March, James G. 2006. Rationality, foolishness and adaptive intelligence. *Strategic Management Journal* 27, 201–214.

McCarthy, Daniel J. 2000. View from the top: Henry Mintzberg on strategy and management. *Academy of Management Executive* 14:3, 31–39.

McKinlay, Alan, & Phil Taylor. 1998. Through the looking glass: Foucault and the politics of production. Pp. 173–190 in *Foucault, Management and Organization Theory* (eds. A. McKinlay & K. Starkey). London: Sage Publications.

Mintzberg, Henry. 1973. *The Nature of Managerial Work*. New York: Harper-Collins.

Noble, David F. 1977. *America by Design: Science, Technology, and the Rise of Corporate Capitalism*. Oxford, U.K.: Oxford University Press.

Person, H. S. 1926a. Basic principles of administration and management: Scientific management. Pp. 204–207 in *Scientific Foundations of Business Administration* (ed. H. C. Metcalf). Baltimore, Md.: Williams & Wilkins.

Person, H. S. 1926b. Basic principles of administration and management: Major problems of management. Pp. 234–254 in *Scientific Foundations of Business Administration* (ed. H. C. Metcalf). Baltimore, Md.: Williams & Wilkins.

Pugh, Derek S. (ed.). 1997. *Organization Theory: Selected Readings* (4th ed.). London: Penguin Books.

Ricoeur, Paul. 1991. Ideology and utopia. Pp. 300–316 in Paul Ricoeur, *From Text to Action*. Evanston, Ill.: Northwestern University Press.

Sandfort, Jodi R. 1999. The structural impediments to human service collaboration: Examining welfare offices at the front lines. *Social Service Review* (Sept.), 314–339.

Scott, William G. 1985. Organizational revolution: An end to managerialism. *Administration & Society* 17:2, 149–170.

Scott, William G., & David K. Hart. 1991. The exhaustion of managerialism. *Society* (March/April), 39–48.

Sheldon, Oliver. 1923. The art of management from a British point of view. *Bulletin of the Taylor Society* 8:6, 209–215.

Taylor, Frederick W. 1911. *Principles of Scientific Management*. New York: HarperCollins.

Thomas, Robyn, & Annette Davies. 2005. Theorizing the micro-politics of resistance: New public management and managerial identities in the U. K. public services. *Organization Studies* 26:5, 683–706.

Townley, Barbara. 1998. Beyond good and evil: Depth and division in the management of human resources. Pp. 191–210 in *Foucault, Management and Organization Theory* (eds. A. MacKinley & K. Starkey). London: Sage Publications.

Waldo, Dwight. 1948. *The Administrative State*. New York: Ronald Press.

Watson, Tony. 1994. *In Search of Management: Culture, Chaos and Control in Managerial Work*. London: Routledge.

Weber, Max. 1947. *The Theory of Social and Economic Organization* (ed. T. Parsons). New York: Free Press.

Wilson, Woodrow. 1887. The study of administration. *Political Science Quarterly* 2 (June), 197–222.

5

WHAT EXECUTIVES KNOW
Expertise as "Being Governmental"

The great theorist of bureaucracy, Max Weber, modeled governmental bureaucracies and their place in the political system as a struggle between instrumental rationality and political non-rationality. Action is rational (therefore efficient) if it is calculable and impersonal. According to Weber (1947, p. 339), "The question is always who controls the existing bureaucratic machinery. And such control is possible only in a very limited degree to persons who are not technical specialists."

The bureaucrat's duty is to place his judgment and skills at the service of higher authority in the execution of assigned tasks. A politician, in contrast, is engaged in a struggle for power, enlisting supporters, acting independently, and taking personal responsibility for his acts (Weber did not envision women in either capacity). Career administrative officials act on the basis of *technical* knowledge, including organizational know-how, which makes them indispensable and therefore powerful, unless those at the top possess equivalent technical knowledge. In contrast, *political* expertise is acquired in the struggle for power (see Bendix, 1960).

In the previous chapter, we examined the ideology of management, which squares with Weber's understanding of administrative officials. Weber emphasized that the duty to follow orders as efficiently as possible is a mark of administrative professionalism characteristic of the career bureaucrats. This model of officialdom was especially appealing to American reformers in the Progressive era, who saw bureaucratic commitment to neutrality as a crucial building block of administrative legitimacy necessary to check the power of political machines.

In this chapter we take a look at people at the top of the bureaucratic pyramid, where the relationship between political expertise and administrative skill is particularly ambiguous, but in practice also particularly stark. In most democratic nations, administrative systems are made up of, at the top, elected executives (such as members of parliament serving as agency heads), and below them career civil servants. In the American system, combining legislative and executive powers in this way is specifically forbidden by the Constitution. The American president is not functionally a legislative leader, nor can the members of his cabinet serve in Congress at the same time as they are serving as agency heads. The same goes at the state and local levels. In the United States the top ranks of government bureaucracies are occupied by officials who are neither fish nor fowl: executive leaders who have neither formal ties to a particular party nor an administrative vocation. Heclo (1988) calls them "in-and-outers," neither politicians nor bureaucrats in the usual sense.

The result is a significant structural characteristic that blunts the rationality of the American bureaucratic pyramid: In the U.S., whether a government (federal, state, local) or a cabinet agency is headed by an elected official (president, governor, mayor) or an executive (such as cabinet secretary or city manager) appointed by such an official and confirmed by the legislature, officials at the top of the pyramid, where politics and administration meet, are most often "temps" (Maranto, 2005). Unlike people who occupy the rest of the bureaucracy—managers and workers who typically spend an entire working life there—public executives come and go according to election results or other political fortunes (especially whether they remain in good standing with the head of the government at that level).

As a result, in the U.S., modernity's rational bureaucratic mechanisms are definitively open at the top. Weber believed that bureaucracies were well defended against unwanted political influence, including by politically appointed executives, because of their monopoly over technical and organizational knowledge. In a power struggle between career officials and a relatively inexperienced leader (that is, inexperienced in governing), Weber thought politicians were at a marked disadvantage. A separated-powers system exacerbates this dynamic by exposing government bureaucracies at the executive level to a politically charged environment that includes a legislature of which agency heads are not members: "For the President, his appointees, and high-ranking bureaucrats, the struggle to control the bureaucracy is usually a leap into the dark" (Heclo, 1977, p. 1).

In this chapter we suggest that the relationship between in-and-outers and the career managers below them is, in fundamental ways, a power struggle between two kinds of expert knowledge—administrative and political. Our task is to paint a picture of that struggle and highlight, in particular, the significance of knowledge differences between careerists and top executives whether directly elected or appointed: the temp on top. We argue that the ideology of managerial science is weakened at the executive level by the necessity appointed officials face: to give priority to politics. We suggest that, in essence, executive knowledge consists of expertise in "being governmental" (Appleby, 1949, Ch. 4).

Executive Action and Dual Rationalities

Weber argued that the political leader cannot live in the same mode of idea-based commitments as does the scientist. Whereas management science can redefine political rationality as instrumental rationality (e.g., by arguing that efficiency is actually a political value, being what most citizens want), the politically appointed or elected leader at the top of a bureaucratic pyramid has to face up to "the fact that political means, ends and consequences very often do not either correspond as intended or ethically justify one another" (Gane, 2004, p. 65). This brings into question the move to treat efficiency/effectiveness as first among ethical principles at the executive level, in the same way that it is routinely deployed by managers.

The political leader, with direct accountability to external stakeholders, perceives what Weber (1978, p. 121) saw: "No ethics in the world can dodge the fact that in numerous instances the attainment of 'good' ends is bound to the fact that one must be willing to pay the price of using morally dubious means" with no possible *guarantee* that such means (e.g. maximizing efficiency) are fully justified by asserting ultimate values (e.g. the public interest). The gap between the two is fundamental. The political executive must try, nevertheless to bring ends and means into as justifiable a relationship as possible: "This form of realistic but ambiguous political leadership ... calls for a combination of value-rational and instrumentally rational action" (Gane, 2004, p. 65). In other words, the knowledge or mode of knowing that should guide the administrative executive has somehow to blend the fact-based, scientific instrumental rationality definitive of bureaucracy with the value rationality of what Weber calls "ultimate ends"—a blend or reconciliation that Weber did not believe was possible.

The upshot: the role of the political executive at the top of the bureaucratic pyramid is a balancing act: not only in being at the meeting point between the organization and its stakeholders, but also between internal instrumental rationality, which promises a match-up between ends and means, and, as Weber says, "the ethical irrationality of the world" (Weber, 1978, p. 122).

The Governmental Quest for Executive Control

Historically, conceptions of the executive role in public administration started with the power of numbers, but real life tells a different story. The drive to rationalize American government began in the late nineteenth century, among reformers determined to wrest control of city governments away from party machines. The political party culture was centered in working-class and poor neighborhood institutions, buttressed by strategic affiliations with well-to-do businessmen, who occasionally provided political cover by serving as mayor. The power of party organizations like New York's Tammany Hall was a direct challenge to elite reformers; the latter often found themselves sidelined as parties prioritized neighborhood-based interests over those of citywide businesses and professionals. To avoid seeming undemocratic by challenging party power directly, municipal reformers came to think of and refer to themselves as "nonpartisan," a term suggesting that their interests were ones all classes shared. Although they had institutional power bases—independent boards that governed schools, parks, and the like, and elite private institutions like the Charity Organization Society and the Chamber of Commerce—the educated and well-to-do longed to dislodge party men from the ranks of government agencies (Stivers, 2000).

Gradually reform efforts crystallized around making government run better by replacing party loyalists with trained experts—educated men like themselves. Evidence suggests that many municipal agencies were already headed by experts, particularly by engineers, and were reasonably well-run (e.g., Teaford, 1984). Nevertheless, the movement to reform and "systematize" city governments gradually gathered steam.

The reform rallying cry was "Municipal government is business and not politics." The city was a corporation and ought to be run like one. City government was not a political mechanism for dealing with conflicting interests; rather it was an administrative entity for carrying out the best policy for correcting a particular urban problem. In business, the need for efficient expertise was self-evident. In the process of making municipal government businesslike, reformers served corporate interests of stability and predictability in the face of threats posed by militant unions, waves of immigration, and incipient socialism. They argued that a stable, efficient system benefited everybody. The reform strategy was to cooperate with top party officials, who welcomed protection from more radical forces like unions and could ill afford to alienate the wealthy and influential. Despite the focus on alliances with men at the top, including mayors and agency heads, reformers couched their efforts as "democratization" and "progress." Efficiency was justified as democratic, since—it was argued—what voters really wanted was not participation but for government to work better. Reformers styled their efforts as in the service of science, in other words, as disinterested search for the truth (Hays, 1964; Wiebe, 1967; Schiesl, 1977; Stivers, 2000).

A key element in the reformers' rationalizing efforts was the campaign to centralize fiscal control by reforming the budgetary process. The first itemized municipal agency budget in the United States was developed in 1907 for the health department in New York City by its chief, Hermann Biggs, in collaboration with Henry Bruere, a director of the New York Bureau of Municipal Research, a non-profit reform organization. Previously, city agencies like the health department had deliberately inflated funding requests to the city's Board of Estimate and Apportionment, which routinely slashed them. When the allocated amounts proved too low, the city would issue special revenue bonds. The health department's newly itemized budget was so persuasive that the Board thereafter required all agencies to do the same. The budget document made the case for funds in terms that sound familiar today. Health needs translate into dollars and cents, it argued: "Briefly, it is a question of how much health the city can afford to buy" (Stivers, 2000, p. 30). This sort of rational "by the numbers" justification required centralized budgeting so that the entire administrative apparatus could be assessed and its needs determined objectively by a calculating pair of eyes at the top rather than through bureaucratic wrangling and politicking.

The key figure in the budgeting campaign was Frederick A. Cleveland, another early director of the New York Bureau. Cleveland, trained in accounting, believed that rational budgeting was the hub of governance. As the Bureau developed and its national influence grew, so did Cleveland's. Eventually he was tapped to chair President William H. Taft's Commission on Economy and Efficiency, which recommended the establishment of an executive budget at the federal level, an idea eventually ratified in the Budget Act of 1921. Thus, from its municipal roots, the idea of budgeting as a tool of executive control eventually made its way to the top, so to speak, of the United States government, with Cleveland lighting the spark.

The Business of Government

Frederick Cleveland (1909, p. 207) believed that "the elements of successful management of municipal enterprise are the same as the elements of successful management of private enterprise." The differences between the two were largely a matter of methods rather than principle. Cleveland's understanding of method, however, covered such fundamental political questions as how city government should be controlled and its benefits distributed. He saw "rules of private thrift" being translated into "principles of public well-being" (p. 107). The problems of city government were largely administrative rather than political. By restricting politics to party wrangling, Cleveland could promote the idea that deciding what administrative moves to make was simply a matter of objective analysis.

During his time on President Taft's commission, Cleveland emphasized the budget as a mechanism to oversee and discipline government, likening it to a conning tower that would lift government executives out of routine complexity and enable them to see the big picture. Although in Washington he presented the budget as a means for Congress to supervise the executive branch, later he came to stress the budget as a tool of executive control. The budgetary vision gradually shifted from ensuring accountability to citizens toward strengthening the executive's ability to manage government operations efficiently. In "Evolution of the budget idea in the United States," Cleveland (1915) argued that the budget was a *plan for governing*, prepared and presented by the executive for legislative approval. The legislature's role was either to approve or reject the budget as a whole (today's "up or down vote") as well as to review executive performance. Cleveland's budget idea was essentially a theory of government that gave power to the chief executive at the expense of the legislature, since the latter would have little or no say over how funds were allocated. In his scheme, the chief executive became the principal policy architect.

The influence of Cleveland's view of government was carried forward by the New York Bureau he led, and later by universities around the country, in the notion that well-run governments at all levels require trained experts, versed in the science of administration, and able to interpret and present government plans, performance, and results *in numerical terms*. Numbers, and science more generally, became seen as the ideal basis for the identification and pursuit of the best, most efficient way to run government because they used (as Cleveland said) a precise, impersonal—in other words, nonpolitical—language of inquiry, producing truths that everyone would acknowledge because of the method by which they were arrived at. In essence, numbers were a language that everyone could speak. Awareness that reality is not so simple persisted, of course, but the idea that expert administration has a political aspect in addition to a scientific one has never been fully acknowledged, at least by administrative experts themselves. The Progressive notion that government can be run like a business persists today, even in the face of testimony from public executives like Commerce Secretary Carlos Gutierrez:

> Running an agency is very, very different from running a company. Some of the skills do transfer, but you have to be careful figuring out which ones. In government, you can't fire anyone. Your board of directors is 435 people in Congress, and half of them want to see you fail.
>
> (Duhigg, 2017)

Business ideology's force is evident in the almost wildfire-like spread of New Public Management, with its insistence on entrepreneurialism, "customer service," and the measurement of results—that is, the power of numbers. If total quantification is at least questionable within the career ranks, it is even more so at the executive level.

What's Good for General Motors: The Business of Government

In 1953, President Dwight D. Eisenhower nominated Charles E. Wilson, president of General Motors (GM), to serve as secretary of defense. At his Senate hearing, Wilson was asked whether as defense secretary, despite his large holdings of GM stock, he would be able to make a decision that would have adverse effects on GM. Wilson answered that yes, he would, but he couldn't imagine such a possibility, since he believed that what was good for the country would also be good for GM, and vice versa. His statement entered history as "What's good for General Motors is good for the country" and resisted further refinement. Wilson served as defense secretary throughout Eisenhower's first term in office (McKinlay & Starkey, 1998).

Wilson's predecessor as head of General Motors was Alfred E. Sloan, who was responsible for modernizing its corporate structure by creating divisions out of largely autonomous satellite businesses. In 1920, Sloan devised a strategy for fending off what seemed to be GM's impending financial ruin. This strategy had a decisive influence on American corporate structure and management for the next half century (McKinlay & Starkey, 1998). Its goal was executive control from the top. For the purposes of our discussion, Sloan and GM illustrate the kind of centralization-by-numbers that Frederick Cleveland idealized. The story will move us toward our claim that what's good for private corporations is not necessarily workable (or desirable) in government. This is particularly true on the issue of whether top public executives, such as agency heads, mayors, governors, and presidents, either can or should be able to exert sufficient control to be the one place where the "buck" either can or should "stop."

At GM, Sloan concentrated on putting in place accounting procedures that were intended to centralize control over all divisional operations. This was a move that gave pride of place to numbers as instruments of executive power. Refining a model developed at DuPont, the Sloan plan left operational control to division executives and concentrated top executive surveillance on divisional financial data, particularly return on investment (ROI). A multidivisional structure combined with a standardized budget approach and a single numerical measure of effectiveness enabled central executives to monitor divisions closely. As Sloan said of his strategy: "Essentially it was a matter of making things visible." The single-minded focus on ROI forced division executives to adhere to central corporate direction. Sloan was dedicated to "the elimination of operation by hunches ... I keep saying to General Motors organization that we are prepared to spend any proper amount of money to get the facts"—i.e. *the numbers* (quoted in McKinlay & Starkey, 1998, pp. 114–115). Sloan saw numbers as undebatable, therefore a buttress for executive authority. Establish numerical standards at the top, then see to it they are met.

Over at Ford Motor Company, its founder had been running the company as his personal fiefdom ever since its founding in 1903. It was a rigid hierarchy, with job design influenced by Frederick Taylor's scientific management and, famously, by the assembly line production process that Henry Ford had pioneered. Ford, however, kept all the reins of control strictly in his own hands. Upon his death in 1945 it became clear that the company was in a disastrous state, chaotic in the ranks and riddled with inefficiency. His grandson and heir, Henry Ford II, recruited a team of business school graduates and World War II Air Force veterans (known as the "Whiz Kids"), headed by Robert McNamara, to rationalize operations. The newbies quickly went from corporate aliens to "overseers of the corporate Panopticon." McNamara's team transformed Ford from a kind of monarchy, controlled by the gaze of the sovereign and his personal representatives, to a form of corporate rule in which management authority was legitimated on objective grounds, replacing orders barked by a superior with *quantifiable* performance objectives—again, numbers as an executive weapon against inefficiency. The end result was a company controlled by the finance department. The key focus was cost control—value for money. Unhappily, the "'normal' outcome" of this system was that "innovation crumpled on impact" (McKinlay & Starkey, 1998, pp. 116–118).

A reader familiar with recent trends in public management thinking, especially New Public Management (NPM), will have no trouble spotting familiar phenomena, particularly the central role played by quantified performance measures in the quest for central control. This reader will also easily see a major difficulty for public organizations aiming at this form of rationalization: the impossibility of measuring "return on investment," given that government agencies do not make a profit and have great difficulty operationalizing, much less measuring, many of the results of their work.

Given the business ideology of NPM, these automotive industry stories have implications for public governance and the nature of the public executive. There are some private-public similarities. For example, to executives at the top of any bureaucracy, control of the ranks below them is a primary concern. This seems the case regardless of sector. Public executives, like private, are held accountable to those to whom they report, whether they are cabinet secretaries responsible to an elected head of state, or the heads themselves, responsible to the electorate. Accountability may or may not be defined in terms of success or failure in the accomplishment of objectives, but political it always is, by definition. As we will see, this presents challenges that are different from, and more complicated than, reporting to a corporate board of directors.

Another question raised by the GM and Ford cases is the role played by numbers. Clearly Sloan and then McNamara saw control made easier and more definite if performance could be measured numerically. Public executives have pinned similar hopes on numbers as a way of taming the career bureaucracy as well as justifying their own performance. For our purposes, one issue is whether quantitative performance accountability is enough to counter the advantage managerial knowledge has over the knowledge possessed by in-and-outers. Can quantitative control strategies like NPM discipline managers as executives would like? The previous chapter called this possibility into question.

The Triumph of Numbers

We have suggested that the trend in public administration has been toward concentrating government authority and power in the top executive for the sake of rational efficiency. Ralph Hummel (2006) examined this trend from a philosophical perspective. He questioned the origin of our "enchantment with numbers," arguing that numerical information is not the same thing as knowledge (p. 59). He cites phenomenologist Edmund Husserl's account of how mathematics came to prevail over knowledge gained from everyday practices and then to transform scientific constructs into pure ideas. To illustrate this trend, Husserl examined the development of land surveying.

Land surveying began with a person "scoping out" (looking) and marking property lines on the earth in a particular place. It changed when surveyors began to use geometric devices, enabling the tracing of property lines on paper. Repetition of the same way of measuring led to method. Method then became something of its own that could be studied, separated from its physical origin. Gradually the surveyor becomes known not for his knowledge of particular plots of land and his purpose in marking them out, but for his geometric method: "Technique orients itself by comparing one procedure against another, not against the ultimate goal or purpose" (Hummel, 2006, p. 66). The ambiguity of particular hills, woods, swamps, and valleys, together with the mundane interests of the property owner, the purchaser, and the surveyor, recede from the understanding of what surveying *is*. In a further transformation, geometry is challenged as shapes on paper are replaced by "pure" numbers. The particular example or situation has transitioned to an idea, as Husserl says, "empty … of its meaning" in the life-world (quoted on p. 68). The actual experience of tramping over the land, scoping it out, has turned into a method for calculating its dimensions, turning the "rough predictions" that are the best real-life experience can achieve, into the predictions of science (p. 69).

As Hummel notes:

> We begin to treat all areas of human life as equally susceptible to being captured in standard units of measurement. A barrier is erected against noticing the particular and the different, innovation and discovery. Eventually, the lack of these goes unnoticed as we all succumb to universal mathematization.
>
> *(Hummel, 2006, p. 73)*

This loss of the substance of administrative action in favor of its measurement is a frequent topic of press accounts, if rarely in academic analysis. The case study to follow this chapter, of the Veterans Administration (VA), examines this issue in depth. But here is one illustration of the unintended consequences of Hummel's "triumph of numbers." As the VA attempted to improve its outcome scores, it launched efforts to cherry-pick patients admitted to hospitals, favoring lower-risk patients over those who were sicker. One hospital director is quoted as saying, "The numbers are indicators of the quality of care …," whereas emergency room physicians disagree, declaring the practice of screening out sicker patients "dangerous." One doctor says, "It's a numbers game. The leadership has figured out the hospital can actually do better by seeing less patients … These numbers show up on the director's report card, so it is very important they look good." Another doctor notes that efforts to track health care system performance have consistently produced perverse outcomes (Phillips, 2018, p. A12).

Thus, public executives can find themselves between an administrative rock and a political hard place, hoping the numbers will be their salvation, yet repeatedly hampered by the inability to substitute mathematical measurement for the practical, hands-on knowledge that is crucial in achieving substantive results.

A Government of Strangers

Another issue complicating executive knowledge is the question of whether it actually conforms to the centralizing, "where the buck stops" ideology that has grown up around it. We argue that political executives have to be looking at the same time in opposite directions. Controlling those below them is one challenge, and for that purpose the appeal of holding all the bureaucratic reins in one hand is obvious. But it fails to solve the political executive's other problem, which is political accountability to stakeholders, including an elected executive, a legislature, interest groups, or the public at large.

The classic work on appointed public officials is Hugh Heclo's *A Government of Strangers*. Heclo argues that there is "no systematic body of knowledge or special training" to prepare appointees for their responsibilities. Instead, their work is based on "craft knowledge—understanding acquired by learning on the job" (Heclo, 1977, pp. 1–3). In addition to executives' usual lack of technical expertise and relative ignorance of the way the bureaucracy works, the brevity of their tenure makes acquiring such knowledge unlikely. At most, they can hope for perhaps three to four years in a post from which they are expected to marshal troops of career bureaucrats toward policy goals. As noted above, Max Weber considered this to be a most unequal contest. He believed the technical expertise of bureaucrats, coupled with their long experience inside the system and their institutional memories, put the appointee at a disadvantage difficult to overcome. As we will see, however, subsequent research on the increasing politicization of American public bureaucracy tends to confirm Heclo and to call Weber's assessment into question.

Heclo notes that:

> without higher civil service support almost nothing sought by political executives is likely to take effect. It is a power that can consist simply of [careerists] waiting to be asked for solutions by appointees who do not know that they have problems.
>
> *(Heclo, 1977, p. 172)*

Appointees need to understand regulations and complex agency rules; they need to be oriented to the needs and practices of key interest groups as well as to internal political dynamics; they need to know the significant historical developments that have helped to make things the way they are when the appointee gets there. In other words, they must gain access to the stock of knowledge acquired by career bureaucrats in the course of their work: not so much the technical training as the bureaucrat's knowledge of "how we do things around here" as well as "what happened the last time we tried something like this." The appointee, who necessarily arrives *in medias res*, is at a considerable disadvantage. As one former state agency head commented, "In many [respects] you really are simply riding a horse in the direction it wants to go" (Chandler & Pratt, 2011, p. 35).

Studies of political appointees suggest that they frequently deal with this challenge by building personal networks, allies who will help them push forward and exert influence, or at least enable them to act with some understanding of the source and basis of the opposition. But the development of mutual trust and confidence takes time, and is subject to ebbs and flows. Therefore, appointees can never entirely depend on themselves and their personal networks. They must reach downward, into the civil service ranks for knowledge of how particular situations have developed and for the kind of technical expertise they themselves lack. One particular local government appointee we spoke with, who had been called upon by both state and local chief executives to rescue several different agencies from near disaster, told of starting a new job at a particularly troubled county institution.

> The first day, the first thing I did was go find the union steward. I didn't talk first to the deputy director or any of the other people at the top. I went to the steward and said, "I believe we both want the same thing—to help this place run better. I'd like to work with to you figure out how to do that."
> *(Personal communication, 2015)*

The former state official mentioned above stressed that every idea for legislation, every budget request, every position re-description, and every contract needed her authorization. Without being able to rely on her staff, "it would be impossible to conduct business"; delegation was a necessity. The upshot is that the executive control exerted by top appointees is not accomplished just by issuing orders. If it happens at all, it happens through effective working relationships (Chandler & Pratt, 2011, 35). As Treasury Secretary Henry Paulson said,

> You succeed in Washington by collaborating; you can't just think about your own agency, or your own goals. You have to please both sides of the aisle, while making sure you're not outshining other officials, and persuading employees who don't have to obey your orders.
> *(Duhigg, 2017, p. B1)*

In the political context, the private sector model of centralized control by means of numerical measures like return on investment appears rather a far cry from the nature of actual executive work in government. As one businessman with long appointive service in government put it, "Dollars aren't the measure of your performance." Another observed,

> If I sweated fat out of my [corporate] organization and increased productivity by 5 percent, I'd be a big man in my company. Here I could do that and be out of step with the secretary or a senator and get zinged every time.
>
> (Heclo, 1977, p. 202)

Many if not most policy objectives lend themselves very imperfectly to outcome measurement or to being understood as "bang for the buck." In many instances, only inputs (such as dollars appropriated) or levels of service (numbers of clients seen) submit to quantification. Thus, there is evidence to suggest that the appointed agency head can rely on numbers neither as sufficient measure of his or her own performance nor to bring the bureaucrats in his agency into line. On the other hand, as Andrew Bacevich (2016, p. 24) observes of the Pentagon, "While words and catchphrases may carry promises of sound decisions, good stewardship, and forward-looking change, it's where the money goes that matters."

What Do Political Appointees Know?

So far in our discussion, it appears that (1) career managers have a grip on pertinent technical knowledge as well as on familiarity with the situational dynamics of their agencies, a monopoly that protects them to a significant extent from control by temporary appointees; (2) the extent to which government appointees can, like leaders at GM or Ford, rely on numbers (such as performance measures) to expand or maintain their own power either internally or externally is at least variable. With these issues in mind, it seems fair to emphasize that public bureaucracies, despite their pyramidal shape, are open, rather than closed and monolithic systems.

We have already seen (in Chapter 3) that frontline work opens the bureaucracy to influence from outside. Arguably, the relative deficit of power at the bottom of the pyramid, where workers are at the lower end of the chain of command, may make openness at the bottom different from openness at the top. Heclo (1977) suggests that the knowledge of top executives is "craft knowledge," i.e. knowledge from experience. We saw that frontline workers and managers also amass and rely on knowledge from experience. We suggest that the power-knowledge dynamic unfolds differently at the top of the pyramid than it does at the bottom, even when workers and managers share with leaders at the top a reliance on experience. In other words, the public pyramid may be imperfectly rational, but power still accrues at the top.

The still widely accepted model of the executive was first offered by Chester Barnard (1966), who spent years as an executive at Western Electric. Barnard argued that the work of the executive was not the work *of* the organization itself (i.e. the kind of work done at the frontline and managed from the middle) but instead maintaining the organization so that it could work effectively. In his view, the functions (Barnard's word) of the executive were to ensure a system of communication throughout the organization, to promote the conditions that would produce effective effort, and to formulate and define the organization's purpose. He said that executive knowledge and skill was an art rather than a science, made up of developing and honing a "sense" of the organization, using (and risking) power in action, and fostering high morale by instilling into workers at lower levels commitment to the values of the organization (which the executive himself defined). As one former assistant secretary of a federal agency put it, "Good leadership here is often equated with being tough. [But] I … sense the amount of both support and resistance … from subordinates, peers, and superiors [in order to] direct people's energies toward my goals" (Cooper & Wright, 1992, p. 197). Barnard, too, emphasized the necessity of *sensing*—the times, the surrounding environment, the character of the personnel with which the executive surrounded him- or herself, and the importance of learning from ultimately unpredictable action. In other words, practicing an art rather than applying a science.

In a classic study, Matthew Holden (1966) called the executive decision-makers described above "administrative politicians," who have both the opportunity and the desire to take care of the well-being of their agencies. Holden suggested that the task of the administrative politician is achieving a favorable balance of constituencies, a constituency being any relevant group or interest, whether external or internal. Like Barnard, Holden sees this task as involving the calculation of explicit and implicit "decision rules"—though, despite terms like calculation and rule, implicit factors by definition must be judged rather than calculated. He notes that the ecology within which administrative politicians act is "a place of confusion and uncertainty, with false signals strewn about like dandelion seeds in an open meadow" (p. 950). What takes place upon this field of action is competition between constituencies: not simply a power struggle, though clearly it is that, but also a "process of clarification," which may "enhance the sense of reality and maintain the fluidity of choice which prevents serious error" (*ibid*.). In other words, Holden, like Barnard, sees executive knowledge as "knowledge of what is required": a form of skillful judgment (a "sixth sense") acquired and honed in the process of doing the executive work of taking care of the organization, which consists of attaining a favorable balance among constituencies (today's "stakeholders").

Norton Long saw this executive task in terms of power "flowing in from the sides of an organization," that is, horizontally (quoted in Durant, 2015, p. 208). For Long, the focus of the executive is on competitive challenges from other agencies; he sees this as a useful check on agency aggrandizement. The inflow of power horizontally, we note, is another mode of openness that tempers the pyramidal rationality of bureaucracy. As Durant suggests, however, the quest for horizontal power has been met by many forms of legislative resistance, including greater oversight, attempts to restrict the exercise of discretion, and most visibly perhaps, shrinking agency authority by transferring responsibility to private entities, through downsizing, devolution, outsourcing, and public-private partnership campaigns. The executive quest for power, then, means achieving a balance of interests that include other agencies, the legislature, interest groups, private entities, and the general public, all in a manner that furthers the mandated goals of the agency (as influenced by the executive him- or herself).

Thus, as Marshall Dimock observed decades ago, the executive strategy is a survival strategy, both for the individual and for his or her agency:

> The executive is a tactician and a philosopher. He [sic] must live by his wits, his competitive instincts, his understanding of social forces, and his ability as a leader. ... He must struggle openly for power and for survival. ... [T]he leadership of an organization ... involves a constant struggle against other wielders of power.
>
> (Dimock, 1952, p. 290)

Executives and Bureaucrats

Although much of the literature emphasizes outwardly directed strategy, a key competitor in the executive struggle for power is always the career bureaucracy. Max Weber believed that the only alternative to concentration of technical knowledge in the career managerial ranks was administration by dilettantes: "By definition, these officials are more knowledgeable and so more powerful than their superiors ... [potentially] usurping the rule-making or decision-making powers that ideally [derive] from the political and legislative process" (Bendix, 1960, p. 452).

We suggest that the power struggle between career bureaucrats and political appointees is essentially a contest between two forms of accountability, each of which is rooted in a different kind of knowledge. Early twentieth-century reformers argued that governing on the basis of scientific and technical knowledge is democratic because what citizens really want from government is that it should run well—effectively and efficiently. Once broad policies have been determined legislatively, the means of implementation can and should be calculated. Rational administration is neutral, objective, and therefore in the public interest. Accountability by career bureaucrats takes the form of *producing results*, rather than, say, consulting with citizens before acting to fix a neighborhood problem. In this light, career bureaucrats defend the legitimacy of their power on the basis of their professional expertise, which they claim is free of self-interest. What counts, politically, is what comes out at the end of the pipeline rather than the means by which it is produced. Professional knowledge, then, is a source of managerial power because the necessity for further defense is lightened or relieved. Scientific-technical expertise has no apparent partisan coloring. As a mayor of Cleveland once claimed, "There is no Republican or Democratic way to pick up the garbage." The ideology of public management is a power tool. At the executive level, the resort to numbers plays a similar but even more idealized role, aiming (but failing) to remove the executive entirely from the sometimes grubby competition for power.

On the other hand, *political* accountability takes a more active form, in recognition that the selection of administrative means is not as cut and dried as its defenders maintain; rather it requires the weighing of relevant factors and the exercise of judgment—a practice that then obliges administrators to give an active accounting. In this understanding, judgment permeates all levels of the bureaucracy, from top to bottom, and accountability means *giving an account* (or being prepared to) of the basis for one's actions, no matter where you are in the hierarchy or to whom you are responsible—an account that remains debatable and requires persuasion rather than proof. Yet the public executive's position at the top means that the decisions he or she is required to make are much more likely to be ones that affect the entire agency and are also more likely to be heeded within the bureaucratic ranks. As one executive interviewed in a study of policy implementation said to a manager: "I am for this (re)organization. I have looked at it and my judgment is excellent. If you don't like it, you have trouble with me" (Olshfski & Cunningham, 2008, p. 68).

This tug and pull between competing accountabilities is a major difference between public and private organizations. It is why President (formerly General) Eisenhower could bark orders, yet nothing might happen. Clearly, private organizations do not operate like machines, with all members marching in lockstep to executive commands. Chester Barnard (1966) understood this, and represented executive leadership as calculating the extent of employees' *zones of indifference*, to avoid giving an order that would be ignored. Yet public executive leadership does seem to be different from private, in that many more interests claim the right to judge what public agencies and their employees do and say. This makes balancing constituencies a vastly more complex undertaking in the public sector than in the private, requiring its own form of expertise.

What Is Executive Knowledge?

In a classic work, Paul Appleby described the unique mix of public executive capacities, all of which reflect aspects of a balancing act between administrative and political demands:

> Ability to *be governmental* enough to discern the national interest and to insist on programs and procedures so sound that they will be an unyielding rock on which the waves of special interest may break their force in vain; ability to *be political* enough to seek those concessions which are needed refinements

of the process of making governmental action equitable and smooth; ability to *be political* enough to read and respond to the messages of public currents; and ability to *use administrators* who can organize and relate agencies so that they produce organized integrated action ...

(Appleby, 1945, p. 44; emphases added)

Let's break this down a bit. The key executive abilities Appleby lists are "be governmental," "be political," and "use administrators." Each requires specific kinds of knowledge:

"Be governmental"	requires	discern national interest + insist on sound programs
"Be political"	requires	seek concessions + read and respond to the environment
"Use administrators"	requires	identifying personnel and processes for effective action

Interestingly, Appleby distinguishes being governmental both from being political and being able to mobilize administrators. Being governmental is fundamental: It entails developing a sense of the broader public interest and of the programs that will address them effectively. This overall capacity requires both political skill—knowing how to engage in compromise and to sense the situation, and administrative perspicacity—being able to enlist competent administrators in the design and accomplishment of implementation strategies. In this model, executive knowledge is political *and* administrative, and both contribute to the overall capacity to govern. The knowledgeable executive is one who meshes politics and administration in the service of the broader public interest as he or she understands it. Because every individual executive's understanding is by definition limited, he or she is both aided and checked by politics (e.g. legislatures, interest groups, the community) and by administration (the career bureaucracy). A further quote will illustrate—this time, from the former head of a state health agency:

> An increasingly demanding [executive] function is achieving a balance between professional/technical aspects of public health and the political environment in which public health must operate ... [M]y tenure as Director has been influenced by one crisis after another, created in large part by the political environment, budget cuts, and reduced capacity in the face of rising expectations ... the constant need to weigh political trade-offs inherent in taking stands on important issues: to decide how hard to push and the price ... to pay, either in substantive policy terms, or personally.
>
> *(Cooper & Wright, 1992, p. 179)*

Another example from the same volume is from a former head of the U.S. Environmental Protection Agency, whose abilities are described as:

> building legitimacy for institutions ... invigorating and liberating the energies of agencies ... creating an ethos and getting good people in place and motivated ... gaining the power and support to protect [the] ability to perform ... [building] the agency's identity ... [maintaining] a commitment to listen and learn from all sides...
>
> *(Cooper & Wright, 1992, p. 242)*

Again, this is a blend of political skills (building legitimacy, gaining power and support, listening to all sides) and administrative capacities (invigorating agencies, getting good people motivated).

A study of state-level executives (Olshfski & Cunningham, 2008) found that commissioners (agency heads) had two primary concerns: avoiding controversy and bad publicity, and implementing policies so that they would endure beyond the commissioner's own tenure. The blend of political and administrative skills necessary to succeed with these twin challenges reveals the forms executive knowledge takes:

1. Problem definition is a key interpretive activity. Situations are filled with competing definitions, and the executive is the one who must decide among them. One commissioner reported that she made the decision "when I had learned everything there was to be learned about it" (p. 68).
2. The decisive definition (interpretation) was influenced by:

    - the commissioner's previous professional experience ("Engineers see engineering problems, retailers see inventory problems") (p. 44)
    - the commissioner's previous experience in government, or lack of it
    - the risk of political exposure ("I was always scared to death that we would become a campaign issue"), the sensing of which requires knowledge of the agency and its environment (p. 46)
    - the need to get those who would implement the decision involved and agreeable ("you go through that process, educating and getting people to buy into the program"), which requires interactional skill (p. 70)
    - the desire to avoid controversy or bad publicity, which again entails sizing up the situation (we would call it judgment).

Commissioners were aware of their positional authority at the top of the bureaucratic pyramid and took advantage of it. They rarely sought advice from subordinates, preferring to consult predecessors, other commissioners, or friends. Although some reported "walking around" within the agency, they tended to find what they already saw, that is, they looked through whatever professional lens they brought with them. By and large they received their appointments because they had been successful managers, so they were confident of their ability to figure out situations and act. They had much more latitude than did middle managers in the study to choose the problems they would attend to.

For these executives, then, *knowing* the situations they encountered was shaped by their previous *experience*, including professional education and employment; by the extent to which, and the directions in which, they gathered *information* that would contribute to their knowing; by their ability to *sense* the decision environment in order to build support for what they came to "know" and reduce various risks their decision might impose on them and their agencies; and by the positional *power* they held, which gave them more freedom to make good on their definitions of problems and solutions. An executive has to hold all these factors in some sort of balance in order to know and to act—to interpret what elements really count and with what strength. These are the elements of political expertise.

Executive knowledge has elements in common, therefore, with both workers and managers. Like workers, executive *experience* matters. Its substantive content shapes what executives see and how they interpret it, including what they are likely to choose as a way forward. Unlike workers, however, they have a great deal more (though not unlimited) power to act as they see fit. Like managers, they have both a concern and a responsibility to see to it that policies and programs are implemented and sustained. But executives' responsibility to build external support and deal with political partisans requires them to give more deliberate attention than middle managers to party politics and publicity. And again, managers report to executives, rather than the reverse. All three—workers, managers, and executives—exercise judgment: that is, they size up situations and act accordingly if they can. The limitations (the "ifs"), however, are more numerous and more likely to be the kind that can't be ignored the lower down in the pyramid you work.

In contrast to both workers and managers, executives have decisive and visible responsibility for meshing politics and administration, for taking the big-picture view, and of course for the positional power they possess. They are the acknowledged leaders of their agencies, therefore their interpretations count in the pyramid-at-large in a way that those below them don't. They speak for their agencies as no one else can. Despite all the ways in which their power is checked, and these are significant, their place at the top of the organizational pyramid gives what they *know* about their agency, its environment, its problems, its capacities, its successes and failures, indeed its very identity, a singular force with which others must reckon. "The higher up the chain of command, the less dense the network of clearances needed to obtain a decision" (Olshfski & Cunningham, 2008, p. 91).

Yet this knowledge is brought to bear in an inherently ambiguous context. According to a recent study of executive decision-making, when public executives were asked to describe a significant decision, they cited not technically complex issues but ones where an unpopular choice was necessary, or ones that entailed personal, political, or organizational risk:

I had to go toe-to-toe with [the Office of Management and Budget] and say, "Absolutely not ... I don't care. You can fire me ..." Or: "I'm going to belly-smacker this thing, and it's either going to work really well or it's going to be really bad." Or: "Well, there were certainly a lot of people that thought we should continue [the program], but in the end, I mean, it was my call ..."

The researchers concluded that there has been too much stress on decision-making as a cognitive exercise, and not enough on the need to risk doing the right thing: "Executives need to be 'ambidextrous,' that is, able to do both" (Kelman, Sanders & Pandit, 2016, pp. 466–470). If cognitive connotes narrowly analytical, we agree. But perhaps not all of what executives know is how to analyze, or read the results of statistical studies. Having a feel for the situation and sizing up political support and opposition, we suggest, are forms of knowledge that underlie the necessarily ambidextrous executive's skillful practice. In this practice, politics and administration reach some sort of balance, if they ever do.

References

Appleby, Paul. 1945. *Big Democracy*. New York: Alfred A. Knopf.
Bacevich, Andrew. 2016. Who runs the Pentagon? *The Nation*, February 8.
Barnard, Chester. 1966. *The Functions of the Executive*. Cambridge, Mass. and London: Harvard University Press. Originally published 1938.
Bendix, Reinhard. 1960. *Max Weber: An Intellectual Portrait*. Garden City, N.Y.: Doubleday Anchor Books.
Chandler, Susan M., & Richard C. Pratt. 2011. *Backstage in a Bureaucracy: Politics and Public Service*. Honolulu: University of Hawai'i Press.
Cleveland, Frederick A. 1909. *Chapters on Municipal Administration and Accounting*. New York: Longmans, Green.
Cleveland, Frederick A. 1915. Evolution of the budgetary idea in the United States. *Annals of the American Academy of Political and Social Science* 62 (November), 15–35.
Cooper, Terry L., & N. Dale Wright (eds.). 1992. *Exemplary Public Administrators: Character and Leadership in Government*. San Francisco: Jossey-Bass.
Dimock, Marshall E. 1952. Expanding jurisdictions: A case study in bureaucratic conflict. Pp. 282–290 in *Reader in Bureaucracy* (eds. R.K. Merton, A.P. Gray, B. Hockey, & H.C. Selvin). New York: Free Press.
Duhigg, Charles. 2017. For Trump's picks, a billionaire guide to running the country. *New York Times* (January 19), B1,B7.
Durant, Robert. 2015. Whither power in public administration? Attainment, dissipation, and loss. *Public Administration Review* 75:2, 206–218.
Gane, Nicholas. 2004. *Max Weber and Postmodern Theory. Rationalization versus Re-enchantment*. New York: Palgrave MacMillan.
Hays, Samuel P. 1964. The politics of reform in municipal government in the Progressive era. *Political Science Quarterly* 80:3, 157–169.
Heclo, Hugh. 1977. *A Government of Strangers: Executive Politics in Washington*. Washington, D.C.: Brookings.

Heclo, Hugh. 1988. The in-and-outers: A crucial assessment. *Political Science Quarterly* 103:1, 37–56.
Holden, Matthew. 1966. "Imperialism" in bureaucracy. *American Political Science Review* 60:4, 943–951.
Hummel, Ralph P. 2006. The triumph of numbers: Knowledges and the mismeasure of management. *Administration & Society* 38:1 (March), 58–78.
Kelman, Steven, Ronald Sanders & Gayatri Pandit. 2016. "I won't back down?" Complexity and courage in government executive decision-making. *Public Administration Review* 76:3, 465–471.
Maranto, Robert. 2005. *Beyond a Government of Strangers: How Career Executives and Political Appointees Can Turn Conflict to Cooperation.* Lanham, Md.: Lexington Books.
McKinlay, Alan, & Ken Starkey. 1998. The 'velvety grip': Managing managers in the modern corporation. Pp. 111–125 in *Foucault, Management and Organization Theory* (eds. A. McKinlay & K. Starkey). London: Sage Publications.
Olshfski, Dorothy, & Robert B. Cunningham. 2008. *Agendas and Decisions: How State Government Executives and Middle Managers Make and Administer Policy.* Albany: State University of New York Press.
Phillips, Dave. 2018. V.A. doctors say rating push hurts patient care. *New York Times* (January 1), A1,A12.
Schiesl, Martin J. 1977. *The Politics of Efficiency: Municipal Administration and Reform in America, 1880–1920.* Berkeley, Calif.: University of California Press.
Stivers, Camilla. 2000. *Bureau Men, Settlement Women: Constructing Public Administration in the Progressive Era.* Lawrence, Kans.: University Press of Kansas.
Teaford, Jon C. 1984. *The Unheralded Triumph: City Government in America 1870–1900.* Baltimore: The Johns Hopkins University Press.
Weber, Max. 1947. *The Theory of Social and Economic Organization* (ed. T. Parsons). New York: Free Press.
Weber, Max. 1978. Politics as a vocation. Pp. 77–128 in *From Max Weber: Essays in Sociology* (eds. H. Gerth and C.W. Mills). New York: Oxford University Press.
Wiebe, Robert. 1967. *The Search for Order, 1877–1920.* New York: Hill and Wang.

PART II
The Pyramid in Action

6

THE VA CASE

Knowledge and Power in a Service Bureaucracy

In the winter of 2016, amid the blare of a national scandal over veterans' health services, U.S. Senator Jon Tester (D.-Mt.) sent his staff out to meet with veterans all over the state. Bobby Wilson, a Navy veteran of the Vietnam War, came to a session in the town of Superior to complain about trying to get his hearing aids repaired. "The VA can't do it in seven months, eight months? Something's wrong … Three hours on the phone … trying to get this thing set up …" Tony Lapinski, former Air Force mechanic, described waiting on the phone for answers from Health Net, a contractor the Veterans Administration had hired to help veterans. "You guys all know the Health Net piano? They haven't changed the damn elevator music in over a year!" Lapinski is concerned about a possible spinal problem; he worries that maybe he should be getting surgery or chemotherapy instead of sitting for months on the phone.

Health Net and another private contractor had been hired by the Veterans Administration to repair the appointments system that had become a national scandal. But the fix was not working. Vets were still spending hours on the phone, this time for referrals to private providers. Meanwhile, private hospitals, clinics, and doctors were waiting for payments. Some had stopped seeing VA patients ("Despite $10B 'fix,'" 2016).

At least part of the problem afflicting the VA administrative system had become clear. As this chapter will explore, studies had been done, hearings had been held, commissions had issued reports. But after two years, little seemed to have improved. Why?

This book's framework aims to understand the dynamics of public bureaucracies like the VA. Or as phenomenologists like to say, to let the things themselves—the meanings people make of their experiences—show themselves. While it does not set aside science, it treats the actual experiences and interpretations of organization members as a source of knowledge as valid and important as any (Hummel, 1991).

Part I laid out the different knowledges within public bureaucracies and made the case for the importance of hands-on, experiential knowledge. In public administration, most frameworks for studying organizations are intended to find answers to problems. Ours starts from the assumption that to tackle organizational troubles, or at least to expose their origins beyond the usual suspects, requires exploring how and why disparate knowledge frameworks or stances are fundamentally at odds. "Each not only fails to share a common set of referents with the others but claims superiority for its own axioms and thereby obscures and suppresses the functioning of other knowledges in their own domains" (Hummel, 2006, p. 61). This conflict runs deeper than personality clashes and competing interests, to root itself in the discontinuity of the different understandings people at different levels of the organization have of the organizational project they supposedly share.

To illustrate this approach, we offer the case of the U.S. Department of Veterans Affairs health service crisis, and the VA's efforts to respond to recent investigations and studies calling for institutional transformation. The case reveals a gulf in perceptions, knowledges, and understandings between the executive level and frontline workers, a gulf management has failed to span. Notably, the investigative reports and recommendations for reforming the VA take this gap for granted rather than calling it into question. We conclude that, behind the headlines, the real VA health service crisis is about different forms of knowledge. We examine how the differences are ignored and/or obscured in favor of oversimplifying the situation, neglecting the entanglement of knowledge and power, and calling for sweeping changes that are (in our judgment) unlikely to work. The public radio program quoted above hit the airwaves two years after the scandal regarding appointment wait times broke in the press. We see this as a sign that perhaps the usual responses to bureaucratic scandals could use—at the very least—an upgrade.

Based on our knowledge-based approach to understanding the situation, we argue that repairing the problems of the current VA health service cannot and should not be driven solely from the top down, since—as the case reveals—the top literally does not know and does not understand the state of affairs at the service delivery level. Indeed, it can be fairly said that the top *seems not to want to know*, preferring to cling to clichés like "more leadership" and to impose sweeping concepts on deeply complicated problems. We point to the current trajectory of reforms, which adopts a "systems" focus that assumes it is possible somehow to balance or integrate macro-level standardization and micro-level flexibility. This assumption, by ignoring the gap between two mutually exclusive understandings, sets them more firmly at odds with one another. Instead of figuring out how knowledges and/or the practices to which they are tied can be productively interwoven, the system perspective forces the VA toward a false choice between reform (actually, more of the same) and radical surgery—i.e., privatization of major service components.

The case description and interpretation are based on documentary review of several investigations and studies, as well as on participant observation by one of the authors (Carnevale, a disabled and decorated combat veteran of the Vietnam War), who has experienced the crisis in the VA first hand. In addition to being a user of VA health services, he has served as consultant to the Voices for Veterans Council in the greater Denver area hospital; as member of the newly created Veterans Research Engagement Board for Colorado; as chair of the Voices for Vets Council; and, finally, as appointee to the planning group for the 2015 annual Summit. Particularly in this latter capacity, he has experienced first-hand the imposition of top-level cognitive frameworks on local-level understandings.

The discussion draws on investigations and studies conducted in the wake of the scandal, including reports by the VA Inspector General, the Government Accountability Office (GAO), and an "independent assessment" led by the MITRE Corporation. The state of affairs in Denver underscores the difficulties service-level understandings have in coming to terms with frameworks imposed from the top, as well as how those at the top miss opportunities at the front line for real reform. We hope that our interpretation sheds light on aspects and sources of the crisis that are not otherwise visible.

The knowledge approach "takes apart an organization's whole knowledge structure in search of the distribution and actions of knowledges and power. It thus offers a knowledge-conflict explanation for the recurrent failures in the giving and taking of orders endemic in modern organizations" (Hummel, 2006, p. 62). It is a type of analysis that attempts to show the processes and practices by which organizational truth and knowledge are produced: what kinds of practices tied to what external conditions have the effect of producing and sustaining what kinds of knowledges. It starts from the bedrock assumption that all human beings "know," that is, they take up various stances toward being in the world. There is not one stance, but many.

The aim of the knowledge approach is to look closely at the distinctive knowledge-producing and sustaining stances at different levels of the organization. The point is to uncover how various knowledges produce truths, and truths in turn produce and sustain norms of behavior. These norms are the source of different resources and types of power. The research proceeds by examining what people are actually doing and saying, pointing out the patterns and where they come from, as well as the results for the organization's structure and dynamics of power.

The knowledge approach aims to unveil the knowledge-based conditions that produce and sustain organizational structures and dynamics. It concentrates on what is actually going on, in particular how the knowledges gained in direct contact with the work get controlled and subjugated from the top down. Michel Foucault, for whom power and knowledge were two sides of the same coin, cited examples of what to look for in actual organizational practices, including the suppression of "little" (e.g., hands-on, situational, tacit) knowledges in favor of synthesizing concepts; normalizing certain kinds of knowledge (e.g., "best practices"); making a value hierarchy of knowledges (e.g., science is the only truth); concentrating knowledge control at the top (orders go down, content flows up) (Foucault, 2003, pp. 180–181).

For our project, we not only strive to document practices, knowledges, truths, and norms, but to raise the issue of how a public organization gets to be what it is, historically and in terms of contemporary practices that maintain the discontinuities between knowledges and accrue power differentials. The point of employing the knowledge approach is to find out how to do what Foucault (1984) said is possible: in what is given to us as inevitable, how is it possible to think and act differently?

The National Scandal

The U.S. Department of Veteran Affairs (VA) oversees the largest health care delivery system in the United States, with more than 1,700 facilities of various kinds and a workforce of more than 300,000 employees. It serves more than eight million veterans each year and is experiencing an upsurge in demand from waves of veterans returning from Iraq and Afghanistan, as well as the growing needs of aging veterans of the Vietnam War. It is a $150+ billion enterprise in crisis, as the result of charges stemming from mismanagement over the past several years: excessive wait times for appointments, accusations of fraud in manipulating performance indicators, marginal levels of workforce morale, lack of trust on the part of veterans, and loss of confidence among members of Congress and the President.

Long-simmering problems finally hit the national headlines. The scandal erupted at the VA Center in Phoenix, Arizona in 2013. Whistleblowers, starting with Dr. Katherine Mitchell and Dr. Sam Foote, accused the hospital administration of "cooking the books" on veteran wait time for appointments, particularly first appointments (Bronstein & Griffin, 2014; Wagner, 2014). They charged that appointment schedules were being manipulated to give the false impression that wait times were reasonable and responsive to veteran needs, when in reality they were not. The whistleblowers blamed the health service center for the deaths of veterans as the result of over-long wait times for appointments. This charge in particular caught the attention of stakeholders and the general public with direct or indirect interest in the status of VA operations.

A VA inspector general's report documented efforts by administrators at the Phoenix branch to manipulate appointment waiting lists, and triggered widened investigations by the VA and the Defense Department. The head of a group made up of veterans of Iraq and Afghanistan declared, "This is not the first scandal. If you weren't outraged [before Phoenix] you weren't paying attention."

The inspector general's investigation found medical records documenting hundreds of patient deaths while awaiting care. A review of more than 500,000 emails and 140,000 network files on encrypted computers turned up details of the massive cover-up of wait list delays. Administrators were keeping two wait lists, an official one that met federal performance standards and a secret one that supposedly kept track of those not on the official list. The report noted that meeting or exceeding federal standards is "one of the factors considered for awards and salary increases" (Munoz, 2014, n.p.).

A national audit reported that 13 percent of VA appointment schedulers said they had been pressured to falsify appointment requests, and schedulers at 90 clinics said improving performance measures was the reason (Peralta, 2014). In Colorado, it was discovered that 3,000 vets were unable to change their appointment times. One nurse-practitioner had a thousand-member caseload. A staffer told David Carnevale that, overall, the Denver VA placed within the bottom ten percent in a comparative study of wait times nationwide.

Members of Congress expressed outrage at the national charges, demanded explanations, held hearings, and aggressively questioned then-VA secretary, Eric Shinseki. After meeting with Shinseki, President Obama accepted his resignation. The President selected a new leader for the VA from the private sector, who promised transformation in the VA health care system.

Several investigations looked into the situation (NVTC, 2014; MITRE Corp., 2015; GAO, 2016; Commission on Care, 2016). Among other discoveries, these probes found that only one high-ranking official in all the nation's VA centers had received a performance rating of less than fully satisfactory over the previous four years, while hundreds of his compatriots in other centers received the highest possible rating. In each rating period these top staffers received repeated bonuses for outstanding service, despite the persistence of unacceptably high appointment wait times.

Scheduling was not the only problem, however, either in the system as a whole or in Denver. Investigations found that the VA had a corrosive culture, a sclerotic bureaucracy, low employee morale, and a lack of innovation. They also found a greatly increased service load without a matching increase in resources. Added on to the steadily growing need for services among aging Vietnam veterans was a quantum leap in demand as vets returning from Iraq and Afghanistan sought help with an array of serious problems. This was a challenge the VA could not meet with existing resources. Veterans with post-traumatic stress disorder (PTSD) and traumatic brain injuries (TBIs) from enemy explosive devices had particularly acute need for skilled treatment, a need that was not being met with adequate response.

The neglected questions raised by the findings were these: if the VA culture was as toxic as the report charged, and its system as strangulated and resistant to innovation, would simply adding more staff resources be enough? Would executive leaders who had been regularly rewarded with cash bonuses and top performance ratings be spurred by the revelations not just to do some "cover your anatomy" work but to take seriously the need for fundamental change?

Down the Line

As David Carnevale's participant observations found, it is almost a cliché that when whistleblowers on or near the service front line reveal festering problems, leaders—especially if they are regularly rewarded for business as usual—tend to see the complaints as disloyalty. Co-workers who agree with the whistleblower may still turn their backs on the whistleblower, or even attack them for embarrassing the agency.

Consider the following examples (Clark, 2015):

Mark Tello, a nursing assistant with the VA Medical Center in Saginaw, Michigan, told his supervisor that management was not adequately staffing the Center, and that this could result in serious patient care problems. In response, Tello was threatened with termination and ultimately suspended. When a facilitated settlement was negotiated and Tello placed in a new position and awarded back pay, the VA again threatened termination.

Richard Hill, a primary care physician at a Maryland facility reported misuse of patient care funds. He demanded that his unit be assigned additional clerical support staff he argued were necessary for better patient care. Dr. Hill was reprimanded for speaking out and forced to retire in 2014. A settlement agreement specified that his personnel record be cleared of negative findings.

Rachel Hogan, a registered nurse, disclosed a patient's rape to higher ups and warned of the need to address the situation in a timely manner. Later, she complained of a nurse colleague falling asleep twice while on duty, once while sitting with a suicide-watch patient. She charged another superior with sexual harassment. She was forced before a review board and given an unsatisfactory performance rating. Eventually she received another assignment and an improved rating.

Coleen Elmers, a nurse manager in Spokane, Washington, who filed a complaint about a fraudulently altered performance evaluation of one of her subordinates, was rated unsatisfactory. Investigation into this situation continues.

And from Lisa Rein (2015):

Troy Thompson, who reported that the kitchen at the facility where he worked was infested with flies and pests, was reassigned to the janitorial staff.

Ryan Honl reported that vets were being overly medicated with prescription opiates and were developing addiction problems. He was removed from duty and locked out of his office shortly afterward.

Joseph Colon-Christensen reported that his boss had been arrested for drunk driving and drug possession. He was fired.

The findings of at least two investigations cited above (MITRE, 2015; GAO, 2016) can be traced to whistleblowing on the part of frontline service providers, including physicians, who brought the problems to light. For their actions, the system response was rarely, if ever, gratitude for valuable information; rather, quite the opposite.

The Section 201 Independent Assessment and Systems Thinking

Section 201 of the Veterans Access, Choice, and Accountability Act of 2014, passed in the wake of the scandal, called for an independent assessment of VA health care services. Conducted by the MITRE Corporation, the Institute of Medicine, and several subcontractors, the study did multiple interviews and surveys, reviewed documents and data sets, and visited 87 VA sites. The study team also interviewed private sector health care executives and organized a "Blue Ribbon Panel" of experts, in order to gain information about "best practices."

The independent assessment is notable for its scope and thoroughness. The Integrated Report (which summarizes findings and recommendations on twelve aspects of the VA health care system, or VHA) reflects a thorough-going effort to examine both the big picture and fine-grained detail, in order to arrive at a "holistic understanding of VHA" (MITRE, 2015, p. xi). The researchers also *reviewed 137 previous assessments of the VHA conducted between 1998 and 2015*. The report notes that many of its own recommendations underscore previous findings; it emphasizes, however, that the unique value of the Integrated Report lies in taking a *systems approach* to understanding how the VA works and what must be done to transform (*sic*) it. The existence of so many previous examinations, all pointing to the same or similar problems as the ones that triggered the current crisis, should give any concerned person pause. There seems to be a structural gap between urgent recommendations and institutional action. One might wonder how a "systems" approach will be different.

The report declares that the VHA must adopt a systems perspective in order to understand how performance varies from site to site, aggregate site-level findings to understand the system as a whole, and still retain "local granularity." The report continues: "Systems thinking views problems within the context of the overall system and avoids isolated solutions to specific problems. It takes into account the interdependencies of the parts to find the best combination of strategies that meet the needs of the whole" (MITRE, 2015, p. 13).

From the perspective of this book, the preemptive adoption of a systems framework is worth noting. For one thing, according to the reference cited in the report, systems theory "is a discipline for seeing the whole ... for seeing interrelationships and repeated events rather than things, ... patterns of change rather than static snapshots" (Frank, 2000, p. 164). The report *assumes* that "system" is a name for the way parts and whole are interrelated, and that by taking a systems stance we can encompass both static and dynamic elements.

As is well known, systems thinking, in public organizations as in the private sector, assumes that to understand an organization one should begin not with its purposes, as they exist in law or in the minds of their founders and leaders, but rather with input, output, and functioning. In other words, regardless of what it is intended to do, the organization is something like an organism with an ongoing feedback loop in which energy comes into the system, is transformed within the system, and results in some sort of output, whether a product or a service. "System" is a metaphor for "organization," or, in Morgan's (1997) terms, it is an "image" (see Chapter 2). In a systems perspective, one's attention is drawn to the macro-level balance between input and output, and to the survival of the organization as a result. Katz and Kahn (1966), pioneering organizational systems theorists, stress the value of the theory in highlighting the importance of the relationship between the organization and its environment. It follows, they argue, that it is crucial to view the organization as an *open* system, that is, as an entity the survival of which depends on constant awareness of and responses to changes in its environment.

Given the definitive managerial interest in "systematizing," which predates by several decades the birth of systems thinking in the 1940s (see Chapter 4), it is no wonder managers have little trouble thinking within a systems framework. And indeed, its holistic perspective has considerable value. From our perspective, though, the Integrated Report's adoption of systems thinking raises questions. For one thing, the report takes it for granted that system is THE way to think about an organization. No alternatives are even raised to be rejected. The implicit choice seems to be, either system or chaos. Second, there is no thought given to what is entailed in following through on the major recommendation that stems from maintaining a systems perspective: that is, improve system performance while still maintaining local flexibility. Local flexibility is seen as an *aspect of the system*. As such, in order to be an asset to the system it has to be "scalar"—that is, it has to have the potential to be *enlarged, replicated*. Nowhere in the report is the necessity for scalability justified. It is assumed to be a good thing (as is systems thinking itself).

If the present knowledge approach is brought into play, however, these questions can no longer be taken for granted. If what frontline workers learn from being in direct contact with the work does not take *conceptual* form of the "scalar" sort required in order to think in terms of "systems," its value is assumed to be nil. The extent to which experiential-situational learning is "scalar" or "replicable" is a question impossible even to raise because the systems conceptual framework does not recognize that it exists. By emphasizing inputs, outputs, and macro-level functioning, the systems perspective—when it is not enriched by other angles of approach—makes it impossible to factor in the knowledges, understandings, judgment, experiences, and values of the human beings (individuals and groups) who make up the system. At some point, we argue, these human factors have to be taken into account.

Making an Appointment

Given that the catalyst that sparked the entire scandal was the charges leveled by whistleblowers at appointment wait times and scheduling issues, it is worth zeroing in on this level of the problem. Let's consider what is involved in setting up an appointment for a new patient. This process was studied in depth in 2014, soon after the scandal over waiting times erupted, at two VA facilities in Virginia (NVTC, 2014). The report described and offered a flow chart of the process (Figure 6.1).

In what follows we quote excerpts from the report description and add comments to bring attention to the knowledges in play. Our point is simply to show how non-mechanical—how *non-systematic*—the appointment process actually is and *has to be* in order to be responsive to individual patients. The geometric clarity of the flow chart does not show this, and discretionary human action does not appear on the chart, yet is crucial to making the process work. The flow chart is intended as a conceptual summary of what actually happens, but it leaves out the in-the-moment judgments that have to be made in order to deal with the many uncertainties that arise. Bracketed material below is represented on the new appointment flow chart but not spelled out in the narrative description. Our comments appear in italics.

- "A new patient requests to receive medical service [by phone or in person] at the primary care clinic. The Enrollment Clerk (EC) receives the request and determines [by what the patient says] if the patient requires urgent care." *How exactly does the EC interpret what the patient says? Does the EC ask whether the need is urgent? Is the patient likely to say "no" given the typical wait times? What are the rules of thumb the EC uses in order to judge urgency? What have previous experiences taught the EC about how to respond?*
- "If the patient does require urgent care and is present at the facility, the patient is sent for Triage. Based on the [Triage] diagnosis [*same interpretive judgment needed as above*], (1) the patient is sent for immediate treatment because the care need is urgent, (2) the patient is sent back to the enrollment department to make an appointment because the care needed is not urgent, or (3) patient is released because care is not needed." *What have previous experiences taught the Triage people about the fall-out from these options? Is it "easier" just to go ahead and treat, or will this action be questioned up the line as an unnecessary expenditure? What if people are already filling the waiting room? Will an EC who sent a patient to Triage really tell someone who returns not having received care that he or she does not need an appointment? How do Triage and EC actually handle a request for urgent care? What are their experience-based rules of thumb?*

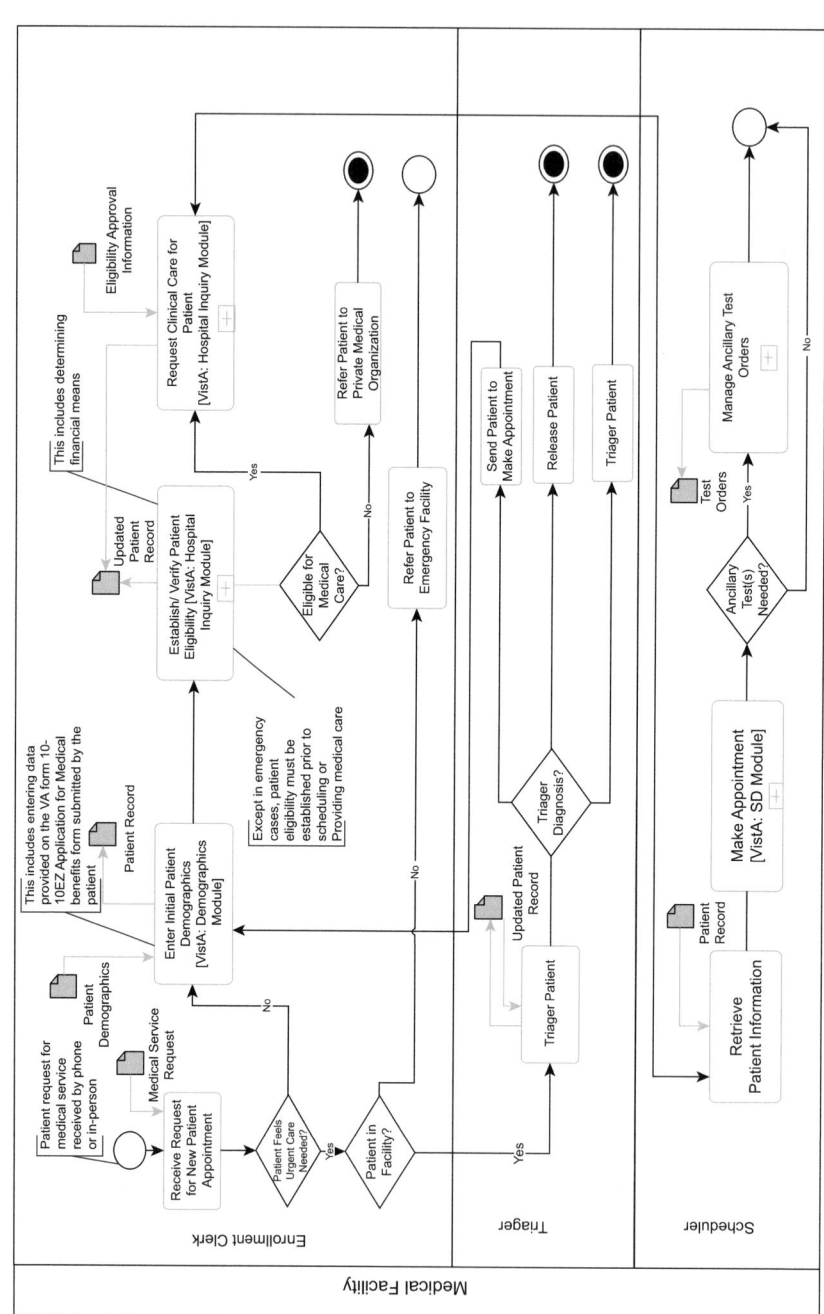

FIGURE 6.1 Flow chart, appointment process for new patient. Source: Northern Virginia Technology Council [NVTC], *Opportunities to Improve the Scheduling of Medical Exams for America's Veterans* (2014).

- "If the patient on the telephone *sounds* in need of urgent care [*How does this sound? Will different ECs make the same determination?*], the scheduler directs the patient to go to the nearest medical facility for care. If the patient does not require an urgent care [*sic*], the EC, which at some facilities also may be the scheduler, enters the patient's initial demographic information and verifies the eligibility of medical care for the patient. If the patient is ineligible to receive medical care at the VA facility, the EC refers the patient to a private medical organization where he/she can receive medical treatment." *Imagine someone acting as both EC and scheduler doing both at once—looking up the patient record, entering information, answering the phone, putting people on hold, telling someone they are ineligible, checking how many people are waiting in line, etc. What kinds of skills are needed in order to do this complicated work? What has experience taught this person about how to handle these multiple functions simultaneously?*
- "If the patient is eligible to receive medical care at the VA facility, the EC requests clinical care for the patient." *It is not clear from the flow chart what is meant by "requests." However, it seems to entail looking through various providers to see which one has an open appointment slot. What does the scheduler know about the different providers? Is the choice automatic, i.e. the first one on the list that has an opening? What kind of judgment comes into play here?* "The scheduler, then, retrieves the patient's information and makes appointment." *The EC, if a different person, has already done this. How do the two coordinate, if they do?* "After an appointment is scheduled, the scheduler determines if any ancillary tests are needed prior to the actual appointment. If so, the scheduler proceeds to schedule necessary ancillary tests for the patient." *How does the scheduler determine the need for tests? Presumably a diagnosis has not been confirmed. Is there a protocol in place on which to base a decision at this point? Just how does a scheduler, who is a clerical rather than medical employee, determine the need for medical tests? Suppose Lab or Radiology are backed up? What skills does the scheduler employ to sort out this potentially complex situation? What has previous experience taught them?* "If no ancillary tests are required the scheduler ends the process."
- "For a specific clinic, the scheduler checks the providers' calendars for availability and capacity in an effort to schedule an appointment within a specified time frame." *How is the time frame "specified?" By whom*? "If a slot is available within the required time frame, the scheduler, then, proceeds to contact the patient and coordinates with the patient concerning their preferences regarding travel and appointment time. If the patient agrees to the identified appointment, their information is entered into the appropriate time slot. Then, the patient is notified of their scheduled appointment. If there is no time slot available within the desired time frame, the patient is added to the Electronic Waiting List (EWL) and their information is entered into the best available time slot. Then, the patient is notified of their appointment information." *Given the complexity here, how much choice about times and distance is the patient likely to have? What are the consequences for the scheduler of adding one*

more patient to the EWL? What skills come into play through which the scheduler makes a judgment about how to balance the patient's needs for a prompt appointment with the lack of available time slots?

The above description, which is already complex, is just the tip of the iceberg. Similar protocols are described (and flow-charted) for scheduling specialty appointments, rescheduling appointments, bundling a particular patient's appointments, cancelling appointments, calling the patient to schedule an appointment, setting up ancillary tests (at this point it is specified that only a provider can order a test), and so on.

The scheduler study leaves at least two impressions. The first is how difficult, how complex, is the job of a scheduler and/or enrollment clerk, given all the choice points in the process; the official rules may be clear but how to follow them cannot be, yet "how" makes all the difference. (As the philosopher Immanuel Kant once said, there is no rule for following a rule.) It seems foolhardy to impose rational protocols on this complex assignment without understanding how actual human beings handle them or what they learn from trying. The second is how rich a trove of hard-learned experiential knowledge lies in the minds and bodies of the people who do these jobs. How do they assess the factors they face at each choice point? What have they learned from pursuing various options, including "make-dos" and "work-arounds"?

Given that judgment must be called into play at each turn in the flow chart, and given (since people are not robots) that judgment by its nature cannot be controlled in the way that the "system" would like to control it, how does an organization make the most of the knowledge and judgment that frontline people have amassed? This is not to say that they routinely, to a person, make the "right" choices. Rather, it is to suggest that unless the executives and experts at the top are willing to assess the frontline openly, non-punitively, and with respect for the work, the VA will never be "transformed." This means that reform needs to be approached inductively, from the ground up, rather than deductively, from the top down, beginning with the recommendation of a systems approach as if it were, on its face, the obvious best choice. It may, indeed, be that frontline workers know things that would help. Someone needs to ask them and involve them in the process of deciding how to move forward.

The Commission on Care Report

The same 2014 legislation that authorized the Independent Assessment (IA) also provided for a Commission on Care (ConC) (2016) to do its own review, based on the results of the IA as well as its own series of site visits, discussion groups, data review, and so on. The ConC issued its report in June, 2016. In most respects it echoed the IA, but it is worth its own look.

Like its predecessor, the ConC speaks the language of system. It describes the current situation in terms that are very close to the rhetoric of President Bill Clinton's National Performance Review in the 1990s, which announced that the federal governance problem was good people trapped in bad systems. In the case of the ConC Report, the finding is that in general the quality of the care the VHA delivers is as good as any in the private sector, but its quality is compromised by access (the most glaring problem), service delivery, operating systems and processes. Recommendation #1 of the ConC Report calls for a system of "high-performing, integrated community-based health care networks, to be known as the VHA Care System." This recommendation, the report says, is called for because the existing system is unable to cope with challenges such as:

> changing veteran demographics, increasing demand for VHA care in some markets, and declining demand in other markets, more veterans being adjudicated as having service-connected conditions, aging facilities, provider shortages and vacancies, and other factors. VHA faces a misalignment of capacity and demand that threatens to become worse over time. … [I]n high demand areas, VHA often lacks the capacity to avoid lengthy wait times and other access issues.
>
> *(ConC, 2016, p. 23)*

We note: A *misalignment of capacity* redirects the focus away from poor performance, including poor management, whether by human beings, machines (e.g. computers), or the system at large. "*Flawed* capacity" might capture inadequate performance, but misalignment connotes that capacity doesn't match demand—that is, the basic problem is *not enough resources*. The report notes that a temporary fix (the Choice Program), authorized by the 2014 legislation allowing greater use by certain veterans of other sources of health care, including private-sector ones, has been flawed both in design and implementation. (Note: The Choice Program is the precursor of the Health Net problem that opened this chapter.) Hence the need for a redesign of the entire system. This first among recommendations, like all of them, is justified on the basis that the situation calls not for "small scale fixes to finite problems," but rather, for "a bold transformation of a complex system that will take years to fully realize but that our country must undertake" because veterans deserve no less. Another recommendation calls for the establishment of a Governing Board to set up a strategy for transforming the system, oversee the transformation, and build a "leadership team." Again, like the IA, the ConC Report is overwhelmingly a top-down approach.

True, both the IA and the ConC Report are the result of considerable efforts to get input from VA employees and veterans, among a wide range of stakeholders. This is commendable, but the hitch from our perspective (as well as a citizen participation perspective) is that people who offer input still have no control or influence over how the input is transformed into policy and strategy (see Foley, 1998). Despite all the rhetoric about transformation, boldness, and so on, no system works well without taking into account the actual work that has to be done at the front lines and elsewhere to make the system go the way leaders and decision-makers want it to. One has only to look at the dozens of previous studies and investigations of the VA and the lists of recommendations going back decades to wonder what happened to all that systematizing and boldness. The statement that it will take "years to fully realize" the ConC Report recommendations is simply a forecast that in a few years there will be another scandal, more reports, and more calls for system transformation—that is, unless concrete steps are taken to build transformation starting from the ground up rather than the top down

The Summit in Denver

In the wake of investigations into VA health care operations, regional hospitals across the country were directed to hold a one-day "Summit" meeting in 2015 to engage with stakeholders. This type of response on the part of an organizational system in crisis is often characterized by specialists in organizational change as "taking the baby's temperature." It is a way to assess the status of the system at a particular point in time, leaving open the question of what if any transformations or reforms will happen as a result. The engagement of stakeholders enables those responsible for change to hear directly from those who use the services and other interested parties, to address from their point of view how the system is currently functioning, what it does best and worst, what needs improvement. In other words, a summit is a form of the well-known strategic planning process, relying on analysis of strengths, weaknesses, opportunities, and threats.

In Denver, the group appointed to plan the summit reflected diverse interests, including staff, veterans, and community members. A large group of participants from the national VA participated. From the outset, the national VA wanted subsidiaries to use the summits to deal with issues that the executive level had *already identified* as of special concern. This starting point, i.e. what national-level executives were most interested in, was biased from the beginning. The most serious issues and problems were already determined before the Denver summit began.

Documents were sent from the central office directing regional facilities as to what steps they should take in putting together the summit sessions (see Attachment, p. 138). The form that centers were given reflects intent from the top to discipline the meetings by drawing boundaries around the planning: what was expected and permitted to be said, making it impossible for stakeholders to give voice in their own words to key problems as they saw them. Such paperwork, developed in isolation from local offices and distributed without local feedback, not only restricts what stakeholders can say, it also sends the clear message about what will and will not be listened to and the format in which it will be taken seriously. This is not to suggest that the national way of dealing with the summits was a *deliberate* effort to constrict the dialogue, although that cannot be ruled out. Deliberate or not, the designated model guaranteed that no new intelligence would be elicited—new in the sense of content not fitting within established executive and managerial perspectives.

Among the Denver group of veterans convened to plan the Summit there (of which Carnevale was a member), the reaction to top-down directives was that they were completely "bureaucratic" and a "not so thinly veiled threat" aimed at those who wanted to be more creative. The already-structured approach from the top seemed not to allow people from the frontline ranks to decide what they wanted to do at the Summit. There seemed to be no room for direct questions to be discussed about that particular hospital. The event seemed to foreclose any chance for *mea culpas* on the part of local staff and no room for the expression of experiential information rather than measurable data. The entire directive seemed to the local group to be out of touch with what ordinary staff and patients face. There would be no expression of fine-grained observations and deeper meanings, no place for negotiations or for recognizing how power influences how services are delivered.

To the Denver vet-and-local-staff planners, the top-down directives reflected lack of trust in their ability to figure out how to define issues, involve the community, fill the room on the day of the Summit, and interact productively. Local staff had local connections and could involve them in planning the event. Not to allow that in a grounded way treated local leaders, they felt, like children.

From our perspective, the executive approach to fact-finding, reflected in the design of the Summit process, is evidence of inability (or unwillingness) to bridge the gulf between the bird's eye view from the executive suite, with its macro focus and interest in measurable results that will please external critics, and the hands-on view from the front lines. Hands-on workers, whether nurses' aides, appointment clerks or physicians, have constantly to cope on the job with unforeseen or never-encountered situations. Clearly both views are important, as is the in-between view of managers, who should be cognizant of the need to sort, analyze, and convey patterns and trends up the chain of command without losing the fine-grained intelligence that can only be gathered at the "street level." Giving institutional preference to the executive level means not only that workers' voices are going to be limited to approved topics, but that executives will seldom if ever find out what is actually going on outside the conceptual boxes they have pre-emptively created.

The overly structured approach to the Summits cut off touch with the know-how of frontline staff as well as with the community connections that vary from region to region. No frank questions from interested parties were allowed, and no local variations in the design of the summit were permitted. Concern about controlling input so that it can be quantified takes priority, while the *quality* and *significance* of individual experiences (staff, patient, and community member) is lost. There is no place for negotiations to occur, and certainly no awareness of the importance of perspectives and experiences at different levels of the organization and among differing interests. The message to those below is that only the executive level has the capacity to think through how a summit should go. Based on Carnevale's participant observations, the implicit message to participants as they saw it was, we don't trust you to figure out how to define issues and draw on your knowledge of the local community. The interest in compiling data from different branches of the VA obliterated the observations to which the Denver group wanted to call attention.

Despite the national level strategy, in Denver a segment the local group inserted, dealing with the crisis in suicides, drew on community members as resources to design that session. The local planning team identified questions to kick off the discussion and ways to make the session as interactive as possible.

Where to Go from Here

President Obama opposed privatization of the VHA, as does the largest union representing VA workers, the American Federation of Government Employees, and the largest veteran service organizations: for example, Disabled American Veterans, the American Legion, organizations that represent Vietnam veterans and those that represent veterans of wars in Iraq and Afghanistan. As this book was being completed, the situation did not look promising (Philipps, 2018). The current director of the Veterans Health Organization promised to heed investigation recommendations, simultaneously claiming that many were already in place within the system. Surveys of veterans regularly document high regard for VHA service quality, and VA employees show a high level of commitment to providing excellent health care. But there is no other system comparable to the VA health system, and veterans are deeply dependent on it, so the basis of such evaluations is tenuous.

The fate of the VA under the Trump administration is murky, but as of early 2018, Secretary David Shulkin was forced to resign because (he claimed) of pressure to privatize VA health services from appointed officials within the department and from outside. Concerned Veterans for America, an advocacy group backed by the billionaire Koch brothers, was pushing to expand the participation of private providers. According to a press report, "Koch-funded efforts have already succeeded in disrupting the consensus-driven veterans community, where policy discussions have long been dominated by congressionally chartered veterans groups" like the Veterans of Foreign Wars and the American Legion. These old-line groups generally support the Choice program and the need for improved administration (Fandos, 2017, n.p.).

No matter who heads the executive branch or sits at the top of the VA pyramid, competing knowledges at diverse levels that make up the VA health system have power implications. To them must be added the political and economic context surrounding the system, including the president, Congress, unions, private service providers, lobbyists, and rank-and-file veterans themselves. Employees are weary of invidious comparisons with the private sector, particularly those that praise it with little or no evidence that it better serves veterans. Most veterans fear transfer of authority to the private sector, the effects of which are currently unknown.

The knowledge approach encourages awareness of the assumptions, particularly those that routinely go unexamined, which underlie any knowledge base. It cautions against acting on the basis of stereotypes about who knows what, and which knowledge should take the lead in dealing with organizational situations and problems. Phenomenology, the philosophical base of the knowledge approach, asserts the value of frontline knowledge that can neither be completely captured nor fully controlled in managerial abstractions and executive commands. Its perspective consciously avoids quick fixes and sweeping generalizations, particularly those remote from where the work is actually performed.

An institution of the size and complexity of the VA is difficult to reform in any sense, but from our perspective massive change efforts imposed from the top are especially likely to have little or no positive effect. Respect for the value of worker knowledge—no matter the size of the organization—leads toward tentative, iterative, fine-grained problem identification and experimentation with small-scale strategies. As we will discuss in Part III, these processes and strategies are circular rather than pyramidal, and offer a logic of reasonableness that tempers linear rationality. Reasonableness suggests that reform must proceed carefully, with attention to the micro level in a myriad of local situations, none of which is exactly like any other. Executives can best serve the VA (indeed any organization) by creating the conditions under which it can *learn* to perform better, starting with decentralized processes designed with the participation of workers, processes that slowly amass experience-based evidence of what works and what doesn't. No more summits are needed that overrule and overpower local staff and local conditions, and that place the goal of service to veterans below commitment to abstractions like a system view.

SEQUEL: BOTTOM UP AT THE VA—THE ENGAGEMENT BOARD

As commissions and other groups studied the U.S. Department of Veterans Affairs and published reports on the crisis, all was not static in the world of practice. Bureaucratic realities and especially bureaucratic practices do not hold still, awaiting the arrival of approved official recommendations. While top-down agendas received important and relevant attention at the national office of the VA, encouraging examples of a "street-level" trend were emerging in the many VA hospitals around the country. One such response serves as an initial answer to the question, "Well, are there any examples of bottom-up programming that are worthy of note as counterforce to the top-down tendencies of the agency?" We can answer in the affirmative.

This sequel to the VA case describes an initiative, an "Engagement Board" at the Denver VA Hospital, that exemplifies what we consider best practices within the bureaucracy: circular actions that generate power up the chain of command, transparency, and veterans' direct involvement at the local level. What results is respect for down-the-line knowledge in VA policy development. Not only, then, is what follows a sequel to the VA crisis as the case described it. It also sounds the overture to Part III, in which we expand on circular perspectives and practices, many of them already at work in public organizations, which if acknowledged and strengthened can temper the linear rationality of classic bureaucracy with the "logic of reasonableness" (Hummel, 1983; Hummel, 1989).

The account that follows is based on David Carnevale's observations as a participant member of the Denver Engagement Board.

Origin of the Initiative

In the Denver VA Hospital, the idea of creating an "engagement board" started among professional staff members in departments of innovation administration and suicide prevention. Right away, this is interesting because the catalyst comes simultaneously from a management-oriented unit ("innovation") and one devoted to a high-priority area of service delivery ("suicide prevention"). As one participant emphasized, "Credit for the creation of the board goes to frontline staff." The idea was to mesh the direct engagement of veterans who have research skills together with VA staff to improve the quality of institutional research into patient needs and preferences, institutional responses to them, and results. Staff within the VA recognized that vets are not simply patients to be served, waiting "patiently" for providers to figure out how to solve delivery problems, but resources who can be involved in improving service delivery. Note that this idea is an inherently circular one, which conceives of solutions as emerging from collaboration among providers and users of services.

The creation of the Denver board was not unproblematic. It was originally referred to as the "Veterans Advisory Board." VA attorneys took the position that the word "advisory" implied that the board would be contrary to federal rules that make an advisory board accountable for its deliberations and recommendations to the U.S. Congress rather than directly to the Denver hospital. This pushback met with resistance from veterans who perceived it as an attempt to kill the whole idea of a board. Finally, the word "engagement" replaced the word "advisory," and the board was able to proceed.

As word of the engagement board spread, about a half dozen more boards were established at VA hospitals around the country. Partnerships among the boards began to form. For example, the Denver board is now partnering with one in Seattle to craft approaches to identifying best practices in service delivery and administration. Board members see the boards themselves as a best practice.

The Denver board developed the following mission statement:

> In order to promote Veteran community engagement, patient-centered research and translation of Veteran Health Administration research findings in practice and community settings, this Board will work in partnership with, and provide recommendations to researchers (Center of Innovation and Mental Illness Research, Education, Clinical Center as an example) throughout the research process, from topic generation to dissemination and implementation of results.

The Denver Veterans Engagement Board is comprised of nine members, all veterans, and all deemed to be both skilled researchers and committed to advancing veteran interests. New members of the Board are selected through an application-driven interview process that involves staff and existing members of the Board in identifying candidates for appointment. The Board is supported by multiple staff with diverse backgrounds and has a full-time consultant facilitator to ensure that the deliberations of the Board are truly participatory, efficient and effective. Participatory processes for the Board itself are highly interactive and made so by the work of the facilitator, who encourages not just internal communicative give and take, but also constructive dialogue between researchers and members of the Board.

It is noteworthy that the Engagement Board was aware of the importance not just of the structural relations between itself and the rest of the VA, but of the dynamics of their work—the processes the structures would generate and be shaped by. By enlisting the services of a facilitator, the members were encouraging collaborative—i.e., circular—relationships among themselves and between the board and its constituencies: contracted and internal researchers, VA staff at all levels, veterans at large, and other members of the public.

Constellation of Values

The Engagement Board is not simply a technical monitor. From its inception, members established their concern that, in all the research studies, certain values be advanced that establish the kind of operational ideals the current and future VA needs to embrace. They are common standards found in organizations seeking to improve customer and client relations, but frequently endangered by lopsided concern over the technical elegance of research designs and methods, at the expense of more fundamental values. Among the values the board has identified are:

- Decentralization
- Transparency
- Participation of staff down the line
- Real engagement among various interests and attentive publics
- Connecting with community providers
- Becoming "Vet-Centric" or involving Vets themselves in program development, design, and policy implementation to create what the agency calls MyVA.

Specific Board Projects

Following are examples of specific research proposals vetted by the Board. In each case, investigators meet with the Board and present ideas for evaluation and feedback. The Board assesses each research scheme and engages in classic dialogic techniques with applicants (assertiveness on the one hand and active listening on the other). The shape of the process is, again, circular. (Based on Wendleton & Fehling, 2016.)

Pain management intervention

Opioid Medication Pain Management Study to survey veterans in Colorado who are on long-term opioid medications, to understand their experiences and views on decreasing and stopping these medications. Convene stakeholder groups of veterans and providers to develop a support program for veterans. Pilot this intervention.

Internet therapy program

Study on the use of computerized cognitive behavioral therapy for insomnia and depression/anxiety.

Vets Helping Vets Pilot

Assign vets with advanced cancer to a veteran peer patient navigator, who will meet with the patient five times to talk about advance care planning, pain management, and hospice and palliative care.

Patient-centered Intervention

Study to get feedback from vets on a shared decision-making and/or patient empowerment intervention that addresses class bias inherent in care; compare with care as usual.

Gunlocks

Go over background on the issue of firearms and suicide, and history of VA firearms safety messaging.

Quit Smoking for Good

Recruit 10–12 vets with PTSD who smoke at least one tobacco device to evaluate a multifaceted smoking cessation program.

Mental Health Coaching

Develop an intervention to help provide support to vets at risk of negative health outcomes, including suicide. Help these vets access self-management strategies to increase their engagement with VA healthcare, by collaboration with their providers, sending caring communications in the mail, and providing phone-based coaching sessions.

Degrees of Engagement

There are different degrees of engagement. The Board evaluates each research presentation in terms of the alternatives listed in Figure 6.2: that is, the degree of connection with the broader community, especially veterans themselves. The idea is that investigators and Board members reach a strong degree of partnership, which then extends to the performance of the research itself.

These concepts reinforce the idea that what is aimed for in theory has actual consequences in practice. The graphic is an evaluation tool that supports and

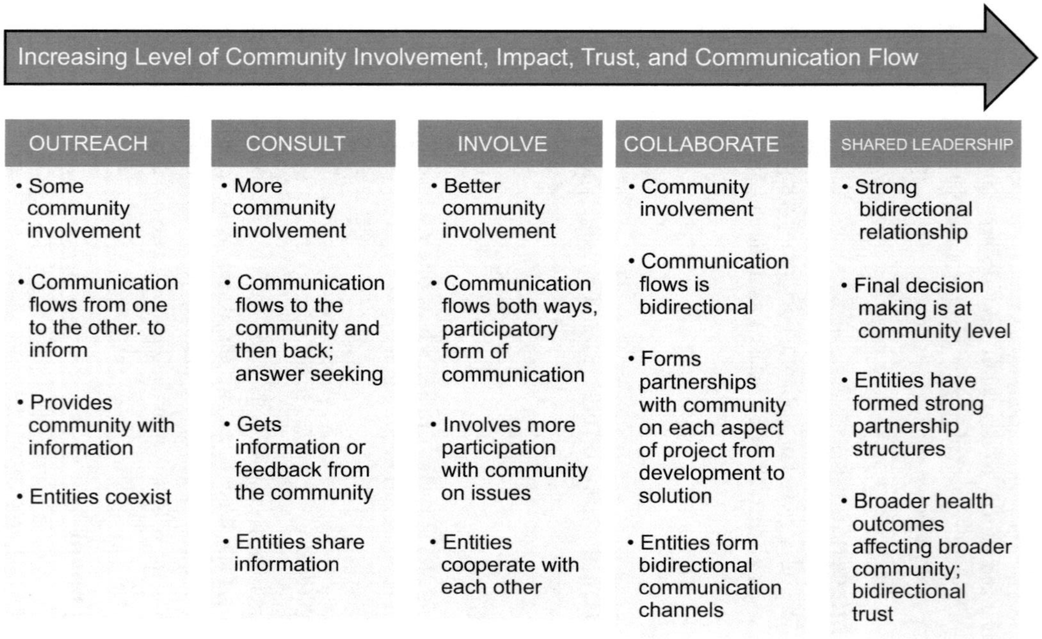

Increasing Level of Community Involvement, Impact, Trust, and Communication Flow →

OUTREACH	CONSULT	INVOLVE	COLLABORATE	SHARED LEADERSHIP
• Some community involvement	• More community involvement	• Better community involvement	• Community involvement	• Strong bidirectional relationship
• Communication flows from one to the other, to inform	• Communication flows to the community and then back; answer seeking	• Communication flows both ways, participatory form of communication	• Communication flows is bidirectional	• Final decision making is at community level
• Provides community with information	• Gets information or feedback from the community	• Involves more participation with community on issues	• Forms partnerships with community on each aspect of project from development to solution	• Entities have formed strong partnership structures
• Entities coexist	• Entities share information	• Entities cooperate with each other	• Entities form bidirectional communication channels	• Broader health outcomes affecting broader community; bidirectional trust

Reference: Modified by the authors from the International Association for Public Participation

FIGURE 6.2 Engagement Board Community Process. Source: U.S. Department of Health and Human Services, National Institutes of Health (2011). *Principles of Community Engagement* (2nd ed.). Publication No. 11–7782.

clarifies the operating values of the ideal VA project, values the Board are determined to realize throughout the national service system. The good news is that all of the research proposals and the interaction between investigators and Board members have ranged on the scale mostly from collaboration to shared leadership. In other words, there is a high degree of circularity.

Overall, the Veterans Research Engagement Board is an experiment, a trial of sorts, to make sure that veterans themselves have a maximum degree of participation in the development of research that is meant to benefit them. To date, the pilot nature of the process is an unqualified success and has served already as a model for other service jurisdictions interested in involving veterans in agency policy making. In this respect, the Board is a best practice that provides a real alternative to investigations without the involvement of veterans themselves.

Examples of Best Practices

First, in addition to the overall fundamental structure and purpose of the Board itself, certain *process* characteristics enable and encourage member participation and interaction with presenters of research ideas. These processes are circular in nature. That is, they are not commanded and energized from the top of the bureaucratic pyramid.

Second, in addition to the veteran volunteers, the Board is peopled by VHA staff, who serve *the Board's* interests. Given the nature of the Board's tasks, certain significant coordination about meeting times and copies of relevant documents are provided in advance of meetings. Follow-up actions by research investigators are also routinely provided to the Board over time. This signals the Board's understanding that humble process elements make significant contributions to the outcomes—for example, meeting when most people can attend, and making sure that they have the information they need to understand issues and make wise decisions.

Third, to ensure active participation of all members of the Board, a facilitator is assigned on a regular basis for all meetings. The benefit of a facilitator is more effective discussions by monitoring the process so that all voices are heard.

Fourth, at the end of each session, the Board evaluates the immediate sentiment concerning instant presentations. In addition to Board scoring, investigators fill out a companion form indicating their assessment of the quality of interaction between themselves and the Board. This mutual evaluative process is circular.

Fifth, as time progresses it is predictable and natural that a certain bonding takes place among and between staff, Board members, and presenters. Circular processes encourage this. Over time the Board becomes increasingly effective in the evaluation of various research endeavors as it improves the way its deliberations take place.

The Interaction of Knowledges

The Research Engagement Board honors in practice what is philosophically argued and illustrated throughout this book: the shared participation of public employees and community stakeholders meaningfully in administration of policies and programs. This narrative presents the practical operation of real work in a major federal agency, which shows that even large bureaucratic enterprises can welcome knowledge from the frontline in policy and research deliberations.

What we learn from the Engagement Board's experience is this: What volunteers, recipients of benefits, and staff know and share with others—both at the basic program level and at the highest levels—is testimony to the value of experiential knowledge, a way of being that validates the core idea of this volume. What people know, at every level, in pyramids and in more innovative circle designs within them, can coalesce to form multi-faceted knowledge of the work in public organizations, the kind that actually produces results. Reasonable participation of direct stakeholders overpowers rigid hierarchical designs with circular processes, and makes for higher quality administration at the employee, managerial, and executive levels of organization. These kinds of experience-based collaborative processes are an improvement over the typical top-down authority that claims the right to control the work based on position power alone, divorced from the actual work of the organization.

Inside Knowledges for Change

Various reports on the state of affairs at the VA leave the Board with ongoing pressure to work toward the desires of competing publics nationally. One idea looming over the VA is privatization of goods and services. The notion is contentious and will provide fodder for heated debate on whether public purposes can be realized by private means.

The Engagement Board notes the relevance of this issue to its activities, but no matter the strength of both sides in the privatization debate, the Board's strategic goals and processes remain the same—to interact with VA researchers and investigators in creating positive conditions of organizational change and development by partnering with like-minded people interested in creating positive experiences for veterans, including veterans themselves.

As this is being written, a hiring freeze has been instituted in the VHA as in other federal agencies. The position of national VA leaders is one of cautious assertion of the obligation to continue to recruit and select, for example, doctors and nurses. Employees in 70 other position classifications have been identified as critical, and agency leaders are requesting waivers to hire in these domains. How that plays out is unknown as we write, but the use of volunteers like the members of the Engagement Board becomes even more valuable in a restricted hiring climate.

In the end, it is a matter of trust. The Board does its work in an environment that presupposes that the VHA cannot be trusted to use its resources wisely, and that there is no real hope for fulfilling democratic ends with bureaucratic means, especially when the goal is reform of a massive, complicated system. Based on Carnevale's direct participation, we perceive, in many quarters, a crisis of faith, an existential failure in practice, plaguing the VA. Substantial transformation is called for. Transformation starts, not from the top, wielding a "systems" view, but at the micro level, with circular processes, such as listening carefully and responsively to the needs of interested publics.

Max Weber, in his classic description of ideal-typical bureaucracy, concluded that strict adherence to rational bureaucracy would inevitably lead to "an iron cage for mankind." His prediction is apt here. Breaking the weight of chains on local practice, as the Engagement Board shows, is just what a good doctor would order.

Afterword: Circle vs. Pyramid—The View from 30,000 Feet

When a traditionally bureaucratic organization like the Veterans Administration is faced with having to transform long-standing structures and practices, it takes a real struggle on the part of those leading the effort to get a fresh perspective on what's happening and what to do about it. Perhaps the hardest thing to see is your own taken-for-granted assumptions.

In our case study of the VA in crisis, we found evidence that despite an institutional good-faith effort, the various reports and analyses had not been able to do enough "consciousness raising" to become aware of deeply held assumptions about what an organization is and how it operates (its dynamics). When the most radical (seeming) diagnosis/prescription is to take a "systems approach," it's time (in our view) to take another look. It's time to get the "view from 30,000 feet"—a popular metaphor these days for *seeing* the big picture—as distinct from imposing a concept on it before looking.

From our perspective, which pictures the bureaucratic organization as a pyramid of mismatched, poorly integrated and even antagonistic knowledges, the problems that plague bureaucratic systems and the repeated failure of management reforms point toward the need to question just what it is that holds the pyramid itself (i.e. the "system") in place. Conventional theory has insisted that the force in question is the century-long faith in the ability of management to control in a top-down manner the actual work of the organization. Yet organizations are always richer than the management perspective is able to see and convey. If the organization is willing and able to encourage and seek out intelligence on what is working and why (in the eyes of those directly responsible—in other words, frontline workers), it can take steps to foster what we call circular processes (see Part III). These can be found already existing within the linear rationality of the pyramid. They can be studied, fostered, and emulated elsewhere.

The most significant aspect of the Engagement Board is its reliance on circular rather than top-down processes, both internally and externally. This encourages discussion among all the members and a decision-making process which, if not totally consensual (i.e., requiring eventual unanimity) is highly integrative, along the lines suggested by the classic process theorist Mary Parker Follett.

Externally, the Board practices a similarly circular approach to interfacing with researchers, committing themselves to a model that moves circularly at all stages: outreach, consultation, involvement, collaboration, and shared leadership.

In our view, efforts like the Engagement Board challenge the age-old response to criticism of bureaucracy: Bureau-pathology is built into the system, and the only answers are either privatization (which assumes that private organizations are not bureaucracies—highly questionable in our opinion) or more of the same: more control, more "rationality," tighter supervision, measurement of results (and forget about the ones that can't be measured), and so on. There is another alternative, and the Engagement Board points the way toward it.

References

Bronstein, Scott, & Drew Griffin. 2014. A fatal wait: Veterans languish and die on a VA hospital's secret list. https://edition.cnn.com/2014/04/23/health/veterans-dying-health-care-delays/index.html Downloaded 9/28/2018.

Carnevale, David G., & Ralph P. Hummel. 2007. Innovation and discovery in the factory and bureaucracy: Theory, art and method of the knowledge analytic. *Public Voices* 10:1, 5–22.

Commission on Care (ConC). 2016. *Final Report*. commissiononcare.sites.usa.gov Downloaded 6/30/2016.

Clark, Charles S. 2015. The Stories of four VA whistleblowers who exposed lapsed patient care. *Government Executive* (January 20).

Despite $10B "Fix," Veterans Are Waiting Even Longer to See Doctors. National Public Radio (May 16). http://www.npr/sections/health-shots/2016/05/16/477814218 Downloaded 8/22/2016.

Fandos, Nicholas. 2017. With fight on health law stalled, conservatives turn to veterans' care. *New York Times*, New York edition (November 9), A18.

Foley, Dolores. 1998. We want your input: Dilemmas of citizen participation. Pp. 140–157 in *Government Is Us: Public Administration in an Anti-government Era* (eds. C.S. King and C. Stivers). Thousand Oaks, Calif.: Sage Publications.

Foucault, Michel. 1984. What is enlightenment? Pp. 32–50 in *The Foucault Reader* (ed. P. Rabinow). New York: Pantheon.

Foucault, Michel. 2003. *Society Must Be Defended: Lectures at the College de France 1975–1976* (eds. M. Bertaini & A. Fontana; trans. D. Macey). New York: Picador.

Frank, M. 2000. Engineering systems thinking and systems thinking. *Systems Engineering* 3:3, 163–168.

Government Accountability Office. 2016. *VA Health Care: Actions Needed to Improve Newly Enrolled Veterans' Access to Primary Care*. GAO-16–328. Washington, D.C.: GAO.

Hummel, Ralph P. 1983. Manager and worker: Phenomenology of time consciousness and rational style. *Dialogue* 6:1 (Fall), 2–12.

Hummel, Ralph P. 1989. Icon and psyche: The circle as emerging symbol for organizational psychology. *Dialogue* 11:2/3 (Winter-Spring), 49–88.

Hummel, Ralph P. 1991. Stories managers tell: Why they are as valid as science. *Public Administration Review* 31:1 (January-February), 31–41.

Hummel, Ralph P. 2006. The triumph of numbers: Knowledges and the mismeasure of management. *Administration & Society* 38:1 (March), 58–78.

Katz, Daniel, & Robert L. Kahn. 1966. *The Social Psychology of Organizations*. New York: Wiley.

MITRE Corporation. 2015. *Centers for Medicare and Medicaid Services (CMS) Section 201 Independent Assessment of the Health Care Delivery System and Management Processes of the Department of Veterans Affairs, Vol. 1: Integrated Report* (September 1).

Morgan, Gareth. 1997. *Images of Organization* (2nd ed.). Thousand Oaks, Calif.: Sage Publications.

Munoz, Carlos. 2014. White House fights to restore veterans' trust. *The Guardian* (June 6). Downloaded 8/19/16.

Northern Virginia Technology Council (NVTC). 2014. *Opportunities to Improve the Scheduling of Medical Exams for America's Veterans* (October 29).

Peralta, Eyder. 2014. Audit finds 13 percent of VA schedulers told to falsify data (June 9). http://www.npr.org/sections/thetwoway/2014/06/09/ 320343022/ Downloaded 8/19/2016.

Philipps, Dave. 2018. VA doctors say rating push limits patient care. *New York Times* (January 1), A1–A2.

Rein, Lisa. 2015. VA whistleblowers, punished for revealing excessive opiate use and infestation, are finally exonerated. *Washington Post* (July 24). http://www.washingtonpost.com/news/federal-eye/wp/2015/07/24/these-va-whistleblowers-punished-for-reporting-problems-were-finally-exonerated/?utm_term=.f08d2d4559d9

Wagner, Dennis. 2014 (May 2). Second VA doctor blows whistle on patient care facilities. *U.S.A. Today.* https://www.usatoday.com/story/news/nation/2014/05/02/va-veterans-phoenix-health-deaths-whistleblowers/8597734 Downloaded 9/28/18.

Wendleton, L., & Fehling, K. (2016). Veterans' Perspectives of Participating on a Research Engagement Board within the Veterans Health Administration. Presented at the annual meeting of the American Public Health Association Annual Meeting, Denver (November).

ATTACHMENT

VA Summit Planning Form

VA Community Mental Health Summit 2015
*Sustaining our
Joint Commitment to
Improve the Mental Health of Veterans and Their Families*

Medical Center Plan Submission
DUE: May 29, 2015

Each VA medical center is required to submit a Mental Health Summit Plan through the facility Mental Health Summit Coordinator.

This initial plan must be reviewed with the VISN MH Liaison prior to submission.

VA Medical Center Summit Plans must be submitted no later than May 29, 2015.

Please reference the attached 2015 VA Medical Center Implementation Toolkit as you develop your Summit Plan.

2015 VA Medical Center Implementation Summit Toolkit

Please identify your **VA Medical Center.**

VISN	▼
VA Medical Center Station Number and Name	▼
VISN MH Liaison	▼

If your facility is not a VA Medical Center, you are not required to host a 2015 Community MH Summit. If you choose to host a summit event, please provide your facility information here.

VISN	
Facility Station Number and Name	

Please provide **CONTACT INFORMATION** for the MH Summit Coordinator, the MH Point of Contact (POC) and Leadership Participants for your facility.

MH Summit Coordinator Name	
MH Summit Coordinator Email	
MH Point of Contact (POC) Name	
MH Point of Contact Email	
VA Medical Center Leadership Participant Name and Title	
VA Medical Center MH Leadership Participant Name and Title	

COMMUNITY PARTNERS should be included as members of the planning team and engaged in all aspects of the 2015 Summits and ongoing partnership activities. A list of types of community partner organizations is provided on page 13 of the 2015 VA Medical Center Implementation Toolkit.

Please identify at least 1 and up to 5 of the community partners you have included in your MH Summit planning and preparation.

	Community Partner Name	Type of Organization
Community Partner 1		
Community Partner 2		
Community Partner 3		
Community Partner 4		
Community Partner 5		

Please provide information on the **DATE** and **LOCATION** of your 2015 MH Summit.

Date (mm/dd/yyyy) [ ]
Duration (in hours) [ ]

Will your MH Summit be held at a VA facility (on-site) or at an alternate location (off-site)?

On-site ○

Off-site ○

PARTICIPANTS

Please indicate the number of participants you anticipate attending your VA Community Mental Health Summit.

	Estimated Number of Participants		
	Total Minimum	Total Maximum	VA Participants
MH Summit Participants			

PARTICIPANT EMAIL ADDRESSES.

Each MH Summit Coordinator is required to ask all invitees to provide their email addresses prior to or on the day of the MH Summit to allow completion of a voluntary electronic survey about their MH Summit experience.

This year, two evaluations will be distributed: One to individuals who attend the MH Summit; and one evaluation to those who are invited but do not attend.

In order to facilitate this process, you will be asked to provide the following information as an uploaded MS Excel file: Invitee's email address and attendance status (y/n).

○ I understand the requirement to provide invitee email addresses and attendance status following our Summit event. I understand I can follow-up with my VISN MH Liaison with any questions.

PUBLIC AFFAIRS OFFICERS (PAO) should be engaged to provide proactive outreach and consistent messaging on the goals, objectives and outcomes of each MH Summit. Has the facility PAO been involved in developing a communication plan for the MH Summit?

- ☐ Yes
- ☐ No. If not, why not?

COMMUNICATION PLAN. This is an opportunity to produce a positive press release related to mental health care at each facility. A communications plan should be developed in partnership with your facility Public Affairs Officer for pre- and post- event publicity which may include use of Facebook, Twitter, and/or other social media outreach tools. Please send copies of any local press releases to the VACOMHSummit@va.gov.

Please indicate what media sources you plan to use to distribute pre- and post- event communications.

- ☐ Newspaper
- ☐ Television
- ☐ Radio
- ☐ Facebook
- ☐ Twitter
- ☐ Direct email / mail communications
- ☐ Other (please specify)

Source:https://vaww.cmopnational.va.gov/CR/MentalHealth/MH_Summit/2014%20Community%20MH%20Summits/NRD/NRD%20Participation%20Policy.pdf

EPILOGUE

The Knowledge Approach to Research

There is no "one best way" to use the knowledge approach. Once you recognize the existence of different knowledges in an organization, there are many paths to explore organizational dynamics. The only bedrock assumption is that no one knowledge is the only kind, or even the best kind. As phenomenologists, we are interested in the substance of people's experience as they themselves describe and use it, as the focus of our interpretations of public bureaucracies. Below, we offer not a methodology but examples of some of the questions that may arise in your mind once you accept, even as a possible starting place, that there is more than one kind of knowledge, and that studying the simultaneous operations of different and perhaps incommensurable knowledges may help us to understand organizational dynamics.

These questions can be asked directly of organization members, in interviews, or posed in the process of interpreting documents, such as reports, evaluations, plans, rulebooks, and so on. They are not the only questions one could ask, but in our experience they tend to come up often. While organizational analysis does not rule out conventional science, what we call the knowledge approach focuses on methods that take into account actual working experiences as they are described by those who have had them (Carnevale & Hummel, 2007). That is, it responds to questions that quantitative science is unable to address.

Work and workers

How does the formal organization define its "work"? Look for statements of purpose/goals, what the enabling legislation requires the organization to do, what activities are measured for "results."

Where did these definitions originate? How did they develop? What sort of assumptions do they make about the nature of knowledge and the nature of an organization?

Where does the work—the human action aimed at fulfilling/carrying out the organizational purposes—occur? Usually, the work is directly performed by workers, usually at the front line of the organization. Is this the case in the situation at hand?

Describe what workers of various kinds actually do, based on observation, reports, interviews, etc.

What do workers know from doing this work? How do they describe what they know? What does it mean, in their view, to be "good" at what they do?

To what extent can the content of their knowledge/expertise be pinned down—measured, patterned, predicted, regularized, summed up in rules, etc.? Especially, what is their own view of how much of what they know can be pinned down?

What evidence is there of worker knowledge that can't be measured—or possibly even communicated? I.e. evidence of "tacit" knowledge, or what Heidegger calls "absorbed coping"?

How do workers describe management? What influence do they see it as having on how they approach their work? What do they think managers know?

Managers

How do managers describe what they do? How do they describe what they know?

The literature and the management profession describe management as controlling and systematizing the work done by workers. Where and in what forms does this control "show up" in the situation? Where do efforts to systematize, make more efficient/effective, etc. show themselves? Rules, handbooks, strategic plans, performance evaluations, manager viewpoints, etc.

How do managers think about/carry out efforts to ensure that workers follow rules that managers have drawn up? Do they use the same strategies on other managers they supervise?

Do managers also acquire tacit knowledge or engage in absorbed coping on the job? I.e. do they also acquire and use experiential knowledge in addition to knowledge from books and theories? What part do they believe this kind of knowledge plays in their sense of their expertise?

Is there a gap between what managers say about their role and the ways they actually do it? I.e., how much of management activity conforms to the ideology of control by abstract concepts, and to what extent is their effectiveness a product of their experience?

Executives

What do executives do? Describe their activities from observation or interviewing.

How do they themselves describe what they do? How do they describe what they know? What does it mean to them to be "good" at what they do? How do they describe what workers know? What managers know?

To what extent are their efforts directed externally versus internally? Is there evidence of tension or mis-match between the two responsibilities? How much of what they "know" comes from outside vs. inside and how do they blend them (if they do)?

How do abstractions and numbers function in executive work? E.g., are they taken and used as "real" or do they function strategically/ideologically? When (under what circumstances) are they real and when are they ideological?

Power/Knowledge

Where in the dynamics of the organization is there evidence of different knowledges approaching situations and problems in contradictory or inconsistent ways? E.g., defining the problem differently, coming up with different ways of dealing with it?

Where is there evidence of clashes between worker knowledge and management or executive knowledge? To what extent are clashes recognized and how are they dealt with? Do managers listen to, respect, accept, etc. workers' experiential knowledge? How do managers think about what workers know? And vice versa?

What about execs? From whom do they get information about the way the work is going? Do they have any direct lines of communication to workers, or is info about the work filtered completely through management?

What are the effects of knowledge gaps and clashes? Especially of worker knowledge being ignored or dismissed by managers and executives?

How might things be different? What do people at the various levels, worker/manager/exec, say should be changed? How might the organization be more effective if different knowledges were recognized, acknowledged, and mutually respected?

PART III
The Circle

7

INTRODUCTION

From Pyramid to Circle: The Power of Process

> For the future of both private and public-sector organizations, much will depend on the creation of functionally mediating work structures that bridge pyramid and circle.
>
> *(Hummel, 1989, p. 82)*

Can any sort of "management reform"—or indeed, any other sort of organizational reform—have a significant impact on modern bureaucracy? This question is important because it seems unlikely that bureaucracies are going to disappear anytime soon, even as the conditions that gave rise to them—the conditions of modernity, including capitalism and industrialism—give way to post-modern and post-industrial societies. Indeed, as "everything solid melts into air" (Marx & Engels, 2008, p. 38), "the pillars of the best-known truths ... today lie shattered" (Arendt, 1968, p. 10) and life becomes "liquid" (Bauman, 2005), the desire for control grows ever more urgent—but with fading hope that control is actually achievable.

In the theory of modern industrial society, centralized command and control of organizations is seen as functional, therefore it is also necessary. It follows that bureaucracy—modernity's chief centralized control mechanism—is legitimate because modern society can't do without it, given the societal value placed on rationality as the efficiency tool. Max Weber viewed both knowledge and control (discipline) as "twin expressions of the overall rationalization of power and technique" (Dandeker, 1990, p. 205). In post-modern times, Michel Foucault, despite a vastly different understanding of power from Weber's, also saw power and knowledge as linked. In fact, he came to treat them as one phenomenon: "Power/Knowledge" (Foucault, 1980).

Weber argued that modern capitalism required a mechanically calculable production process; rational public administration; a formal guarantee of contracts by the political authority; and maximum possible separation of the capitalist enterprise (and its public administrative partner) from the household and its property interests. Hummel (2006) argued that these requirements can be read as entailing different kinds of knowledge, rational/legal versus traditional/household, or science versus feeling one's way. The need for certain kinds of knowledge led to devising certain kinds of structures. If you want calculability, then there must be routines. If efficiency is needed, then jobs must be designed/engineered to be as efficient as possible. Responsibility for deliverables leads to structures that promote predictability. The question, as modernity shows signs of receding into the past, is how firmly we must cling to Weber's belief that with bureaucracies, there is little choice: either the linear rationality promised by modernity's great machine, or "dilettantism." But what happens when the machine's warranty expires? (See Hummel & Stivers, 2010.)

With this history in mind, it is easy to see why so-called reforms have made relatively little headway within modern organizations, since virtually all of them were measures that reduced, or threatened to reduce, the level of rational efficiency and therefore what Karl Marx called surplus value—profit in the private sector, budget maximization or deficit reduction (familiarly, "more with less") in the public. At least since the dawn in the late nineteenth century of self-aware public administration driven by business values, repeated proposals to reform dynamics between managers and workers, as well as external dynamics between citizens and bureaucrats, inevitably ran into the (usually undeniable) charge of inefficiency. This has always been public administration's kiss of death, as if working quality of life and citizen involvement could only be justified if they didn't cost anything. The longstanding bargain sacrifices worker and citizen political strength for tenuous economic rewards: "Autocracy at work as the unavoidable price for 'Democracy' after hours" (Waldo, 1948, p. 75).

As Waldo (1952) noted, Progressive-era reformers who developed public administration thinking claimed to be concerned about democracy, but they saw it as external and inimical to the achievement of efficiency. They linked political democracy to parties and policy formulation, not to administration. According to Woodrow Wilson (1887, p. 214), "Self-government does not consist in having a hand in everything, any more than housekeeping consists necessarily in cooking dinner with one's own hands"—perhaps unconsciously turning bureaucrats into hired help and citizens into dinner guests.

Once the theoretical border wall between political and economic values comes down, however, and the political implications of business ideology are revealed, fresh ideas about public administration flood in. Part III is devoted to exploring some of these ideas. This part is inspired directly by Ralph Hummel's (1990) article, "Circle managers and pyramid managers: Icons for the post-modern administrator." Systematically comparing pyramid ideas with circle ideas in the public organizational context, Hummel advises: "The first step on the way to becoming a circle manager ... is to recognize the ways of [circular] understanding where they already exist" (p. 214). He argues that *circular thinking and acting do not necessarily cancel scientific investigation and rational explanation, rather good judgment connects science to practice in a circular process of reasonableness.*

The idea of circular processes is useful as a potential basis for envisioning a way of bridging the gap between experiential, hands-on knowledge and abstract, conceptual knowledge. Can this gap be bridged? Can different knowledges be interwoven to produce joint action? If there is such a bridge, as we argue below, it is built in a circular, iterative process that works simultaneously on two levels, understanding and practical action. The key ingredients, we will suggest, include (1) back-and-forth movement between part and whole, between center and periphery, between idea and action, and (2) a focus on *situation* as the encompassing phenomenon that, when collaboratively studied, enables integrated action.

In the balance of this introduction, we lay out theoretical underpinnings and research results that support the circle-enabled organization. We consider several aspects of life and practice in today's public bureaucracies that could be improved with the help of circular thinking. We follow the guidance offered by Richard Harvey Brown (1978) in his essay, "Bureaucracy as praxis": Public bureaucracies can be understood in other terms than as materially concrete, impervious monoliths populated by faceless officials. Taking another stance, as we do in this book, bureaucracies can be seen as organizing processes enacted by persons who generate and keep in place understandings of their situations. In other words, as we suggested in Chapter 2, bureaucracies are life-worlds. As such, they "serve as paradigms that govern permissible conduct" (Brown, 1978, p. 371). People who care about administrative governance have a choice of stance. Clearly, bureaucratic life-worlds can be seen, as they typically are by those at the top, as constantly in need of narrowing, systematizing, and disciplining. Alternatively, they can be seen as rich resources of lived experience, creativity, and fresh perspectives informed by awareness of the nexus between ideas and actions.

Why Circles?

In twentieth-century philosophy, the circle idea grew from hermeneutics, or the interpretation of texts. The theory of textual interpretation held that understanding a text was a circular movement, starting with the meaning of some part of it, then moving back to the text to place that meaning within a larger chunk of text and then repeating the process. Circling back and forth between text and interpretation, one could develop an understanding that was true to the text but also gave a fresh reading of it. Notice that hermeneutics resists the notion that there is "one best way" to read anything. This is not the same as "anything goes."

As Dreyfus (1991) notes, Martin Heidegger drew on the idea of the hermeneutic circle to argue that we always begin any interpretation (of text or life) from within the very circumstances we aim to understand—in other words, we begin (find ourselves) within some already existing understanding of a situation, and work from there. Since "there" includes a lot of taken-for-granted or even unseen assumptions, understanding it means approaching the situation so as to let fresh elements show themselves. We start from where we are, move toward being able to see new elements, form a fresh understanding—and repeat. This circular process is the nature of knowing-being. Heidegger argued that all interpretation *must* start with the taken-for-granted (you have to start where you are), which limits the kinds of questions that can be asked. This could mean that any circular approach is a vicious circle, one in which interpretation is trapped. The reason we are not trapped is that what we are aiming to understand is not a closed arena but *being itself*, which can never be made completely explicit, and can always be "called into question." In other words, being-in-the-world itself has a circular structure (Dreyfus, 1991, p. 201).

This understanding of the nature of being may seem arcane, but it has direct relevance and usefulness for organizational action. If, as the hermeneutic circle suggests, there is no knowledge without starting from what is given to us in the existing situation, the task is not to try and exclude all of what makes up the situation except the one preconception we want to test, but to approach it critically in the course of inquiry. The philosopher Hans-Georg Gadamer advises that we put ourselves in dialogue with what we do not understand in the situation, risking and testing our prejudices, and seeing what we might be open to: "It is true of every conversation that through it something different has come to be" (Gadamer, 1976, p. xxii; see also Bernstein, 1985, pp. 128–134).

John Dewey (1998a) said that acquiring knowledge means acting into the situation to see what it will put up with and what it won't. In other words, interpretation is not a process that permits you to ignore reality, but rather to come to terms with it—to understand it and potentially to change it. This suggests that members of organizations who want to get something done can and must learn the art of trying to understand the perspectives of others, in order to get a full understanding of the situation:

> participate or share in them, listen to them, open ourselves to what they are saying and to the claims to truth they make upon us. ... The hermeneutical attitude supposes only that we self-consciously designate our opinions and prejudices and qualify them as such ... In keeping to this attitude, we grant the text [or the person] the opportunity to appear as an authentically different being and manifest its own truth, over and against our own preconceived notions.
>
> *(Bernstein, 1985, p. 138)*

One of the present authors (Stivers), as a grad student listening to a panel of theorists, asked: "What does this mean for us practitioners?" The late Fred Thayer, perhaps the most unforgettable PA theorist ever, a retired Army colonel turned academic, replied: "What it means is, when you are faced with a decision of any moment, get out of your office or your cubicle and talk to somebody else. Don't decide in isolation."

Mary Parker Follett and Circular Response

Perhaps the best-known administrative thinker to draw out the practical implications of circular understanding was Mary Parker Follett. As the editors of her talks to business groups note, she had two basic concepts. The first was "circular or reciprocal response" (Fox & Urwick, 1977, p. xxiii). This was based on an understanding about the nature of reality. Follett believed that the behaviorist stimulus-response theory was a gross oversimplification of what actually happens:

> Reaction is always reaction to a relating. ... I never react to you but to you-plus-me; or to be more accurate, it is I-plus-you reacting to you-plus-me ... In the very process of meeting, *by* the very process of meeting, we both become something different.
>
> *(Follett, 1924, pp. 62–63)*

Reality, then, lies in the "in-between"—two or more people in conversation, activity shaping situation and situation shaping activity: "There is no result *of* process, but only a moment *in* process" (p. 60).

Follett's second basic concept, "integration," follows from the first. The outcome of the circular process (to the extent it can be said to have an "outcome") is the meshing of differences: You + Me becomes a whole: you-plus-me. Something new has come into being, which immediately continues to evolve. Follett believed that the process of change inevitably produces conflict, but if it is approached with open minds and in a supportive milieu, conflict *could* lead to productive change. She was no Pollyanna: She didn't claim that integration could always be achieved (once she remarked, "I don't say there is no tragedy in life"), only that the possibility was there and was worth striving for.

The important thing about integration for our argument is that Follett saw it as an alternative to top-down control. In her well-known talk, "The giving of orders," she observed that nobody likes to take orders from someone else, to be put in the subservient position of being bossed around: "People do not like to be ordered even to take a holiday. I have often seen instances of this" (Follett, 1977 [1925], p. 32). The key to successful management is to depersonalize authority by studying the situation collaboratively and taking orders from *it*. Follett was not advising us to stand back and listen to a disembodied voice from objective reality. Rather, she was urging us to approach the situation hermeneutically, by engaging with it tentatively, trying something and seeing what emerges—and repeat. By doing this collectively, everyone concerned would then be responsible not to some remote authority figure but, collectively, to the situation itself, and what their study of it had concluded it required. Follett's model of what is now often mis-called "collaboration" is *circular* (reciprocal relating of all the situational factors), made up of *direct and personal* contact of everyone responsible, and *ongoing* (not ginned up in an emergency, but practice-as-usual).

Given the recent enthusiasm for collaboration among devotees of New Public Management (NPM), it is worth noting that Follett's circular process was a tangible person-to-person activity and not an abstraction. In the NPM literature the focus has been, almost without exception, on collaboration as contractual arrangements between government agencies and their private institutional partners, such as nonprofits and private corporations. In NPM the institutions are the actors. But abstractions can't collaborate, only people can. If Agency A contracts with Nonprofit B to provide designated services ("deliverables") to some subset of Agency A's client base, this in itself is not actually the stuff of collaboration, only the conceptualization of it. The relentless emphasis in this line of thinking on end results ("deliverables") ignores the circular processes between A people and B people that make the difference between getting good results and bad. This research frequently tells us *what* happened (how many clients served, how much money spent or saved, etc.) but almost never *how*. Who interacted with whom? How did they figure out how to translate abstract contract terms into real-life actions? Were they able to integrate their respective understandings of the situation, and if so, how did that happen? These kinds of process questions remain inside what is often referred to as "the black box," as if process cannot be observed, studied and learned from. (We hazard the guess that the contents of the black box have landed there because they can't be quantified.)

This neglect of process has meant that despite all the "reinventing government" rhetoric, the continued existence of bureaucracies has been taken for granted—but that's okay, it is said, because now they are partners in a network. Networks are studied for how they link up different organizations in a kind of tinker-toy structure, but the actual interest is in justifying shrinkage (devolution, privatization) in government activities, so the tangible processes of collaboration between government and private organizations remain a mystery. Collaboration happens between and among real live people, not organizations.

Hummel observes that typical manager complaints, such as "Why don't our workers take pride in their work? Why is there so much absenteeism? Why aren't workers inventive?" all turn on the neglected fact that workers have so little control of their work. Their ability to size up a task, design a line of action, and exercise their own interpretive skills toward it—all have been devalued by the organization, for fear that things will get out of control, or threaten the existence of so many managers:

> Intentions are separated from actions. ... technology (the way the work is done) is separated from organizations (the way jobs are structured). Work and job are no longer integrated. ... All conflict in organizations can be

traced to the struggle between [the worker] who knows what the work is and [the manager] who is separated from [it] and yet has the power to control the jobs. ... [B]oth management and workers are working with only half a deck.

(Hummel, 1982, p. 9)

Let's consider a different model, one in which the logic of reasonableness (Hummel, 1983) supports and is reflected in wisdom in practice, the ability to exercise judgment in particular situations.

The heart of circular logic (reasonableness), now in danger of being smothered under scientific management models re-booted, is judgment: figuring out the right thing to do in the given circumstances. "Right" in this instance implies more than technical or scientific correctness, though this can be one factor. Judging means deciding what fits a given situation best; in fact, the ancient Greek word for judging or justice, *diké*, means "fit." Judgment is what public servants must deploy in order to figure out what is the public "thing," the *res publica*, in the situation at hand.

Judging is at the center of governance, including all aspects of the administration of agencies, from frontline to executive, because public life deals not with isolated technical correctness but with the public good. Public servants must decide how to join correctness with goodness. Few if any decisions are purely technical, because they have public consequences beyond the achievement of rationality. They serve some interests or needs and undermine others. Clearly, scientific studies and quantitative data provide important information, but never do they tell us what to do all by themselves. John Dewey (1998, p. 281) once said: "Many people seem to suppose that facts carry their meaning along with themselves on their face. Accumulate enough of them, and their interpretation stares out at you." Dewey took an alternative view, that the task of interpretation, *if shared widely enough in dialogue*, could use facts to find the fitting solutions to particular public problems.

Hummel's logic of reasonableness corresponds to the notion of wisdom in practice. It entails a circular, dialogic process of interpreting situations to find the action most likely to serve the public interest. When administrative theorists talk about the *exercise of discretion*, they tend to neglect the details of how this happens. Typically, discretion is treated as rational decision-making by an isolated individual (e.g., Simon 1945), though even Simon recognized that individual rationality is bounded. We argue that the logic of reasonableness better fits the practice of administrative discretion. The discussions to follow expand on this position. Wisdom in practice requires being able to judge, a cognitive skill that cannot be taught but can be learned in practice, that is, through experience. Further, wisdom in practice is communal, that is, it is dialogic rather than abstract.

Actually-existing Circular Organizations

The central core of a circular organization, as distinguished from a pyramidal bureaucracy, is that in a circular organization, as in democracy itself, "anyone who has authority over others [is] subject to their collective authority" (Ackoff, 1989, p. 11). Authority is a circular process. Although there are few if any examples of a fully circular organization, except perhaps some very small ones, our goal here is not to argue for the possibility of transforming pyramids fully into circles. (With Follett, we don't say there is no tragedy in life.) Rather we aim to consider how pyramidal dynamics can be tempered and the worst of the domination they exercise be eliminated. Real-world examples can be learned from, and proposed strategies explored.

Ralph Hummel argued that, logically, management has to have a certain minimum of cooperation from workers. The evidence is what happens when workers follow the rules to the letter; as a senior police officer told a researcher, "A department depends on the exchange of information and if people aren't talking to each other, there's not a thing you can do" (James Q. Wilson, *Varieties of Police Behavior*, quoted in Hummel, 1979, p. 11) The key words here are *exchange* and *talking to each other*. Cooperation is not a one-way street: "He who would induce cooperation must agree to be shaped in turn" (Selznick, 1949, p. 64). "Performance" is not a solo but an ensemble. Therefore, attention to reciprocal processes is functional, not frivolous.

Romme (1995) notes that traditional organizational decision-making relies on linear processes, commands flowing down, and frontline intelligence trickling up. But, as we have argued, this traditional model falls way short of circular, because management concepts aim to control what happens on the firing line, rather than to be "shaped in turn," so that the gap between hands-on knowledge and management concepts never really closes. In contrast, in circular organizing, each functional work group manages its own work area, based on consent arrived at by collaborative study of the situation: "A circle assigns its members to functions and tasks required by the common work objective." The members of the circle are collectively responsible for gathering measurement data to ferret out problems and potential improvements. Circles at lower levels of the organization are linked to circles farther up the hierarchy by means of common members: for example, a line manager at a lower level is also a member of a circle at the section level: "Thus the flow is circular, and the link to the hierarchy is maintained" (pp. 213–214). Such a structure sets up the enabling conditions for the kind of processes Follett called "integration"; it is congruent with her model of democratic process (Follett, 1998 [1919]).

Romme notes that, in practice, so-called "quality circles" are not typically integrated into the hierarchy, so they have less influence on policy-making at higher levels than they might. Links between and among the circles at different levels ameliorate typical top-down processes by enabling useful intelligence about frontline work processes to influence the entire enterprise. Individual learning on the firing line (or elsewhere) can become organizational learning. Romme also advises that consent at the individual circle level is crucial, and salary equivalence promotes its success. His model has been applied in both public and private organizations. A similar model is offered by Ackoff (1989), who observes that in circular organizations, "the principle responsibility of a manager is to manage over and up, not down; to manage interactions within their units and between their units and the rest of the organization and its environment, not the actions of their subordinates" (p. 13).

Eric Trist, one of the grand old organization theorists, developed with his research partner, Fred Emery, the sociotechnical school of organization theory. The core of this theory is that different sorts of organizations function well in different environments, from placid to turbulent. According to Trist, placid environments are a thing of the pre-industrial past. Modern bureaucracy worked reasonably well in the "disturbed-reactive" environment of the industrial age that favored expertise and large scale. But the post-industrial environment is "turbulent": causal strands among events and processes are mixed in with one another, producing much greater complexity and uncertainty. In a turbulent environment, independent action on the part of technological bureaucracies, with their "authoritarian control structure and tendency to debase human resources," are unable to cope with the nature of their surroundings. As Trist notes:

> Emergent social processes must be able to cope with new levels of interdependence, complexity, and uncertainty. Collaboration rather than competition is a basic requirement for this purpose. Acceptance of interdependence is founded on a willingness to align one's own purposes with those of diverse others and to negotiate mutually acceptable compromises rather than always trying to coerce and dominate in order to get one's way ...
> *(Trist, 1977, p. 272)*

Trist goes on to point out the importance of new strategies for problem-solving in a turbulent environment, in particular, a synthetic process in which parts and wholes are brought into relationship with one another (e.g., as Follett suggested, by studying the situation). Since the magnitude of complexity is too great for any one mind (or for one perspective shared by a group), collaboration is essential. Uncertainty demands flexibility in the quest to understand and solve problems; rigid structures and rules discourage the needed flexibility and creativity. In other words, organizations need to pay attention to the everyday social processes that are where collaboration (now understood as Follett's integration) takes place, if ever it does:

> Successful organizations will be socio-ecological rather than bureaucratic, with much local autonomy and a good deal of participation and democracy.

> Their parts will be mutually articulated rather than arranged in strict hierarchies. ... At the corporate level any thoroughgoing change toward the new model would appear to involve the working out of an explicit management philosophy consonant with the new direction.
>
> *(Trist, 1977, p. 15)*

That is, the management thinking that will be successful in the future will not be yet another "reform" that is basically Taylorism dressed up in new robes. It will take seriously the virtues and potential rewards of circular processes. In what follows, we explore possible ways of re-thinking certain aspects of the practice of public administration along circular lines.

References

Ackoff, Russell. 1989. The circular organization: An update. *Academy of Management Perspectives* 3:1, 11–16.

Arendt, Hannah. 1968. *Men in Dark Times.* San Diego, Calif.: Harcourt Brace.

Bauman, Zygmunt. 2005. *Liquid Life.* Cambridge, U.K.: Polity Press.

Bernstein, Richard J. 1985. *Beyond Objectivity and Relativism: Science, Hermeneutics, and Praxis.* Philadelphia: University of Pennsylvania Press.

Brown, Richard Harvey. 1978. Toward a political phenomenology of formal organizations. *Administrative Science Quarterly* 23:3, 365–382.

Dandeker, Christopher. 1990. *Surveillance, Power and Modernity.* Cambridge: U.K.: Polity Press.

Dewey, John. 1998a. Search for the public. Pp. 281–292 in *The Essential Dewey, Vol. 1* (eds. L.A. Hickman & T.M. Alexander). Bloomington & Indianapolis: Indiana University Press. Original work published 1927.

Dreyfus, Hubert L. 1991. *Being-in-the-world: A Commentary on Heidegger's* Being and Time, Division I. Cambridge, Mass.: M.I.T. Press.

Follett, M. P. 1924. *Creative Experience.* New York & London: Longmans, Green.

Follett, Mary Parker. 1977. The giving of orders. Pp. 21–41 in *Dynamic Administration: The Collected Papers of Mary Parker Follett* (eds. E.M. Fox & L. Urwick). New York: Hippocrene Books. Original presentation 1925.

Follett, Mary Parker. 1998. *The New State: Group Organization the Solution of Popular Government.* University Park, Penn.: The Pennsylvania State University Press. Original publication 1919.

Foucault, Michel. 1980. *Power/Knowledge: Selected Interviews and Other Writings 1972–1977* (ed. C. Gordon; trans. C. Gordon, L. Marshall, J. Mepham, & K. Soper). New York: Pantheon Books.

Fox, E.M., & L. Urwick (eds). 1977. *Dynamic Administration: The Collected Papers of Mary Parker Follett.* New York: Hippocrene Books.

Gadamer, Hans-Georg. 1976. *Philosophical Hermeneutics* (ed. & trans. D.E. Linge). Berkeley & Los Angeles: University of California Press.

Hummel, Ralph P. 1979. On the human condition: being in the company of others and satisfying human needs. *Dialogue* 2:1 (Sept.-Oct.), 11–16.

Hummel, Ralph P. 1982. The nature of work: Philosophy, psychology, and productivity. *Dialogue* 5:1 (Fall), 2–12.

Hummel, Ralph P. 1983. Manager and worker: Phenomenology of time consciousness and rational style. *Dialogue* 6:1 (Fall), 2–12.

Hummel, Ralph P. 1989. Icon and psyche: The circle as emerging symbol for organizational psychology. *Dialogue* 11:2/3 (Winter-Spring), 49–88.

Hummel, Ralph P. 1990. Circle managers and pyramid managers: Icons for the postmodern public administrator. Pp. 202–218 in *Images and Identities in Public Administration: Discourses on Governance* (eds. H.D. Kass & B. Catron). Newbury Park, Calif.: Sage.

Hummel, Ralph P. 2006. The triumph of numbers: Knowledges and the mismeasure of management. *Administration & Society* 38:1, 58–78.

Hummel, Ralph P., & Camilla Stivers. 2010. Postmodernism, bureaucracy, and democracy. Pp. 324–348 in *Oxford Handbook of American Bureaucracy* (ed. R.F. Durant). New York & Oxford: Oxford University Press.

Marx, Karl, & Friedrich Engels. 2008. *The Communist Manifesto* (3rd ed.) Pathfinder Press (www.pathfinderpress.com).

Romme, A. George. 1995. The sociocratic model of organizing. *Journal of Strategic Change* 4, 209–215.

Selznick, Philip. 1949. *T.V.A. and the Grass Roots: A Study in the Sociology of Formal Organization*. Berkeley & Los Angeles: University of California Press.

Simon, Herbert. 1945. *Administrative Behavior*. New York: Free Press.

Trist, Eric. 1977. Collaboration in work settings: A personal perspective. *Journal of Applied Behavioral Science* 13:3, 268–278.

Waldo, Dwight. 1948. *The Administrative State*. New York: Ronald Press.

Waldo, Dwight. 1952. Development of the theory of democratic administration. *American Political Science Review* 46:1, 81–103.

Wilson, Woodrow. 1887. The study of administration. *Political Science Quarterly* 2 (June), 197–222.

8

THE LOGIC OF REASONABLENESS

Experience, Judgment and Dialogue in Administrative Practice

> Come now ... let us reason together.
>
> *(Isaiah 1:18)*

In this chapter we explore what Ralph Hummel (1989) called the "logic of reasonableness" as a basis not just for the bureaucratic front line but for administrative practice as a whole. Having argued in this book that government bureaucracies are structured as pyramids of rational knowledge, we are aware of the need to make a case for singling out another form of knowledge as the foundation for governance. This is especially true since the prevailing view among public administrationists is that the logic of rationality, not the logic of reasonableness, is the proper basis of administrative practice. Much of this book has criticized managerial domination on the basis of science; does the notion that experience should take pride of place make any sense? Isn't this a poor attempt at a workers' power play? Should not our argument be taking the form instead of "Can't we all get along?"

Actually, we do favor all of us in bureaucracies getting along. The problem is that the scientific mindset rules out getting along with other forms of knowledge (beginning by denying that there are any such alternative forms). In reply, experiential knowledge accepts that all knowing starts from somewhere—from the situation and perspective that particular individuals and groups find themselves in at the current moment. This stance recognizes not only the existence but also the value of scientific investigation and its results; it simply sees science as not the only stance from which to understand and act in situations. On this basis, the logic of reasonableness that grows out of experience may be the only way for all knowledges in bureaucracies to "get along"—to work effectively together.

In public service and particularly in public administration, science claims pride of place because being unarguably right justifies the power that unelected administrators exercise, internally and externally. Scientific truth becomes the counterweight to political irrationality and self-interest, and promises to bring argument to a conclusion. As a public health leader once said to Stivers, "We get the facts and the facts tell us what to do." Granted, in the Donald J. Trump era in which we write, facts seem to have lost some of their automatic allure among many members of the public, evidently because they have been persuaded that there is no such thing as a fact. As philosopher Hannah Arendt (1972, p. 4) observed in a discussion of the Pentagon Papers, "Truthfulness has never been counted among the political virtues, and lies have always been regarded as justifiable tools in political dealings." Little did Arendt realize the depths to which her observations could reach.

Public administration has always seen rationality in the classic linear sense as a way of countering self-interest, obfuscation, and deception in politics. Scientific findings promise to enable public managers and analysts to speak truth to power, as the old saying goes. The problem is that, as has become increasingly clear, the facts, well-documented as they may be, do not automatically tell us what to do; if they were ever accepted as true on their face, the last few years have wiped that face away. The public does not have access to the evidence on which most assertions of public fact are based, so their ability to judge is handicapped. Worse, what a George W. Bush-administration aide once called "the reality-based community" is in danger of disappearing entirely: "That's not the way the world really works anymore ... we create our own reality ... We're history's actors ... and ... all of you will be left to just study what we do" (quoted in Stivers, 2008, p. 48). As we now know, this statement was just the tip of an iceberg looming in the path of the American ship of state.

But if not on truth claims based in science, then on what grounds are public debate and governance to be guided? Arendt, who deeply valued politics as a peculiarly human form of life, argued that we need a different understanding of the role of *public* truth, one that can serve as an alternative to what she called "official double-talk," the manipulation that has silenced authentic public dialogue and put the public space in darkness.

In this chapter we argue that experiential knowledge is a crucial, indeed fundamental, resource for everyone in public life, not only bureaucrats at every level of the pyramid but elected politicians, judges, and ordinary citizens. The key experience-based capacity, now in danger of being starved out of existence, is judgment, or as Aristotle called it, *phronesis*: practical wisdom.

Judgment, practical wisdom, consists in being able to figure out the right thing to do, the right action to take, given the circumstances, the situation facing you. "Right" thing in this instance does not mean technical or scientific correctness, though this can be a factor weighed in the judgment. Judging means deciding what *fits* a given situation best—in fact the ancient Greek word for judging or justice, *diké*, means "fit."

Judging is at the center of governance, including the administration of agencies, because public life and politics deal with the debatable, with particular situations. Administrators are called upon most every day to decide what comes next in one situation after another. They must exercise judgment—that is, they must decide what fits, what is appropriate in terms of the public good. This is never a *purely* technical decision! Clearly, scientific studies, quantitative data, can provide important information, but never do they "tell us what to do" all by themselves. John Dewey (1998 [1927], p. 281) once said: "Many people seem to suppose that facts carry their meaning along with themselves on their face. Accumulate enough of them, and their interpretation stares out at you." Dewey took an alternative view: that the task of interpretation, *if shared widely enough in dialogue*, could find the fitting approach to solving particular public problems.

Hummel's logic of reasonableness, we believe, corresponds to Aristotle's practical wisdom. In governance it entails a circular, dialogic process of interpreting particular situations, with the aim of finding—judging—the action that seems most likely to serve the public interest. When administrative theorists talk about the exercise of administrative discretion, they tend to neglect the details of *how* this exercise takes place. The process remain murky. Typically, discretion is conceived of as a rational decision-making exercise engaged in by an isolated individual (e.g. Simon, 1945; Friedrich, 1940; Finer, 1940). In our view, a logic of reasonableness best fits the *practice* of administrative discretion, which lies at the very heart of what it means to "administer" in the public sector. The discussion to follow takes up these elements: We will argue that practical wisdom is the constitutive knowledge required for governing. Practical wisdom entails being able to *judge* wisely, a cognitive skill that cannot be taught but can be learned through experience (that is, *in practice*). Further, the nature of judgment is *communal*: that is, the standards by which it is validated are *dialogic* in origin.

We start by discussing *practice*: what it means to be an administrative practitioner, how administration itself, which is the exercise of *discretion*, requires experiential learning. What one learns as an administrator, or must learn in order to be effective, is how to judge the fitting thing to do in particular situations, how to exercise *practical wisdom*. And practical wisdom is a skill that cannot be acquired through contemplation, but only in situations that involve other people, that is, by means of *dialogue* that produces shared sense of the right thing to do.

What Does It Mean to Practice?

In public administration, academics often refer to people who are actually doing administration, rather than studying it or talking about it, as "practitioners." We believe this way of speaking comes from that old culprit, the Cartesian model of science that separates the knower from the known—what Cook and Wagenaar

(2012) call the "received view" of practice. Science does experiments and comes up with theories, which can then be applied. Practice is understood (at least among scientists) as the *application* of some tested assertion: following theory A in order to get results B. To motivate employees (B), pay them more (A). To improve employee compliance with rules (B), make sure the rules are clearly written (A). And so on. This all sounds smooth, but the application process has always been problematic, if not for theorists, then definitely for applicators. Hence the old saying, "It may be good in theory but it doesn't work in practice." The scientific model of practice discounts the knowledge that comes from doing the activity itself rather than studying it. Could it be that practitioners know something that didn't originate in a scientific study?

The experiential understanding of practice is actually a very old idea, though obscured by the centuries-long march of science. Bringing it back into its own gives us an understanding that helps to bridge the gap Cartesian science opened up, which created the application problem in the first place. The experiential view also re-introduces the ancient notion of practice as fundamentally normative, guided and shaped by shared moral and aesthetic standards, as Aristotle held with respect to *phronesis*.

Both these neglected features of practice are useful in making the case for a more wholistic, circular understanding of what goes on in administrative agencies. In particular, it offers a more fine-grained interpretation of what it means for an administrator to "exercise discretion" when faced with a situation that requires action. If uncovered and recognized, practice newly understood presents a potential alternative to hierarchical domination. Given the ubiquitous assumption that there is no such alternative, there is value in suggesting that something that looks natural and inevitable may not actually be so.

Practices as Practical Wisdom

In public organizations, as elsewhere, patterns can be observed in daily activities, and in fact are a definitive feature of bureaucratic life (see Chapter 2). People in organizations share explicit and taken-for-granted understandings of "how we do things here," which take the form of meaningful enactments of relevant rules or norms. These can be explicit, as in deliberate following of laws, regulations, agency protocols and precedents, or they can be more or less tacit assumptions. In both cases, practice entails judging what the rules (written or otherwise) require in particular situations. This sounds fairly straightforward, but it is not. Philosophers as different as Immanuel Kant and Ludwig Wittgenstein agree that there is no rule for following a rule. If you try to write down such a rule, you find yourself in infinite regress. In principle, no action being justified as following a particular rule can be rejected on its face. Justifications for actions have to be judged by others as reasonable or not. Often, in bureaucracies, an individual's exercise of discretion in following a rule is accepted on the basis of precedent: "I did what the records show others did before me." But not necessarily: "I decided the way I did because previous decisions neglected this particular feature of the situation."

Another bump in the road of bureaucratic decision-making is that many regulations try to balance conflicting political values, say individual rights versus community needs. Take this example, which came up in a class: An individual who owns a tract of forest land wants to log it off in order to raise money. But he discovers a bald eagle nest on the tract, and it is against the law to disturb the nest because bald eagles are a protected species. The official who has to decide is faced with choosing between public values. The property owner, in theory, has the right to use his land. But there is significant public interest in keeping a dwindling species from becoming extinct. What is the practical wisdom in this situation? What factors should the official consider?

Eventually a discussion of the practice of public administration encounters a definitive feature of exercising discretion: *There is no right answer, in the scientific sense!* No amount of factual examination will resolve the issue in the way that an experiment resolves the question of the causal relationship between two variables. Administrative decisions are essentially contestable. That is what makes them political, in the generic sense, and why they require judgment. Reasonable people can reject any such decision without the rejection being irrational on its face. If I decide that the property owner can log his land despite the eagle's nest, because individual rights come first, reasonable people can argue that I made the wrong decision. The same is true for the opposite decision; it is not irrational to argue that the broader public interest in saving endangered species outweighs an individual's property rights. Practice, then, is virtually never a matter of rote application of scientific findings. Reasonableness has to be justified rather than proved.

Aristotle (1976) argued that judging wisely is the key skill for public life, not only on the part of people in government but citizens as well. The interesting thing about this skill is that, as Aristotle said, *it can be learned but it cannot be taught.* Practical wisdom is acquired in experience, or not at all. It is the most important intellectual virtue, because excellence lies in the practice itself, rather than in anything that results from it. In other words, it is not instrumental, even though it may have consequences. For political excellence, everything depends on being able to read the situation, seeing what it requires. In doing so, the person of practical wisdom has already made something of it. So practical wisdom merges knowing and acting. Thus, it erases the gap between theory and practice.

Advancing a vision of governance as practice does not imply that uniformly good results will ensue. Practice is not the "one right way" that Frederick Taylor promoted. It is inspired by commitment to the public good, and as such it cannot escape uncertainty, disagreement, or the possibility of failure. It may be that practical wisdom is "no more than a commitment to do our best under uncertain and thus more or less unpredictable circumstances" (Kemmis, 2012, p. 152).

Practical Wisdom as Judgment, Judgment as Dialogic

If practical wisdom or judgment cannot be taught but must be learned in experience, how does this happen? One can bring to bear facts, or precedent, or principles, but what it comes down to is having to apply whatever ammunition seems relevant in particular case after particular case. It is beneficial to study what someone else did in another situation, as Ralph Hummel concluded in suggesting that the stories managers tell each other are as "valid as science." Hummel talked to managers, asking them why they tell each other "war stories," and how they decide whether someone else's story is useful, relevant, trustworthy. Why would managers find someone else's story applicable to their own situations? One manager said, "You're looking for somebody that has the, that shares—this is a contradiction in terms—that shares a unique experience" (Hummel, 1991, p. 37). A similar argument was made by Eugene Gendlin (1973), phenomenologist and practicing therapist. You can use any situation to help make sense of any other situation. This does not mean that all situations are the same. It means that the very act of comparing two situations engages you in relating one to the other, in the process of which similarities and differences show themselves. You find what is the same in what is different, or vice versa. This could be seen as a sort of dialogue between two cases.

Hannah Arendt (1982), following Kant, saw judging as an intersubjective process because it can only be validated communally. She saw the process as one that relies first on the imagination. Studying the situation, you imagine yourself occupying some other position than your own. You put yourself in someone else's place, not to "feel their pain," but to experience how you yourself would feel in those circumstances. Arendt called this "training your imagination to go visiting" (p. 43). You compare your initial view with the possible viewpoints of others. This is a way of testing your assumptions and whatever existing interest you have in the problem. The more viewpoints you consider, the more likely you are to reach a kind of generality from particulars. This process brings you to some sort of changed perspective, but how can you be sure that this is the "fit" one? (See also Disch, 1994.)

As a public servant, even if you have the authority to act on your own, you are obligated to be able to give reasons for your decision and try to persuade others that you made the right choice. Arendt called this "wooing" the agreement of others. Sometimes they will agree, sometimes they won't. This process is important, regardless of the outcome, because it captures the heart of democratic politics. Public servants give reasons for their decisions, or are prepared to give them if asked, because what they do has binding consequences for others. You seek to persuade, in the hope of coming to agreement. This is the final step in arriving at a valid judgment: to court the agreement of others. Thus, judging is fundamentally circular and plural.

Best of all, however, is not settling for experiencing the views of others in your imagination, but rather creating the conditions for actual, face-to-face dialogue.

This is the heart of democratic politics. The very word "public" connotes what we experience in common when we "appear," as Arendt put it, to one another in conversation about issues for which we share concern. The way the conversation unfolds is completely unpredictable because every human being is unique, someone who has never lived before and never will again. When people come together around common concerns their talk both unites and separates them. It unites them by linking their differences around a shared issue. It separates them on the basis of their unique perspectives, which keep the group from turning into a crowd or a mob. Arendt believed that there is no public space absent occasions when people with different perspectives come together to discuss them. It is this process that lights up the light of the public space.

Dialogue in Bureaucracies

Dwight Waldo (1948, p. 75) once said that public administration had made a bad deal: "'Autocracy' at work as the unavoidable price for 'Democracy' after hours." Administrators spend their working days taking orders from superiors further up the pyramidal ranks, while the practice of democracy is exiled to the selection of political representatives. The bargain is unavoidable, according to the early thinkers on public administration (Wilson, 1887; Goodnow, 1900); politics in administration inevitably corrupts it, if not literally, through patronage and pay-offs, then procedurally, by tainting the scientific rationality that was thought necessary to achieve maximum fairness and best results. Waldo was talking about the notorious "politics-administration dichotomy" that was a prominent feature of the early days of theory. The dichotomy was issued a death certificate in the mid-twentieth century but seems to have resuscitated itself in New Public Management emphasis on results rather than on how they are achieved.

It may be the contemporary insistence on performance measurement—in other words, measurement of results and neglect of the process by which they have been reached—that accounts for neglect of the issue of the interactive processes by which bureaucracies *act*. We pursue some of the particulars of circular dialogue in chapters below.

References

Arendt, Hannah. 1972. Lying in politics. Pp. 1–48 in *Crises of the Republic*. New York: Harcourt Brace.
Arendt, Hannah. 1982. *Lectures on Kant's Political Philosophy* (ed. R. Beiner). Chicago: University of Chicago Press.
Aristotle. 1976. *The Ethics of Aristotle: The Nicomachean Ethics* (trans. J.A.K. Thompson). New York: Penguin.
Cook, D. Noam, & Hendrik Wagenaar. 2012. Navigating the eternally unfolding present: Toward an epistemology of practice. *American Review of Public Administration* 42:1, 3–58.

Dewey, John. 1998. Search for the public. Pp. 281–292 in *The Essential Dewey*, Vol. 1 (eds. L.A. Hickman & T.M. Alexander). Bloomington & Indianapolis: Indiana University Press. Original work published 1927.

Disch, Lisa Jane. 1994. *Hannah Arendt and the Limits of Philosophy*. Ithaca, N.Y. & London: Cornell University Press.

Finer, Herman. 1940. Administrative responsibility in democratic government. Pp. 247–275 in *Public Policy* (ed. C. Friedrich). Cambridge, Mass.: Harvard University Press.

Friedrich, Carl J. 1940. Public power and the nature of administrative responsibility. Pp. 221–245 in *Public Policy* (ed. C. Friedrich). Cambridge, Mass.: Harvard University Press.

Gendlin, Eugene. 1973. Experiential phenomenology. Pp. 281–322 in *Phenomenology and the Social Sciences*, Vol. 1 (ed. Maurice Natanson). Evanston, Ill.: Northwestern University Press.

Goodnow, Frank. 1900. *Politics and Administration: A Study in Government*. New York: Russell & Russell.

Hummel, Ralph P. 1989. I'd like to be ethical but they won't let me. *International Journal of Public Administration* 12:6, 855–866.

Hummel, Ralph P. 1991. Stories managers tell: Why they are as valid as science. *Public Administration Review* 31:1 (Jan.-Feb.), 31–41.

Kemmis, Stephen. 2012. Phronesis, experience, and the primacy of praxis. Pp. 147–161 in *Phronesis as Professional Knowledge* (eds. E.A. Kinsella & A. Pitman). Rotterdam: Sense Publishers.

Simon, Herbert. 1945. *Administrative Behavior*. New York: Free Press.

Stivers, Camilla. 2008. *Governance in Dark Times: Practical Philosophy for Public Service*. Washington, D.C.: Georgetown University Press.

Waldo, Dwight. 1948. *The Administrative State*. New York: Ronald Press.

Wilson, Woodrow. 1887. The study of administration. *Political Science Quarterly* 2 (June), 197–222.

9

THE DIALOGIC CIRCLE IN THE BUREAUCRATIC PYRAMID

Conflict Resolution and Collective Bargaining

In this chapter we discuss how moving toward dialogue and away from counterproductive conversations marked by avoidance or competition or confrontation can strengthen circular relationships inside the pyramid. Our focus is on relationships internal to the bureaucracy, though much of what we have to say can be applied to relationships that cross the organizational boundary, such as interactions with citizens and community groups.

The word dialogue comes from *dia* (through) and *logos* (the word). Dialogue is the flow of meaning between or among us when we listen and respond to each other. As such, it fills in the gaps between different experiences found in bureaucracies. At its best, dialogue aims to engage us in a collective present-tense telling, where no one person's position or thought dominates, but where larger questions and new frontiers are laid bare for exploration.

As we noted in the introduction to Part III, interpretive philosophy sees interaction among human beings as somewhat like a text, in that understanding in both cases is a circular process, a reciprocal movement, either between human beings, or between human being and something in writing—for example, a rule. The philosopher Hans-Georg Gadamer (1976, p. xxii) captures the importance of dialogue when he says, "It is true of every conversation that through it something different has come to be." Dialogue is the *logic* of understanding, and that logic is circular. It is mutual: it involves genuine seeking to understand the other person, and the willingness to risk our own opinions through the encounter. As Bernstein notes:

> If the quintessence of what we *are* is to be dialogical ... then ... it should give practical orientation to our lives. We must ask what it is that blocks and

prevents such dialogue, and what is to be done ... to make [it] a concrete reality.

(Bernstein, 1983, p. 163, italics added)

Hierarchy is the enemy of dialogue because it tends to fracture and fragment human interactions in organizations by making them seem one-way, usually top down. Domination gets in the way of communication in the issuing and receiving of orders, and efforts to dig more deeply into whether the order is actually the best way to proceed can trigger conflict. At its best, dialogue enables people to approach each other in an exploratory way, starting with give and take, then reflection, then exploration of what can be found in differences, with the hope of real engagement. In other words, dialogue is circular. As Giddens (1990) has said, dialogue is "facework," direct back-and-forth interaction that is the foundation of faceless commitments such as trust in the legitimacy of the chain of command.

Typically, efforts to start dialogue where it is lacking are seen as threatening and overwhelming, and a lot of people bail out without giving it a real chance. As a result, genuine dialogue rarely happens. People at different levels of the organization bring different experiences, understandings, beliefs, and experiences to it. The hierarchical physics of the bureaucracy attempts to resolve differences by means of position power. Issuing orders prevails, and listening means complying. There is little genuine participation; rather there is "buy-in" or going along. This is the virtual definition of inauthenticity.

Dialogue and Conflict Resolution

Dialogue is a resource to achieve consensus in a situation that can all too easily default to win-lose dynamics. Genuine dialogue is oriented to win-win, or integration in Follett's (1924) terms. Here we consider the role of dialogue in conflict resolution. The model embraced here has its roots in the dialogic negotiation of differences when people in organizations disagree on the nature of the problem and courses of action going forward. Consider Figure 9.1.

Two positive vectors are evident. One is "assertiveness," or the extent to which individuals or groups are willing to stand up for their sense of the situation The other is "circularity," or the willingness to consider the interpretations of others about the same situation. Dialogic conflict resolution meshes standing up for one's own view and making room for the views of others. The typical problem comes when the two vectors get out of balance with each other and head towards conflict. Assertiveness turns into refusal to hear another viewpoint, or open competition, or outright power moves. Circularity can lapse into compromise or acceptance of the "other side," not because it is more persuasive but because it appears more powerful. Ideally, dialogue is both high on assertiveness and high on circularity. This balance is what Follett called "integration." In

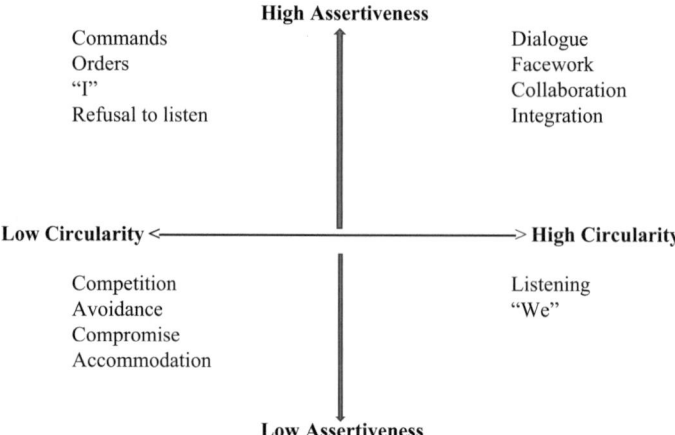

FIGURE 9.1 Vectors of Dialogue: Assertiveness and Circularity (by David Carnevale)

practice, trying to achieve integration is often the last resort, after competition, avoidance, compromise, or accommodation have failed.

Mary Parker Follett's (1977) notion of "integration" offers a process by which assertiveness and active openness to the views of others can actually take place. She recommended depersonalizing the situation, in other words, shifting people's focus from what they personally stand to gain or lose to what the situation itself requires. She held that compromise was not the best possible outcome, because it was inherently unstable. If you have to give up a chunk of what you really want, you walk away unsatisfied. There was an even better aim: integration, a new understanding among everyone concerned, in which all would come away feeling that they actually got what they wanted.

The basis on which integration could potentially work was what Follett called "circular response." As she said, "I never react to you but to you-plus-me; or to be more accurate, it is I-plus-you reacting to you-plus-me ... By the very process of meeting we both become something different" (Follett, 1924, pp. 58–59, 63). Study of the situation starts with recognizing that ordinary ways of coping have stopped working, or have been called into question. The situation now calls for paying attention, which may entail coping with the conflicts in the working relationship itself. Studying the situation means not just staring at the problem but engaging in some new activity, which could include a conversation that changes the relationship among the participants. Conflict resolution enables them to take a meaningful step-in-common, which in and of itself changes their understanding of what they are engaged in.

Conflict resolution opens the process beyond the objectified aspects of the problem itself to the participants' differences in beliefs and interpretation of experiences, as well as the emotional baggage that blocks openness to exploring new ways of working together (new ways of Being). But the process takes work. It would be ideal if everyone could move right away to high levels of assertiveness and listening, but in reality people tend to deploy negotiating behaviors such as the following (see Figure 9.1):

- *Competing*: unilateralism, focused almost entirely on what is good for me or us; it is high on assertiveness, on win-lose or zero-sum, low on listening.
- *Avoiding*: refusal to engage the other; it is low on assertiveness, low on listening. It can be positive, such as refusing to be baited, letting the attack pass by.
- *Accommodation*: low on assertiveness and high on listening. It can be positive, such as letting go of a minor issue for the sake of moving forward, but at its extreme it is appeasement.
- *Compromising*: horse-trading, "splitting the baby." It is intermediate between assertiveness and listening. It works if the issues are not very important to the parties, but not if the issues are large and difficult. In these cases, the deals that are struck don't hold up.
- *Collaboration*: high on assertiveness and high on listening. It is the place on the grid where "win-win" happens. It matches Follett's "integration" in that nobody walks away feeling that they gave up something important.

There is no single action that fully addresses resolving the differences among people. There is no one best way. In the end, a skill set that includes all the moves on the board may be necessary. But dialogue, whatever form it takes, ideal or imperfect, is transformative. Something different comes to be.[1]

Example: The Mental Health Commissioner and the Union Rep

>Commissioner: You say you are for good government but every time I try to evaluate individual performance of union members, you file a grievance if the net result of the evaluation process is less than fully satisfactory to you. How do I teach good conduct if it makes no difference to you whether the employee is a good or poor performer? What would you have me do?
>
>Union Rep: We end up appealing low performance ratings because, first of all, we have a duty of fair representation if the evaluation process, not just in terms of technique but also in terms of process, is not fair in the minds of our grievance committee, or job stewards are not fair. When your people have not done their jobs in terms of the idea of progressive discipline but have run roughshod or blindsided our member with an off-the-wall negative appraisal, we have no choice but to file a complaint with your office. Your folks have a duty as well, to effectively supervise or manage people in more sophisticated ways than what we are seeing throughout your shop, then complain we must.
>
>Commissioner: I see what you mean and we are working on training people to do righteous evaluations but many are reluctant to follow the spirit and letter of

performance appraisal ideals when they know that if they stick their heads out and counsel an employee to improve performance they will get confronted by the union, your union, and make the appeals process so onerous that it is not worth the hassle to honestly assess performance consistent with our shared ideas about progressive discipline. You say you are for the merit system and merit-based principles but want to arrest the process of employee performance appraisal such that no merit can be reasonably be developed over here. You can't have it both ways.

Union Rep: Yes we can, it is all about paradox and dialectics if you will indulge me here. I agree you have every right, management rights, to administer your shop in concert with an affection for merit principles but, at the same time, you must manage fairly when it comes to really dealing with individual performance. You can't have it both ways either. You must hit both notes, honest and open feedback provided to our members, and if you do that you will win grievances, which arbitrators lately have found you failing to do, doing what you are doing in fair ways to the employee, not just proving that you are in charge in some authoritarian way.

Look, we do steward training which we are obligated to do according to our current agreement and you have management training in human resources administration for your people. We are obviously not hitting the mark. Perhaps we ought to do some joint training of people on both sides of this argument and see if we can come up with better ideas about what progressive discipline really means in practice. We are willing to do that, even on an exploratory basis and see how the trainees from both sides of the table can agree with the legitimate needs of both parties in making judgments about employee performance. Both parties have an obligation, not just in terms of their sides of the table, but in dealing with both sides reasonably in these kinds of disputes, about making righteous and open methods of judgment as relates to an individual's overall functioning.

The above discussion is win-win: It seems a solution that really satisfies the interests of both parties in a dispute. It is strong on assertiveness and also strong on listening.

There is no single action that can address the resolution of differences between people. In one negotiation or path toward settlement, all the moves on the board may be necessary. In public administration terms, there is no one best way. In the end, a skill set that includes all the possibilities is necessary. And the essence of dialogue is that through it something different comes to be—that is, it is unpredictable. To be clear, dialogue is more than a transaction, it is a transformation. It transcends simple paradox. It entails building trust and represents the courage to be, embracing freedom and real, if inevitably limited, democracy in bureaucratic life.

Collective Bargaining

It is impossible to write these days about government bureaucracies without acknowledging the virulent negativity that abounds among some members of the public against governments and their employees. Anti-government feeling encompasses public employees, their unions, and the process of negotiations itself, creating mistrust that warps interactions between governments, their employees, and citizens.

Public employees are caught in a vise not of their own making, made up of partisanship, performance failures, especially in crisis situations, dwindling support for wars and other foreign ventures, and the widespread feeling that "government is not us" (Hummel & Stivers, 1998). The list is not exhaustive. Most ordinary public employees do their jobs as well as can be expected despite failures born of the zero-sum interactions that crush true dialogue among relevant parties to a problem situation.

We believe that experiential knowledge on the front lines, the knowledges born of intelligence that arises by doing public work, are the key to improving everyday problem solving in government. But knowledge is power only when power allows knowledge to be consequential. What typical public employees know from experience does improve managerial and even executive knowledge if the structural nature of the government problem-solving system is open to listening, to hearing possibilities not normally welcome in bureaucratic, autocratic, and hierarchical arrangements.

There needs to be healthy sharing of power from the top to the bottom of the organizational pyramid. This happens through facework, or not at all. The absence of good faith, bilateral relations sanctioned by law leads only to "telling" or high task and low relationship methods as the primary leadership method that is about control of persons, places and problem solving. This tendency is evident in collective bargaining. If the 1960s were the "time for the public employee," as bargaining rights exploded in the public sector, now the time is away from dialogue and towards a retrenchment of management interests at the bargaining table. The focus is still on the unionized public employee, but today in a decidedly negative direction.

There is always a need for a certain kind of information-sharing, given that there are alternative kinds of knowledges in organizations. The gaps between them can be filled or at least bridged with meaningful exchange between and among parties. We believe that collective bargaining can best be understood as one among many forms of circular dialogue. Collective bargaining is collective learning. It is a process in which the nature of the information flow is exploratory, as is the hermeneutic circle, within but tempering the pyramid. It is a process of unfolding, revealing itself through open activities. The absence of dialogue is a kind of sickness that distorts and obscures. In the end, facework is a communication between equals. Collective bargaining is dialogic when the duty to bargain in good faith is fulfilled.

Tough negotiation periods come and go as the economy over time rises and falls. Tough bargaining contexts can become the rule rather than the exception. This is where the parties find themselves today, with the added burden that bargaining rights themselves are under threat in many jurisdictions across the country. Public employees are being reassured that their opinions still matter and that they can still participate in governance of the workplace. But the good faith of employers is increasingly difficult for workers to believe in.

Good faith standards have always been a rock-bottom awareness that made collective bargaining meaningful. But structures that are the foundation of good faith are being undercut and removed, in what appears to workers as a power move on the part of management to regain unilateral control.

Hard bargaining by either party is not unfair, and employers, like unions, can take their concerns to the bargaining table, where integrative negotiations are still possible. To refuse to come to the table is pure folly, as both sides will come to realize. Relationships will only become more confrontational, "talks" will be more aggressive than assertive. And yet the possibility of circular dialogue, in which each goes out to meet the other, as Barrett (1990) says, is still there: "[M]eaning in life happens in the area between person and person in that situation of contact when one says *I* to the other's *Thou*" (p. 17).

As Follett (1924) said, fear of conflict is dread of life itself. Collective bargaining is a way of being in administrative organizations such that greater equality comes from willingness to listen and to hear what can be translated from the other's experience. This is at the core of democracy. Collective bargaining tempers the arrangement whereby higher place in the pyramid means superior knowledge and superior significance. Otherwise, persons below accept oppression because society says do what you are told. This is why knowledge of doing the work is not power unless power is willing to let it be so.

Conclusion: The Movement Away from Democratic Means and Ends

The creation of conditions for meaningful give and take on actual work requires ongoing dialogic practices within pyramidal bureaucracies. We believe managers and workers can engage in circular study and refinement of the work in partnership, exchanging information and studying the situation. This is perhaps the same as saying that working in bureaucracies may not be as much of a Faustian bargain as Waldo (1948) feared. Our optimism does not extend to the disappearance of bureaucracy itself, but to a different way of visualizing what it takes to make it work better for the good of all, including citizens, that is, recognizing that democracy can inhabit the bureaucratic pyramid to a greater extent than has been thought possible. As Waldo argued, administration is political theory in action. Whereas the dominant ideology is still autocratic, the fact of so little progress over the decades in the ongoing reform efforts to increase management control may have something to teach us.

Hierarchical thinking asserts that the know-how of frontline staff is limited and must be shaped and controlled by managers. Power is brought to bear not only on work processes but on mentalities, so that inhabitants of the pyramid are lulled or trapped into believing (or at least going along with the idea) that what they are ordered to do is natural, realistic, even scientific. Yet, even as they go along to get along, workers—perhaps even without realizing it—*interpret* the orders they receive even as they act on them, and the gap between ideas and actions remains. The power of circular processes will remain untapped until people begin to see their situations in different ways.

Note

1 Readers interested in evaluating their own conflict style can Google "Thomas Kilmann Conflict Style Questionnaire" and take the survey, which is also helpful in teaching about conflict resolution and in organizational consulting. See also Fisher & Ury (2011), *Getting to Yes* and Ury (1993), *Getting Past No*. Both explain "principled negotiations" and "interest-based bargaining" styles, which are relevant here.

References

Barrett, William. 1990. *Irrational Man: A Study in Existential Philosophy*. New York: Doubleday Anchor Books.

Bernstein, Richard J. 1983. *Beyond Objectivism and Relativism: Science, Hermeneutics, and Praxis*. Philadelphia: University of Pennsylvania Press.

Fisher, Roger, & William L. Ury. 2011. *Getting to Yes* (rev. ed.). New York: Penguin.

Follett, Mary Parker. 1924. *Creative Experience*. New York: Longmans, Green.

Follett, Mary Parker. 1977. The giving of orders. Pp. 21–41 in *Dynamic Administration* (eds. E. M. Fox & L B. Urwick). New York: Hippocrene Books. Original work 1925.

Gadamer, H. G. 1976. *Philosophical Hermeneutics* (trans. and ed. D.E. Linge). Berkeley, Calif.: University of California Press.

Giddens, Anthony. 1990. *The Consequences of Modernity*. Stanford, Calif.: Stanford University Press.

Hummel, Ralph P., & Camilla Stivers. 1998. Government isn't us: The possibility of democratic knowledge in representative government. Pp. 28–48 in *Government Is Us: Public Administration in an Anti-Government Era* (eds. C.S. King & C. Stivers). Thousand Oaks, Calif.: Sage Publications.

Ury, William L. 1993. *Getting Past No* (rev. ed.). New York: Bantam.

Waldo, Dwight. 1948. *The Administrative State*. New York: Ronald Press.

10

CIRCLES OF TRUST IN PUBLIC ORGANIZATIONS

The Power of Facework

Do managers in a public bureaucracy *trust* the frontline workers they supervise to do the work the way it needs to be done to accomplish agency objectives? Do executives *trust* managers to organize the work effectively? Consider the following voices from an agency charged with responsibility for public housing:

> Managers make us do their dirty work while they sit at head office, safe from the wrath of tenants. If a tenant walked into the foyer of head office, senior managers would crap their pants. [Yet] the majority of staff [at all levels] talked to me about the importance of a "good management style."
> *(Public housing service officer, frontline; Chalkley, 2012, p. 167)*

> Off the record, I think that the [elected executive], then the director, and finally us, the managers, have been under increasing pressure to be seen to be fixing the "crisis" with public housing, without actually understanding what the crisis is, or even if there is a crisis.
> *(Manager, head office, Housing; Chalkley, 2012, p. 183)*

In this situation, frontline workers see managers as hiding in the head office while workers take the flak from tenants. Ironically, workers are urged to practice a "good management style." At the same time, head office managers feel stuck with solving a public housing crisis that nobody at the executive levels has defined. It appears that trendy concepts like "management style" and "crisis" are not enough to bridge the gaps between different bureaucratic levels: worker, manager, executive.

Can workers in a public bureaucracy *trust* managers to deliver on the promises they make to workers about improvements in working conditions? Again, listen to voices from the same public housing agency:

> The managers identified [by frontline staff] as respected for "good management style" were physically present in the local offices … or had frequent telephone interaction with the front line … would "help" on the front desk, have a coffee in the tea room and would rarely email. … [They] "always called you back, even with shitty news."
>
> *(Chalkley, 2012, p. 170)*

> Over a coffee, [a retired housing manager] told me that one of the most difficult things … was the arrival of the professional public servant; bred in captivity and trained from birth to be an arsehole … [They were] often referred to as "the suits."
>
> *(Chalkley, 2012, p. 180)*

> What becomes immediately apparent … is the entrenched adversarial relationship of head office versus local office. … Staff told me that "head office doesn't listen to what we say" and that they "mostly take the orders from head office with a grain of salt."
>
> *(Chalkley, 2012, p. 190)*

Here, voices from the various levels begin to sing similar tunes: In the eyes of workers, "good management" is not just a "style," it's about being physically present, lending a hand when it's appropriate, returning phone calls asking for help. Good managers "listen to what we say." By the same token, managers are suspicious of "suits," head-office professionals trained to ignore the realities of situations. It appears that worker, manager, and executive not only know differently, but that these conflicting knowledges result in mutual distrust.

This chapter explores what has been learned and said about trust in organizations. It argues that the existence of different forms of knowledge at different levels of the bureaucracy produce differentials of power and understanding that get in the way of building basic trust. We mean the kind of trust that solidifies collaborative work dynamics throughout organizations and makes possible the accomplishment of basic purposes. Knowledge gaps can be bridged, power dynamics tempered, and trust built, by circular human practices like conversations that build mutual respect—in other words, by facework.

Trust and Facework

Trust is faith that the intentions and actions of a person or group are ethical and dependable. In social exchange relationships, such as in public organizations, trust is the expectation that consensual norms or reciprocal obligations will be lived up to, especially when the rights and interests of others are involved (Carnevale & Wechsler, 1992, Carnevale, 1995, 2003). Trust means one's needs are secure in the good faith hands of someone else. In general, trustworthy conduct is a matter of respect and honor. These definitions may seem idealized, but they are bedrock assumptions in the social fabric of organizational life, supporting all of an organization's rules, roles, and relations.

The consensus running through the literature on organizational trust is clear: The significance of trust for organizational performance is difficult to overvalue. Studies claim that individuals, groups, and organizations perform at higher levels where trust abides (cf. Covey, 1996; Peters & Waterman, 1982). Many find that trust is a direct and positive correlate of productivity. For instance, trust is associated with ethical conduct, open communication, fairness in the administration of rewards and punishments, encouraging employee involvement and participation, managing power, ethical politics, principled leadership and the quality of supervision (Carnevale & Wechsler, 1992).

The links of trust enable individuals, groups, and organizations to know and to learn interactively. Learning organizations are fundamentally based on trust of self and others. Consider the following, summarized from the organizational trust literature:

- A willingness to trust disposes people to take the risk of relating to interdependent others.
- If the act of trusting is reciprocated, people reveal more, share information, consider alternative points of view, work problems in the spirit of partnership.
- Greater learning—for the individual, group, and the organization—is fashioned as the self-reinforcing open communication increases psychological safety cycle, encourages meaningful dialogue, reduces resistance to contrary beliefs, and thinking is synthesized into fresh ideas.
- Better decisions are reached when mutual confidence as opposed to mistrust permeates the decision-making process.
- When high levels of trustworthy conduct are realized, a self-heightening cycle of mutual adjustment is formed, intensifies and repeats.

Anthony Giddens (1990, pp. 83–85) argues that *"the nature of modern institutions is deeply bound up with the mechanisms of trust in abstract systems,"* especially trust in expertise (italics in original). The ability to trust beyond the realm of direct, face-to-face contact among members in the institutions lies at the heart of the modern.

No institutional member—whether frontline worker, manager, or executive—can opt out of abstract trust, or "faceless commitments." Just as we trust the physician and the attorney without having to see their diplomas, we trust professionals in general because particular expertise marks them as what they are. Yet Giddens insists that what makes abstract trust viable, what holds these trust relationships in place, is whatever direct, face-to-face interaction takes place between them and us: "[A]ccess points carry a reminder that it is flesh-and-blood people (who are potentially fallible) who are [the system's] operators. Facework ... [relies] upon ... the demeanor of system representatives or operators" (italics in original).

In current political and organizational climates, much attention is devoted to creating "zones of trust," sanctuaries where people can find safety in their lives. The central idea is that the foremost condition of safety is trust that there are places where opening up, bringing expression in the open, being authentically and assertively true to oneself and others are the conditions from which trustful leaps of faith emerge in the face of contrary pressures to use, to exploit, to manipulate. The popular idea in social dynamics is "transparency" or high trust assumptions about the world of being and action. The existence of realms where facework is not only possible but encouraged holds the whole organization together, if Giddens' argument is accepted.

The Trust Literature

The significance of trust is made clear in the research literature by the many different variables with which it is associated. Trust is linked to productivity (Golembiewski & McConkie, 1975), group performance (Zand, 1972), cooperation and (in its absence) conflict (Deutsch, 1958), leadership styles (Likert, 1961), managerial assumptions (McGregor, 1960), need satisfaction (Maslow, 1954), organizational development (Carnevale, 2003), communication (Mellinger, 1956), psychological contracts (Argyris, 1957), the quality of labor-management relations (Armshaw, Carnevale, & Waltuck, 2007, Carnevale, 1995), perceptions of government and politicians, and, when it is missing, with the existence of administrative evil (Adams & Balfour, 1998). These links are not exhaustive.

According to this literature, people trust based on previous direct experience and the amount of information they have about whether the required leap of faith is warranted. There is no doubt that deep-seated self-protective human instincts play a role in how humans react to fear, dependency, and uncertainty, which leads to how willing they may be to take risks based on another's promise of good faith. However, people have the ability to learn to behave in ways that transcend basic dispositions. So it is with trust.

For our argument, a key assertion from the literature is that *trust is a learned behavior*. That is, it is built and maintained in facework. Individuals, groups and organizations make choices with varying results when it comes to trust. Over time, experiential learning either reinforces primitive, self-protective instincts or encourages engaging the world in more optimistic ways. People do not come to organizations as blank slates when it comes to trust. They have predispositions of every kind. Organizations choose whether to encourage healthy trust or low trust work cultures. It is more difficult to plant seeds of trust than mistrust. Individuals bring attitudes about trust with them when they join an organization, born of their previous experiences at work or in life generally. Research results, we conclude, support the claim that building trust is not something that can be done in the abstract, such as by relying on management concepts like "good management style." Trust among people at different levels of the organization is achieved by means of facework—dialogue and teamwork, for example—if at all.

Much is written these days about "transforming organizations" without regard to the facts that transformation is change at the highest degree, and changes that only award points for style will fail. Transformation means deep change, fundamental alterations instead of superficial half measures. All change is not transformational. We have argued that the failure of management reforms can be traced to superficial change, failing to take up deeper issues of authority and power. Most management reforms are only empty talk, changing the surface nature of the conversation and leaving underlying power relations untouched.

Organizational trust has a rich scholarly knowledge base. The question we address here is: If trust is a "learned behavior," how does this learning happen, and how does trust get built across the experiential, cognitive and power gaps created by the division of labor and the differing knowledges it engenders? Put more sharply, if trust is learned from experience, how does it find its way into the operating practices of managers who have been accustomed to the ideology of management, which discounts experiential knowledge and concentrates on maintaining control of workers?

The quotes that began this chapter, from a study of public housing offices in Victoria, BC, illustrate what we believe are common tensions among staff at various levels: frontline officers, middle managers, and top executives. To our ears, they reveal how people at different levels see those at other levels as *not understanding their situation and worse, unable or unwilling to try*. They also suggest, however, that the key to establishing trust is interaction of a particular kind.

"The Whole Organization Was in the Room"—a Case Example

The whole organization was in the room in the federal social security organization in a large southwestern city. The director, judges, other professionals and administrative support personnel came together to talk about the manifest differences in trust or sense of safety felt by the various parties about their work. We were the outside consultant, facilitators aimed to get issues on the table and owned by participants, in full view calling for dialogue: assertiveness on one hand and active listening on the other.

We asked the following question: "If there were one issue in this operation that could be settled, what would that be?" One idea came up time and again from frontline staff: Who should staff the welcome desk to greet clients? Frontline staff pointed out that, instead of having a full-time person staffing the desk, the duty of coverage fell piecemeal to them. Not incidentally in their eyes, all the frontliners were female, and the majority were black or brown, whereas upper-level staff, who were not tasked to help with coverage, were mostly white males. Upper-level employees did not have their work interrupted to do short hits on the welcome window. Frontline workers interpreted having to drop their other duties to staff the desk at a moment's notice as indifference to the importance of their work. They also saw it as racist and sexist.

We began to probe the welcome desk issue, trying to understand what it was all about and how it had wounded general trust among different levels of staff, depending on who was called to staff the window, or not. As the consultants pressed the issue, the director told people to stop talking about such a mundane subject, wasting the consultant's time and eating away valuable opportunity for "dialogue." Interesting to the consultants was the director's failure to see staff discontent over the welcome desk as "dialogue."

All consultants have their own standing and trust in play during organizational interventions. To agree with the director, to shut off the resentment and dissent, would have been fatal to meaningful change and would leave the consultants seen as not honoring the real sentiments in the room. The consultants—wisely, as it turned out—contradicted the chief executive and used this seemingly minor issue as a sign of deeper divisions in the group as a whole. Feelings ran high but the welcome desk came to be a central issue, symbolic of larger emerging questions. The consultants gained the trust of down-the-line staff, the director learned that no matter what an issue might seem in substance, workers decide to attach meaning to a situation in their own way, to fix their own weight to events, and if this not respected, trust goes out the window. Nothing is too small to be evidence of trust or mistrust.

A related case that illustrates the link between reform and trust involved police officers in a mid-size city in Oklahoma. At the first meeting, the consultant tried to engage with the group but there was no feedback at all from police union officers. Finally, after about two hours, when not a single officer had embraced the process at hand, one spoke out: "Who are you, who pays you, what are you doing here, why should we participate with you?" Consultants have to overcome the mistrust of rank and file organization members, given that their contract with agencies comes from top leadership. Their connection with the top makes consultants look like agents of change bought and paid for by the highest levels of the organization. In short, the boss buys the facilitation and expects the results he or she wants.

These are awe-inspiring questions not easily managed from the stance of the outsider hired by those in charge. It took weeks of meetings and participation in department events for the consultant even to begin to open up organization members to the most basic kinds of trust and cooperation.

Mistrust

When mistrust and betrayal are embedded in an organization's social system, assorted pathologies reign (Reina & Reina, 1999):

- High levels of stress are created as the social context is seen as threatening.
- Performance at every level is impaired as considerable time is spent on self-protection and self-sealing conduct.
- Innovation is damaged because of the essential dishonesty and inauthentic behavior that abounds as what is truly known or felt is withheld.
- Blaming cultures are created as people distance themselves from responsibility and accountability.
- People want psychological safety all the time and the workplace is no exception. Workers are hyper-vigilant about who can be trusted and who is unreliable.

Sonneberg (1994) sums up the consequences of low trust organizations: Just as high levels of trust reduce friction among employees, bond people together, increase productivity, and stimulate growth, low levels of trust adversely affect relationships, stifle innovation, and hamper the decision-making process. Employees in organizations marked by low levels of trust usually cooperate at higher levels of stress. They spend a great deal of effort covering their true feelings, justifying past decisions, and conducting witch hunts or looking for scapegoats when something doesn't work out. This prevents them from focusing on the work they should be doing and the free exchange of ideas that result in innovative solutions.

When trust is violated, mistrust is obviously one result, but not the only one. People feel they have been "handed over," "given up," and "let down." Their ability to enter into other trusting relations is crippled. Many just want to get even. People, at the heart of things, learn about organizational life and develop degrees of commitment to trust or not to. This makes it harder to reconcile differences in knowledges that are inherent in bureaucratic affairs. Even a small thing, like what counts or doesn't count as dialogue, can either build trust or undercut it. To breach trust is to deny the worth of others, to shake the very foundation of their being.

Employees who feel mistrusted tend to paint with a wide brush. Typically, when people feel deceived, they withdraw into submission and conformity or attack the fraudsters to restore their dignity and esteem. Either way, victims of untrustworthiness are not fully committed to working collaboratively with the perpetuators of the psychic assault. Restoring a trusting relationship takes a healthy measure of sensitivity and a fair amount of time.

Bargaining Impasse—a Case Example

Why do parties to an organizational dispute resort to feigning interaction because of institutionalized roles playing out in real time with one another? In this example, the parties in a bargaining impasse were the union representing the staff and a statewide utility company. The union reps came to the table ostensibly to argue faithfully in their classic role: as internal outsiders, feeling responsible to speak truth to power. We may call this a "distributive bargaining" or traditional stance: high on aggressiveness and low on cooperation. Management on the other hand played its own traditional hard-nosed role: high on aggressive response and low on cooperation. The mediators could almost predict all of the positions that would be taken between the parties in the negotiations, issue by issue—a logjam, obstructive to any attempt by either party to engage in a higher level of trust with the other.

The mediators suggested to the parties that the talks were not getting anywhere and that a higher trust approach was crucial to avoiding a statewide strike. Strict compliance with hierarchical roles was taking everybody to the brink of disaster. The mediators took a page from the book of the old TV and movie spy, Maxwell Smart. When pressed to give restricted information, Smart would go to what he called the "cone of silence" for advice and instructions. The mediators suggested, and parties agreed, that when the conflict was predictable and the classic playing out of institutionalized roles seemed inevitable, they would go to a "zone of silence" where real, prejudicial talk could occur without penalty. The process actually worked. Time after time, the parties would go to the penalty-free zone; gradually traditional postures became less and less evident. Slowly, people moved from low trust to high trust behavior. After a while, the worst name anyone could be called was "violator of the zone of silence." The union, for instance, moved from "slow-dragging the customer" to a stance that was downright managerial.

The Pyramid and Trust

The pyramidal structure of bureaucratic hierarchy means that those at the top develop and rely on a different form of knowledge than those they command; thus, they are bound to be on trial when it comes to worker trust. The same can be said for worker knowledge and the willingness of managers and executives to trust in its efficacy (recall Chapter 6 and the VA).

According to Hummel (1990), the pyramidal shape of modern organizations shows itself in the well-known "org chart," with boxes representing various subsections arrayed in a triangular shape and the head office or chief executive at the top. Yet everyone within the organization knows that this formal structure does not capture the way things really work, that is, the actual dynamics of interaction that people depend on to get their work done. The chain of command and its built-in mistrust among people at different levels, and the reciprocity that not only builds trust but facilitates high performance, remain hidden, or even blocked.

The possibility of creating respectable levels of organizational trust may be constrained by hierarchical work roles, but organizational authorities are not helpless in the face of reality. Much can be done by organizational leaders to create high trust work cultures, even within a hierarchy. Forms of organizational structure are not destiny when it comes to trust formation. It is how personnel are treated within any structure that is determinant when it comes to employee attitudes like trust. In other words, through good facework the pyramid can be made to give way to a certain extent to the circle (Hummel 1990).

A Circle within the Hierarchy—Case Example

An example of the dynamics of trust within the pyramid comes from a statewide public health agency. The director of the agency was concerned with what he perceived as pervasive mistrust among his immediate staff, as well as reluctance to trust the central office among staff in the various field offices throughout the state. The consultants called in by the director started meeting with individuals at the top of the pyramid and in small groups of mid- to higher-level administrators, to get a sense of how people felt at the various levels and between center and field offices.

Over time the meetings between the mediators and people in the managerial ranks were running at about 30–40 participants per session. At the same time, the mediators visited each of the field offices. It became clear that not only was there low trust among the organization's leadership, but the mistrust of headquarters among field staff was far worse. Tension between field office and headquarters, of course, can be found in almost every organization on the planet that has branches and a central office.

The mediators recommended establishing a way of bringing together the field and central office by including them in more information from headquarters about a wide range of strategic matters. An organization was created within the organization to do this. Each field office was encouraged to elect delegates to a statewide conference of rank and file members of staff to talk about issues of primary concern to them. At that initial conference, participants communicated directly with the agency's director, who came to the gathering. He proved to be open to dialogue in the truest sense, and when the group voted to have the internal group made permanent, he agreed. In effect, the mediators, with the support of the director, created a union inside the organization, which took the views of line staff more strongly into account. Again, traditional hierarchical roles were still in play, but they were no longer as controlling. Line staff got more and better information from the top—essentially a sharing of knowledge—and a stronger presence going forward in determining the organization's strategic choices. This is an example of how, through good facework, circular processes can be nurtured inside a hierarchy, with greater mutual trust as a result.

A year or so later, at the closing of the mediators' contract with the health agency, one of the mediators was speaking at the Governor's Leadership Conference. Spotting a couple of participants from the health agency, he set his prepared remarks aside and indicated that he was sorry more had not been accomplished during the intervention in terms of overcoming individual and institutional mistrust in the agency. The representatives responded that the consultancy had been a success: The employees' council still existed and was playing an important role in various agency deliberations. Trust was increasing throughout the unit because people had more access to information and employee voice had a new-found legitimacy in what had previously been a hierarchical and stifling imposition of rules and power on the job. When there is a modicum of good will, it is amazing what some facework can do!

Pyramids, Circles, and the Building of Trust

Trust is embedded in an organization's rules, roles, and relations (Fox, 1974). However, organizations cannot sanctify them enough to escape the truth that constructive organizational process operates a good deal in the spaces where formal arrangements cannot reach. In the gaps where formalization does not impose dominion, i.e. in the myriad experiences that cannot be fully shared by talking, organizational members can build circular trust relations that have a powerful bearing on what is done. This lesson is especially relevant for bureaucratic institutions whose pedigree is rooted in low trust assumptions and highly regulated work practices (Carnevale, 1995). We believe that the move to reduce pyramidal interactions and supplement them strategically with circle interactions is the secret.

The pyramid's organizational chart receives lots of attention, usually at the top levels. But the chart is an abstraction, not real life. For example, at one public union, a leadership position was held by a person who was from the private sector. He had his staff spend lots of time massaging the organizational chart searching for efficiency and effectiveness. Everybody at the top level had a power stake in how the most recent "shakeup" would increase or lower their authority. No matter the outcome, the latest design of the organization at the top, there were no boxes representing people who were not in the room for these discussions. Rather than efficiency, the real issue was the politics, who got control of what functions, how scores were settled, how coalitions were formed, how horse trading influenced the various parties to the exercise, and who would get more, not less power. The executive group would go to "retreats" to hammer out details on their own or sometimes hired consultants to facilitate the process. The point here is that the boxes on flip charts told one story beginning with the genesis of the "teambuilding," but behind the scenes, it was the actual politics of the organization that was in play. It was in these underground places where real work got done, where real power was manipulated, that the truth of things was created. The maps were not the territory, and trust was always in play as a key activity in the negotiations, no matter how visible: Circle relations were hidden by pyramidal conveniences.

Bureaucratic organizations aim for a high degree of control—the kind of management that leaves little to chance. The aim for predictability is understandable in complex, open systems. There are limits to control, however, and they begin where workers are robbed of the opportunity to use what they know from experience, to be free to make judgments, to act in ways that fit the situation, and to rely on relationships that may veer outside the formal chain of command. In other words, true control requires a basic level of management trust in workers' knowledge and good faith.

Bureaucracies remain the most common form of organizational structure and have hardly yielded in the face of assault from one management reform to another, all supposedly based on a critical stance toward the bureaucratic. We believe that the repeated failure of management reforms can be traced to management's lack of trust in the efficacy of worker knowledge and its fear of losing control. Despite its virtues, then, the fundamental assumptions of bureaucracy, all of which revolve around controlling work processes to meet political expectations, are antithetical to crafting trust and therefore to the very accountability they seek to ensure. Classic features of bureaucracy, even when put in place for good governance reasons, reek of a lack of trust in workers: detailed job descriptions, standard operating procedures, strict reporting requirements, an arsenal of regulations, and maintenance of files and records are all aimed at restricting the discretionary judgment of workers—in other words, the use of their experiential knowledge. Despite all of these control measures, or rather because of them, bureaucratic institutions breed mistrust without guaranteeing high performance. The more the physics of restraint are imposed, the more countervailing forces emerge, not the least of which is alienation among the people who do the work.

If the necessary understandings associated with all the interdependencies at work could be codified, trust would be irrelevant. Having examined the different forms of knowledge at different organizational levels, however, and understanding the lack of mutual comprehension and mutual trust they produce, we can now see the importance of processes of interaction and dialogue that are the only mechanisms by which trust and mutual understanding can be generated. The question becomes, to what extent, and through what means, can the pyramid's negative effects be tempered or reduced through the encouragement of circular dialogue, teamwork, and mutuality?

Organizational Reform – Some Lessons

One author (Carnevale) had completed work on a change effort in a large public organization. The first meeting was designed to initiate a series of discussions with employee groups about how they felt about their jobs. One fellow wore a baseball cap throughout the meeting and, finally, invited the facilitator's attention to it. "You see this?" he asked. "Well, they [management] had us all down for a cookout and speeches about improving the way things were here and they gave out these hats. That was three years ago and all I've got to show for those promises is this hat." He then asked, "What makes you think things are going to change here?" This is now Carnevale's "you see this hat?" story, but the man was right, and illustrates not just the cynicism of staff, but the futility that numerous citizens everywhere feel when it comes to invitations for "involvement" or providing "input" into other people's machines of governance. It is at the center of the crisis of trust in government.

Recall the observations of Giddens (1990) that in modern society, we are expected to trust a lot of people we hardly know, or don't know at all. When we are asked to trust someone purely because of his or her role ("this is your boss," or "this is the head of personnel"), we are basically being asked to trust an abstraction, an embodiment of expertise and/or authority. These are faceless commitments, essentially trust in the role rather than in the individual who fills it. Recall the workers at the bottom of the Teton Dam face, with a felt sense that the grout strategy did not fit the situation, saying to one another: Well, those guys at the top must know what they're doing. Then the dam collapsed.

Giddens argues that person-to-person trust is built on the basis of *facework*, interchange with others. A large organization cannot function unless the people in it are willing to trust abstractions and expert systems. They must therefore calculate, in particular circumstances, the benefits and risks of trusting. And, as Giddens notes,

> expert knowledge does not just provide that calculus but actually creates (or reproduces) the universe of events ... One of the things this means ... is that no one can completely opt out of the abstract systems involved in modern institutions.
>
> *(Giddens, 1990, p. 84)*

One's very sense of the situation is shaped by previous faceless commitments; therefore, ambivalence is at the heart of all trust relations.

Carnevale's "hat" guy embodies the organization member whose experience tells him that the expert system in which he is embedded is not going to make good on the promise symbolized by the training session he's attending.

> Trust is only demanded where there is ignorance—either of the knowledge claims of technical experts or of the thoughts and intentions of intimates ... Yet ignorance always provides grounds for skepticism or at least caution. ... Trust is much less of a "leap to commitment" than a tacit acceptance of circumstances in which other alternatives are largely foreclosed.
>
> *(Giddens, 1990, pp. 89–90)*

The Consequences of Fighting Back

In low-trust work environments, employees feel helpless, powerless and replaceable. They share their misery with each other, but they may not trust each other to step out and speak out. They neither trust management nor each other. Even to consider speaking spikes their anxiety. There is not enough trust to fight back, and until they understand their common standing and experience, they cannot begin to speak truth to the power that has them in its grip. Admittedly, faceless commitments are a lot to ask of anyone in an economy where jobs are insecure and a reasonably peaceful career is out of reach for many people. The reluctance is not without reason.

Most well-known management reforms aim to strengthen faceless commitments rather than facework: commitments to "improving human capital," "empowerment," "the learning organization," or "teamwork," rather than circular practices like dialogue that experiment with dropping organizational roles in a "zone of silence." People don't learn to collaborate and trust one another by listening to a Power Point presentation or participating in a canned training session. And in fact, circular facework, according to Giddens, is the means by which faceless commitments are sustained. Commitments based on roles, on rules, on abstract ideals like "mission," are not self-sustaining. "Facework generates trustworthiness" (Giddens, 1990, p. 87).

Giddens argues that collaborative work teaches people more than simply how to join their efforts to get the job done. They learn more than how to divide up the technical requirements:

> What is learned in the formation of basic trust is not just the correlation of routine, integrity, and reward. What is also mastered is an extremely sophisticated … practical consciousness … [T]he sustaining of basic trust is accomplished through the chronic monitoring of the gaze, bodily posture, and gesture, and the conventions of orthodox conversation.
> *(Giddens, 1990, p. 99)*

This tacit mastery is the glue that cements faceless commitments through patterns of circular action over time within an institutional framework.

Conclusion: Does Training Do any Good?

There is an ideal organization that has been pursued for a century or more. The idyllic image strikes several integrating chords:

> The new authority will be: member led, officer driven, customer focused; a team environment where the whole is greater than the sum of its parts; a flat management structure where employees and managers are fully empowered

and decisions are devolved close to the customer; a culture of learning rather than blame; a clear sense of direction and purpose. A firm commitment to deliver high quality public services through a combination of direct provision and effective partnerships.

(Micklethwait & Wooldridge, 1996, p. 1)

Despite its familiarity, this vision still represents an ideal worth striving for. But people become weary of the push toward deceptive enthusiasms and processes that hide more than they reveal. Given their experiences, how can workers trust in persons who come with fool's gold and a mountain of reform-oriented language in hand? In other words, does training do any good?

All the people who "bought in," "thought outside the box," went to the ropes courses, watched the films, met with facilitators, adopted the new language *du jour*, got the flip charts on the wall, debriefed the themes that began to emerge, and played group games, are in too many cases terribly let down as change doesn't gain a foothold that can be sustained.

Frank Sherwood, one of Carnevale's mentors, wisely dealt with organizational change efforts this way: All we really do is change their language, he observed, and not their management style. Soon the change mentality, even if it takes hold to some effect, will dissipate, as we always only get a handful of people in our training-for-change programs. For those who don't attend, the new language is ignored as one of those marginally useful things that come from retreats that other people went to. We go right back to what we were up to before. We are always running uphill against the high-control, ideal bureaucratic institutions that reduce our free-floating anxiety.

What, then, should we do?

The key to opening up an organization is to trust people to risk the tougher choices. It is important that leaders of organizations understand the need to liberate staff to take risks, if they really want to know what people think and how far they will go to make changes. Organizations are not transformed by allowing staff to plan the agency picnic this year. Some measure of real power has to shift, to be moved away from elites. That shift takes trust on the part of leaders.

Authoritarian work systems have some virtues, but none that expand opportunity for workers to be creative, none that are flexible enough to deal with the chaos in the world. People are readier to trust if they receive messages from leaders that encourage the "killing of the Dragon" inside—the fear of risk—that likely holds them back (cf. Quinn, 1996).

People have as much capacity to trust as not to trust. The issue is, what choice will they be encouraged to make? The core idea is what people think they know from experience about the motivations of others. As Giddens concludes:

> All knowledge claims, in conditions of modernity, are inherently circular. ... The social sciences presume a circularity in a twofold sense ... The

knowledge claims [modern institutions] produce are all in principle revisable, but they also become "revised" in a practical sense as they circulate in and out of the environment they describe.

(Giddens, 1990, pp. 176–177)

In other words, the bureaucratic promise of full control over people and processes has not and will not be fulfilled. Social reality is fundamentally produced and sustained by human relationships; therefore, the quality of those relationships, and especially the trust they are able to generate, is crucial to the patterns modern institutions display and to what they are able to accomplish. It is perhaps harder to eliminate human freedom than it once looked. Used strategically and democratically, this stance could ground circular dynamics within the bureaucracy.

References

Adams, Guy B. & Danny Balfour. 1998. *Unmasking Administrative Evil*. Thousand Oaks, Calif.: Sage Publications.

Argyris, Chris. 1957. *Personality and Organization: The Conflict between System and the Individual*. New York: Harper & Bros.

Armshaw, Jim, David G. Carnevale, & Bruce Waltuck. 2007. Union-management partnership in the United States Department of Labor. Pp. 366–378 in *Public Personnel Administration and Labor Relations*. An ASPA Classics Volume (ed. N.M. Riccucci). Armonk, N.Y.: M.E. Sharpe.

Carnevale, David G. 1995. *Trustworthy Government: Leadership and Management Strategies for Building Trust and High Performance*. San Francisco: Jossey-Bass.

Carnevale, David G. 2003. *Organizational Development in the Public Sector*. Boulder, Colo.: Westview Press.

Carnevale, David G., & Barton Wechsler. 1992. Trust in the public sector: Individual and organizational determinants. *Administration & Society* 42:1, 471–494.

Chalkley, Tony. 2012. *An Ethnography of Housing: Public Housing Work in Victoria*. https://researchbank.rmit.edu.au/view/rmit:160252/chalkley.pdf Downloaded 11/8/16.

Covey, Stephen. 1996. *The Seven Habits of Highly Effective People: Restoring the Character Ethic*. New York: Free Press.

Deutsch, M. 1958. Trust and suspicion. *Journal of Conflict Resolution* 2, 265–279.

Fox, Alan. 1974. *Beyond Contract: Work, Power and Trust*. London: Faber & Faber.

Giddens, Anthony. 1990. *The Consequences of Modernity*. Stanford, Calif.: Stanford University Press.

Golembiewski, Robert, & M. L. McConkie. 1975. The centrality of interpersonal trust in group processes. Pp. 131–155 in *Theories of Group Processes* (ed. C.L. Cooper). New York: Wiley.

Hummel, Ralph P. 1990. Circle managers and pyramid managers: Icons for the post-modern public administrator. Pp. 202–218 in *Images and Identities in Public Administration: Discourses on Governance* (eds. H.D. Kass & B. Catron). Newbury Park, Calif.: Sage Publications.

Likert, Rensis. 1961. *New Patterns of Management*. New York: McGraw-Hill.

Maslow, Abraham. 1954. *Motivation and Personality* (1st ed.). New York: Harper & Row.

McGregor, Douglas. 1960. *The Human Side of Enterprise* (anniversary ed.). New York: McGraw-Hill.

Mellinger, G.D. 1956. Interpersonal trust as a factor in communication. *Journal of Abnormal & Social Psychology* 52:3, 304–309.

Micklethwait, John, & Adrian Wooldridge. 1996. *The Witch Doctors: Making Sense of Management Gurus*. New York: Times Books.

Peters, Thomas J., & R. Waterman. 1982. *In Search of Excellence: Lessons from America's Best Run Companies*. New York: Harper & Row.

Quinn, R.E. 1996. *Deep Change: Discovering the Leader Within*. San Francisco: Jossey-Bass.

Reina, Dennis, & Michelle Reina. 1999. *Trust and Betrayal in the Workplace*. San Francisco: Barrett-Koehler.

Sonneberg, F. 1994. *Managing with a Conscience: How to Improve Performance through Integrity, Trust, and Commitment*. New York: McGraw-Hill.

Zand, Dale E. 1972. Trust and managerial problem-solving. *Administrative Science Quarterly* 17:2 (June). 229–239.

11

AUTHENTIC ETHICS IN THE BUREAUCRACY

Perhaps the biggest difference between public organizations and private ones is that, despite the bureaucratic chain of command (or maybe because of it), people who work in the public sector are ultimately accountable to the public-at large. That means that the last-word ethical standard for people in public service, whether frontline worker, manager, or executive, is what is good for the republic—as the Latin origin of the concept says, the *res publica*, the "public thing." In this public context, the word "good" introduces an element of complexity that is foreign to private enterprise.

Many public servants, as well as people who write about public administration, assume that clear standards for the public good can be articulated, even measured. Hence the proliferation of so-called codes of ethics, which tend to set forth rules of behavior for bureaucrats to follow, such as, "Don't take agency office supplies for home use," or "Don't let a contractor treat you to lunch." As bureaucrats we know have argued, if you don't have basic rules in place, some people will try anything (Stivers, 2008). On the other hand, occasional bureaucratic scandals in the headlines illustrate that some people will try anything no matter how many rules there are.

A less simplistic understanding of ethics has to do with how bureaucrats use administrative discretion. There are few if any jobs in public service that are so clearly defined that no judgment is necessary. This is because, as the philosopher Immanuel Kant once said, there are no rules for following a rule. You're in a situation, you know that there is a big book of rules you are supposed to follow, but you still have to figure out which rules apply to this situation, and in what way. There is more than one way to "follow" a rule, depending on the circumstances. So how do you decide what you should do?

Then there is the problem one of Ralph Hummel's (1989) articles pinpointed. As the title put it, "I'd like to be ethical but they won't let me." That is, most bureaucratic employees do not have complete freedom to make the judgments necessary to exercise discretion according to how *they* see the public good. Nevertheless, they are held personally responsible (not only by the bureaucrats above them but by the public and its representatives) for the way they exercise whatever authority they have. The chain of command tells you that, in most cases, the decision as to which rule applies and how it applies is above your pay grade. But placing final authority at a distance from the situation violates a key element that virtually all ethical philosophies insist on. The worker directly connected to the situation at hand is obedient, but prevented from pursuing his or her own understanding of the public good. He or she is responsible to the boss giving the orders. But as Dwight Waldo (1952, p. 100 fn. 4) said of democracy, ethics are not served "by delegating to foxes all decisions about chickens." Some may point to Max Weber's argument that the highest ethical standard for a bureaucrat *is* precisely the orders of the superior, but enough water flowed under the bureaucratic bridge during the twentieth century (let alone since) to call that view into question.

We believe that most public servants chose the work they do because they believed in the possibility of serving the public good. But turning that commitment into day-to-day guidance is a complicated challenge, as Hummel suggested. Despite having to follow orders, there are few if any situations in which all discretion is eliminated. Even the determination to follow orders "exactly" is a choice. Since there is no rule for following a rule, this chapter offers instead some food for thought. Running through the public administration literature for the last half century has been a thread devoted to existentialist thought and what it offers in the way of basic understandings of what it means to be ethical. In this chapter, we discuss certain aspects of existentialism especially in relation to key issues like trust and authenticity. We explore the exercise of discretionary judgment and how circular processes can temper the bureaucratic pyramid.

What Is Existentialism and Why Do We Need It?

Ethical action in public administration is one form of practical wisdom, or what Aristotle called *phronesis*. According to Aristotle, practical wisdom (acting ethically) does not consist in applying abstract rules that are handed to you. In this respect, he and Kant agree, since Kant's view (no rule for following a rule) led him to conclude that practical wisdom (judgment) was making the morally right choice given the particular situation. In other words, it is *the situation itself*, rather than a rule, that seems to call for a specific kind of action. "And that means that everything depends on one's ability to see the situation. Such seeing is not theoretical, precisely because to see what a situation calls for, is already to act" (Bernasconi, 1989, p. 133). Being ethical, then, starts with "making something."

What you make is not a tangible product but something of the situation you are in. You understand it in a particular way, acting toward it in some way to make clearer what it requires: for example, by talking to someone else to find out how they see it, or by gathering further information or data.

Given the above basic characteristics of administrative practice—that it is situational, not abstract, that it requires informed action—one match between administrative ethics and existentialism comes to light. Existentialism is a philosophy that asserts that the meaning of human existence is found *in* existence, and not on some higher transcendent plane. In other words, human beings have no defining qualities or characteristics except that they exist and will someday die. We make our own existence at any moment. "A person is fundamentally not what he or she has been or is already, but what he or she is not yet, for at every moment I face diverse possibilities, among which I must choose" (Bender, 1989, p. 263). That means it is up to us human beings to define ourselves through our actions during whatever time we have here in existence. John Dewey (1998/ 1932) argued that when we make moral judgments (What does the good consist of here?), we are not simply deciding what to do, we are also deciding who we want to be.

If that is all there is to being human, then we are free to choose (indeed, we *must* choose) what we do and become during our lifetimes. That freedom is a mixed gift, because the lack of sure underpinnings for ethical action can and does produce anxiety. Each of us is responsible for what we do; even if we are given orders by a boss (or a god) it is up to us as to how we respond. Thus, in our bureaucratic lives we are never just "things" or the roles we occupy, such as "worker" or "manager." Anxiety is produced by this having to choose, regardless of orders and in the absence of certainty that the choice is the right one. Obeying what seems to be the "letter of the law" is itself a choice.

What we strive for in the existential mode is *authenticity*. Existentialists contend that authenticity consists of accepting responsibility for your own life, rather than living (without much reflection) according to rules that are handed you by someone else or by society at large. Existentialists recognize that people are necessarily embedded and immersed in the world, which distracts them from awareness of their own individuality and responsibility: "We tend to drift along into public ways of acting, doing what 'one' does, and we assume that our lives are justified so long as we are conforming" to the norms and expectations of our social world (Guignon & Pereboom, 1995, p. xxxi). This statement should sound familiar to readers of the first part of the present volume, in which we discussed Heidegger's notion of being-in-the-world and the tendency to go along to get along, taking for granted much of what we encounter. For Heidegger (1962), authenticity is choosing oneself rather than conforming to conventional wisdom (what "they" say) or identifying with a role (e.g. "manager"). Authenticity means owning up to the reality that deciding the right thing to do is up to you. This is what Heidegger meant by "taking a stand."[1] We never exist or act in some abstract way but always in particular circumstances that we understand in particular ways (Dreyfus, 1991, p. 27). Accepting that is the core of authenticity. As Zingale and Piccorelli (2012, p. 213) observe, existentialism defines authenticity as "healthy individuals willing to accept the burden associated with individual freedom and who take responsibility for working, loving and reasoning from their center by respecting their own needs and those of others."

This existential understanding of authenticity points the way to a deeper understanding of organizational trust. As we have discussed, trust is confidence and faith in others to honor agreements, behave ethically and meet moral and social obligations (Carnevale, 1995). Trust expands the social horizon and discourages purely self-protective behavior. Since mutual trust encourages people to find meaning in their own lives and some measure of psychological safety in the face of anxiety, trust is itself an existential issue. Many, perhaps even most, organizations can lapse into mistrust, bad faith, and unexamined sense-making that relies pervasively on what "they" say. We pursue this concern in what follows as we explore the possibility of authentic bureaucratic relationships and the gap between actuality and potentiality in working lives inside bureaucracies. As Rollo May observed,

> Perhaps the most ubiquitous and ever-present form of the failure to confront nonbeing in our day is in conformism, the tendency of the individual to let himself be absorbed in collective responses and attitudes, to become swallowed up in *das Man* (the mind of the group), with the corresponding loss of his own awareness, potentialities and whatever characterize him as a unique and original being. The individual temporarily escapes the anxiety of nonbeing by this means, but at the price of forfeiting his own powers and sense.
> *(May, 1983, p. 107)*

Existentialist thinking is an antidote to the purely rational and scientific postures dominant in public organizations as well as to the ubiquitous pressure to conform and follow orders—neither of which relieves the individual from responsibility or offers escape from discipline.

The Escape from Freedom

Especially in our working lives, most of us tend to drift along in public ways of acting, doing what "one" does, and we assume that our lives are justified as long as we are conforming to the norms and expectations of the social world, the work world. When we suppress the uniqueness of our personal lived experiences for the illusion of safety in group inauthenticity, we can lose our integrity as individuals.

It is a poor bargain to abandon the truth of self in order to satisfy the illusion of safety and personal development by clinging to group norms, those that in practice are taken for granted rather than adopted after reflection and choice. Authenticity would urge people to accept responsibility for their own values (stances) and push back against community demands for mere conformity. As we noted above, practical wisdom (*phronesis*) consists of finding an authentic way to understand and deal with particular situations.

The retreat into the conforming group mind is "an escape from freedom" (Fromm, 1965). Fearful people seek safety in traditionalism and try not to stand out. Escape into the group, Fromm says, is a comforting veneer. Conformity replaces trust. The escaping person abandons freedom, the right to say, to feel, and to be what resides deep within the authentic self.

Paolo Freire (2000) concurs. Although he was writing about freeing a colonized populace from the effects of imperialism, his view of how to humanize (his term) oppressed peoples is not irrelevant to bureaucracy. Freire believed that the basic relationship between oppressed and oppressor (we could substitute the relationship between ordinary bureaucrats and the chain of command) was *prescription*: imposing one's choice on someone else, transforming their consciousness into conformity. The lower-down bureaucrat follows the prescriptions of the higher-up, and in so doing becomes afraid of freedom. To *be* becomes to *be like*—like the higher-up, or like what the system demands. Freedom, on the other hand, requires that the individual be active and responsible, not "a well-fed cog in a machine":

> The oppressed suffer from the duality which has established itself in their innermost being. They discover that without freedom they cannot exist authentically. Yet, although they desire authentic existence, they fear it. They are at one and the same time themselves and the oppressor whose consciousness they have internalized. The conflict lies in the choice between being wholly themselves or being divided; between ejecting the oppressor within or not ejecting them; between human solidarity or alienation; between following prescription or having choices; between being spectators or actors, between acting or having illusion of acting; between speaking out or being silent, castrated in their power to create and re-create, in their power to transform the world. This is the tragic dilemma of the oppressed …
> (Freire, 2000, pp. 8–18)

For people in public service, positioned somewhere in the chain of command, this duality is structural. Daily life in bureaucracy is a constant struggle to balance, if not to resolve, this dual consciousness.

Authenticity and Trust

The organizational pyramid is a structure that claims righteous power up the line, and at the same time is fearful of those who toil at the lower levels. Authenticity is diminished by the belief among higher-up bureaucrats that the practical, experience-based knowledge of the front line is a threat to management orders. This fear gets in the way of trust. As Robert Kramer notes, for those "on the proverbial bottom ... fear of exploitation and the nagging suspicion they are being treated unfairly by those above them are real and recurring concerns in many organizations." In turn, those on the top suspect that those lower down, for whom they are responsible, are shirking or sabotaging the organizational effort (Kramer, 1996, p. 217).[2] The organizational norm, then, is mutual mis-trust. Existentialism would suggest that the place to start doing something to alter this structural relationship is with oneself, that is, by being able to trust oneself. As Rogers (1961, pp. 16–19) says, "I find I am more effective when I can listen acceptingly to myself, and can be myself. ... I can trust my experience ... I have learned that my total organism sense of a situation is more trustworthy than my intellect."

How the dualities Freire expressed play out in the individual personality says much about the kind and amount of freedom a person consciously chooses in constructing his or her life. Relevant considerations include the ability to be assertive when it comes to one's own aims and purposes—to believe that even though control over your own organizational situation has limits, you can still write parts of your own story and push back against the claims of hierarchy. Having an opinion and offering it during discussion does not constitute deviance.

Trust at its heart is a commitment to self-consciousness, to self-awareness, and to potentialities to be filled by action. The core of freedom is to choose and to enable others to choose, to create the conditions for authentic being-in-the-world of diverse knowledges that is the bureaucracy (Bugenthal, 1965). Issues of trust are a strong undercurrent in organizational life. One cannot study "organizational behavior," a prominent focus of administrative research, and not see how the notion of trust lies deep beneath commitment, loyalty, motivation, conflict, power, communications, organizational citizenship, teamwork, and organizational change. The more trust, the more these dynamics are realized—or so it is believed or hoped for, despite evidence to the contrary in the form of pervasive top-down relations on the job (Carnevale & Wechsler, 1992; Carnevale & Hummel, 1992, 1993).

Trust is an expectation organizational members have of one another. In some instances, it is a self-fulfilling prophecy: you get what you choose to give. Communicate authentically, for example, and the chance for further open communication is enhanced. Deal with conflict recognizing the legitimacy of others' interests, and others are more likely to recognize your own. Give a team authority to transcend pseudo-participation and they are likely to be more creative. Asking is different from telling. Putting a group in a room to announce new things is not participation, nor is taking a few questions and calling that "dialogue."

Despite good intentions, organizational reforms, as we suggested earlier, are typically disappointments. Reforms come on the scene with great fanfare, but they are soon supplanted by other quick fixes. If anything, such efforts have only reduced trust on the part of employees who are weary of being asked to buy into the new, new deal. People carry real wounds as the result of what is, in the final analysis, existential betrayal of the potential relationship of Selves with Others. In his *Critique of Dialectical Reason*, Sartre characterized bureaucracy as "a total suppression of the human." Its defining characteristics are "mistrust, inertia, the suppression of initiative, and the dissolution of identity" except in relation to higher authority. But despite the power of bureaucracy, Sartre believed in the constitutive possibility of group resistance—of anti-bureaucratic struggle even within the iron cage (quoted in Bender, 1989, p. 269).

As Weber argued and our project acknowledges, bureaucracy has very deep roots in the overall conditions of modernity—conditions that post-modernity has not displaced (Hummel & Stivers, 2010). Yet, existential philosophy offers possibilities for envisioning resistance to bureaucracy, and possible deconstructive infiltration by non-bureaucratic group and individual actions. Such vistas arise as we occupants of bureaucracies take seriously the existentialist assertion that, no matter what the circumstances, we are responsible for our own fate, and for the fate of the groups and societies of which we are members. Perhaps bureaucracy cannot miraculously disappear, but still we can develop authentic practices that promote freedom, and awareness of the freedom we already have.

Humans are not just thrown into the world, but thrown into the company of others. This means that our wants and needs must co-exist in some way with the actuality of others, their needs and interests and their quest for authenticity as deep as our own. This commitment is a form of trust, for without it there is nothing left but existing in the conventional state. Organizations force us to choose between different aspects of ourselves. In the end, the existential view promotes trust in ourselves and in our power to pursue our own projects even where linear rationality and managerialism prevail. If you cannot be true to yourself, you will have little chance to be true to the public interest. Authenticity is the ground on which ethical public service takes a stand.

Practical Wisdom

One element blocking the way toward authentic ethical action in public bureaucracies is the increasing focus on tangible results as the ultimate measure of success. The idea has a long history (see Chapter 1), dating back to the earliest management writings, but it has gone into high gear in recent decades with the New Public Management campaign to make public organizations as much like businesses as possible. Since capitalist businesses are measured by their profits, and profits are generated by products (or services), the idea that government agencies are businesses despite the fact that they don't produce profits is equivocal at best.

Critics have observed this much, but failed to take the next step toward a deeper understanding.

Measuring the success of public organizations and of their employees in terms of the products and services they produce warps an understanding of the meaning of public service that goes back at least 2,500 years. Aristotle's writings on politics and ethics distinguished between various kinds of human endeavors. There are three kinds of knowledge-acquisition, each supporting or furthering a distinct kind of action (Aristotle, 1976):

- The "highest" form of knowledge is *episteme*, or seeking truth—that is, necessary truth or science—for its own sake, no matter whether it was useful or applicable. The relevant activity is *theoria*, or contemplation of the nature of things. The clearest examples today are pure mathematics and logic, and perhaps some kinds of philosophical speculation. These do lend themselves to use in practical activity, but they are not defined by being useful or having specific outcomes.
- *Techne*, or skill achieved by acting according to craft rules, is acquired in *poiesis*, or making, an instrumental activity towards the achievement of a known outcome. The skill of producing a product (or a defined service) is centrally shaped by its objective. One acquires *techne* by practicing *poiesis*, making something, following the rules for learning the craft until mastery is achieved. Much of public administration (or management) thinking and writing today views administration as implementation, a form of *poiesis*, employing *techne*, or skill that produces a defined result.
- *Phronesis*, or practical wisdom, means knowing the right thing to do given the circumstances, acting wisely for the good of everyone without being constrained ahead of time to only certain specified outcomes. *Phronesis* comes out of and supports *praxis*, doing right in the given situation. Right and good are not defined by products but *by the practice itself*. We argue that the interweaving of technical skill with concern for the public good is the essence of *public* administration, as we discuss below.

Since its invention, the notion of management has centered on technical skill supporting and furthering the production of defined outcomes. The catch is that the publicness of the public sector is about more than the old cliché of "who gets what, when, how." Publicness is also defined by debate over what government should do, whose voice will be heard in that debate, what rights members have to participate, and what a just outcome is. So, results cannot be limited to tangible products or services, and skill in governing cannot be restricted to knowing how to organize technical production processes. Government excellence is not *measured* but *judged* by its practical wisdom. Public administration is not simply an instrument, it is a form of life, a *praxis*. People who govern are thus not only producing material goods and services, they are also "producing" *government itself*.

That is what makes government different from business, and why governments cannot be judged on tangible results alone.

Bureaucrats who "would like to be ethical" find themselves adrift when they are told that the worth of what they do is translatable into numbers, especially into dollars and cents (Hummel, 2006). Like all human beings, their deepest commitment is to leading a life that has meaning, and few human beings arrive at the end of life convinced that the "most toys" or the "most deliverables" are the best measure of what their lives have meant.

An emphasis on practical wisdom as the foundation of ethics in public service signals the importance of maintaining a modicum of critical distance between the requirements of the role you occupy, on one hand, and on the other your sense of yourself and the project of public service as you understand it—with the proviso that this understanding changes and grows more nuanced with time and acquired experience.

Accountability

The literature of public administration has always concerned itself with relations between bureaucrats and those to whom they are answerable. This means that individual public servants exist in relationship to other selves. Your sense of self always encompasses your sense of the nature—the "feel"—of those relationships. Government of others and government of the self are intertwined. An ethical climate in a public organization encourages people not only to think for themselves (even when they are unable to carry out their conclusions), but to consult with others. This is often difficult in public agencies where employees are saddled with total responsibility for what they do but also expected to obey orders from above. That is why "I want to be ethical but they won't let me" resonates. Nevertheless, people don't come into public service just to have a safe job and obey orders. So the question of ethics doesn't go away.

Nevertheless, working in an agency is, in this respect not so different from life itself. We are all thrown into it, into circumstances we didn't choose, and faced with the reality that life is finite. One can try to evade the circumstances, ignore the inevitable outcome, or one can open oneself to the possibility of building a meaningful life with what is at hand. You take responsibility even though, ultimately, you are not in control.

Rules and codes of ethics are inadequate guidance, as we have suggested. But if life is being-in-the-world, it is fundamentally *with* others. The public realm is a common world, a shared world in which we are accountable to one another for what each of us does and what we do together. This web of relationships we have with others is the ground on which public action takes place. In this respect, the pyramidal structure of bureaucracy is tempered by circular, reciprocal engagements between and among members. Thus, the issue of how we account to others and to ourselves for our actions is central to the question of ethics and to public service itself.

No consideration of public sector ethics can neglect hierarchical accountability as a key structural feature of bureaucracy. The chain of command is an accountability mechanism that emphasizes the formal roles of members and defines accountability as obedience to commands from above. Yet most members, when they have the opportunity, can produce critical and reflexive accounts of the dynamics of their working lives. Few if any bureaucracies are oppressive enough to stamp out all internal feelings of disaffection, disagreement, and resistance. And, as we suggested in Part I, public organizations are permeated, indeed maintained and carried forward, by routine sense-making that attempts to account for what is going on. This aspect of organizational life underscores how "giving an account" to someone else is as much interpreting or sense-making as it is explaining or justifying.

The philosopher Maurice Merleau-Ponty points out that dialogue—everything from routine sense-making to justifying to debating and arguing—constitutes a common ground between another person and myself. He sees dialogue as circular. Our thoughts interweave and feed into some sort of shared action that neither of us created alone:

> We have here a dual being, where the other is for me no longer a mere bit of behavior in my transcendental field nor I in his; we are collaborators with each other in a consummate reciprocity. Our perspectives merge into each other, and we coexist through a common world.
>
> (Merleau-Ponty, 1962, p. 354)

This form of circular, mutual accountability draws fellow members of the bureaucracy together and surmounts, if only for a limited time, my perception of them as instruments for the accomplishment of my own objectives. The fact that circular organizational talk exists within hierarchies is both a constant threat to power concentrated at the top and a persistent challenge to instrumentalism, which can never be as perfectly rational as it is cracked up to be. To the individualizing mode of accountability encouraged by hierarchy, circular and reciprocal dialogue signals the "practical interdependence of action: an interdependence that always has both a moral and strategic dimension" (Roberts, 1991, p. 367).

Conclusion

Public service, like life itself, is fundamentally ambiguous. You didn't choose to be born, nor did you choose the circumstances. Yet life is essentially about choosing who to be. People who work in government have chosen to "go where the action is, … the arena of greatest confrontation with problems of moment and opportunity for effective action" (Richter, 2001, p. 472). Public servants are daily faced with great opportunities and great challenges. They have taken seriously the work of leading a meaningful life, and that is already the ultimate source or possibility of authenticity. As Sartre said, "Existentialism must be lived to be really sincere. To live as an existentialist means to be ready to pay for this view and not merely to lay it down in books" (quoted in Kaufmann, 1975, p. 47).

Notes

1   This aspect of Heidegger's thought makes his moral failure before and during World War II particularly stark. He failed to live up to his own sense of what it means to live morally.
2   During a chat about the impact of Reinventing Government within the federal bureaucracy, Kramer once remarked to Stivers that "bureaucrats have holes in their souls."

References

Aristotle. 1976. *The Ethics of Aristotle: The Nichomachean Ethics* (trans. J.A.K. Thompson). New York: Penguin.
Bender, Frederic L. 1989. Bureaucracy: Toward an existentialist critique. *Social Philosophy Today* 2, 259–272.
Bernasconi, Robert. 1989. Heidegger's destruction of phronesis. *Southern Journal of Philosophy* 28:S1, 127–147.
Bugenthal, J. 1965. *The Search for Authenticity: An Existential Analytic Approach to Psychotherapy*. New York: Holt, Rinehard & Winston.
Carnevale, David G. 1995. *Trustworthy Government: Leadership and Management Strategies for Building Trust and High Performance*. San Francisco: Jossey-Bass.
Carnevale, David G., & Ralph P. Hummel. 1992. Managing smart work in the public sector. Working paper, University of Oklahoma. Norman, Okla.
Carnevale, David G., & Ralph P. Hummel. 1993. The soul in the machine: quality, power and the future of work. Paper presented at the 54th National Training Conference, San Francisco.
Carnevale, David G., & Barton Wechsler. 1992. Trust in the public sector: Individual and organizational determinants. *Administration & Society* 23:4, 471–494.
Dewey, John. 1998. The moral self. Pp. 341–354 in *The Essential Dewey*, Vol. 2 (eds. L.A. Hickman & T.M. Alexander). Bloomington & Indianapolis: Indiana University Press. Originally published 1932.
Dreyfus, Hubert L. 1991. *Being-in-the-world: A Commentary on Heidegger's* Being and Time, Division I. Cambridge, MA: MIT Press.
Freire, Paolo. 2000. *Pedagogy of the Oppressed*. New York: Continuum.
Fromm, Erik. 1965. *Escape from Freedom*. New York: Avon Books.
Guignon, C.B., & D. Pereboom. 1995. *Existentialism: Basic Writings*. Indianapolis: Hackett.
Heidegger, Martin. 1962. *Being and Time* (eds. J. Macquarrie & E. Robinson). New York: Harper Perennial.
Hummel, Ralph P. 1989. I'd like to be ethical but they won't let me. *International Journal of Public Administration* 12:6, 855–866.

Hummel, Ralph P. 2006. The triumph of numbers: Knowledges and the mismeasure of management. *Administration & Society* 38:1 (March), 58–78.

Hummel, Ralph P., & Camilla Stivers. 2010. Postmodernism, bureaucracy and democracy. Pp. 324–348 in *Oxford Handbook of American Bureaucracy* (ed. R. Durant). New York: Oxford.

Kaufmann, Walter (ed.). 1975. *Existentialism from Dostoevsky to Sartre*. New York: Penguin.

Kramer, Robert. 1996. Divergent realities and convergent disappointments in the hierarchical relation. Pp. 216–245 in *Trust in Organizations: Frontiers of Theory and Research* (eds. R. Kramer & T. Tyler). Thousand Oaks, Calif.: Sage Publications.

May, Rollo. 1983. *Man's Search for Himself*. New York: New American Library.

Merleau-Ponty, Maurice. 1962. *Phenomenology of Perception* (trans. C. Smith). London & New York: Routledge.

Richter, Anders. 2001. The existentialist executive. Pp. 464–475 in *Democracy, Bureaucracy, and the Study of Administration* (ed. C. Stivers). Boulder, Colo.: Westview Press. Originally published 1970.

Roberts, John. 1991. The possibilities of accountability. *Accounting, Organizations & Society* 16:4, 355–368.

Rogers, Carl. 1961. *On Becoming a Person: A Therapist's View of Psychotherapy*. Boston & New York: Houghton-Mifflin.

Stivers, Camilla. 2008. *Governance in Dark Times: Practical Philosophy for Public Service*. Washington, D.C.: Georgetown University Press.

Waldo, Dwight. 1952. Development of the theory of democratic administration. *American Political Science Review* 46:1, 81–106.

Zingale, Nicholas, & Justin Piccorelli. 2012. Chains of freedom: A view from Erich Fromm on individuality within organizations. *Administrative Theory & Praxis* 34:2 (June), 211–236.

12
COMPETING KNOWLEDGES AND PUBLIC SERVICE EDUCATION

Public service education is a central factor in any discussion of the nature of administrative knowledge. The issue of education is not just philosophical, it is also political. There is a link between particular ways of knowing and the kinds of political life each way makes possible. Rules of knowledge shape rules of political practice (Fay, 1975), including practice within government bureaucracies. In light of this, administrators can no longer be taught that practice is simply a matter of applying theories or tested hypotheses, assuming that somewhere down the line their political implications (if any) will play out. To be more pointed, the rules of knowledge that the academy adheres to and its members impart to students not only have built-in political implications but influence the terms of thought and action within the bureaucracies that many of its graduates occupy (Stivers, 2010).

In public administration, ever since Woodrow Wilson and Frank Goodnow, administrative knowledge has routinely been equated, at least by many academics, with whatever results from the scientific method; knowledge is viewed as a control mechanism in the hands of practitioners, as in the ubiquitous claim that quantitative research can reveal the sure path to results. In Wilson's (1887) eyes, science made it possible to limit the influence of "the democracy." In other words, science expanded administrative power. As education for public service developed and university-based programs proliferated throughout the twentieth century, an early interest in hands-on learning disappeared in favor of classroom training of expert professionals. William E. Mosher, dean of the first graduate school of public administration, declared that a democracy "could only be protected from the divisive forces of the modern world by a system of careful administrative management and control" (Johnson, 1975, p. 12). Public administration educators came to define administrative knowledge as the product of systematic study by scientists, applied by trained administrators to achieve maximum control over work processes—and workers. The question today is Foucault's (1984, p. 48): "How can the growth of capabilities be disconnected from the intensification of power relations?" Can education for public service take a form that expands administrative skill without expanding bureaucratic power over members of the public?

Teaching Administration: The Search for Reality

How, then, to prepare students to enter public service or enhance their capabilities as already-practicing civil servants? The issue is an enduring one, for students and instructors alike. Teaching is made even more daunting these days by the fact that many, even most, students are already on the job. The question for instructors is: How do we support students' learning in a way that fits their real needs? How do we share experiences (theirs and ours) that shed light on the dynamics of the workplace and enhance their ability to work effectively? The challenge is great, given the rigor of bureaucratic and methodological rules: abstract, often unvalidated, and biased toward control and dominance—operational moves that seem void of heart.

Direct experience with the working situation may not guarantee skill in problem solving. It is, however, the only way people can see and feel the actuality of the work. No one studies a problem situation from nowhere. Yet rationalism and science deny the relevance and validity of direct experience. Can academia persist in its commitment to knowledge solely from computer simulation or scientific examination? How can academics help future and current managers appreciate and rely on direct working experience gained from the situation? How do teachers relate what happens in the classroom to the real issues students face when they are no longer within the secure environment—the safe space—of the university?

What people learn in the classroom or the training center faces countervailing pressures in the work setting. Scientific generalizations buckle under resistance from operations-as-usual. The classroom learning of a few people, even the best people, has a short shelf life back on the job. The intra-organizational and extra-organizational fresh possibilities cannot survive the sheer weight of organizational denial that persists no matter how good the training or other developmental initiatives. The bureaucratic culture finds ways to suppress and destroy thinking that is contrary to the seeming good order of the dominant machinery.

The classroom, in contrast, is a place where problems are served up in neat bundles. Reality is left behind. The data are already objectified. The best "case" is the one with the numbers. Here, drilling students remains too common. In neither the reasoning of computer programming nor the detached methods of scientific observation do students experience the personal stake that takes hold when they are called to make judgments on the job. The artificial, unrealistic world we create for them in the classroom feels, and is, not the one where everything they do *counts*: "The practitioner must choose. Shall he remain on the high ground where he can solve relatively unimportant problems according to prevailing standards of rigor, or shall he descend to the swamp of important problems and nonrigorous inquiry?" (Schön, 1987, p. 1).

University classrooms are idealized places; out of touch, as many participants observe, with "the real world." How do teachers of public managers establish a realistic learning environment? It must be one where people exist in actual situations rather than in the abstract. In life and work, people are not detached observers of events, but part of them. In the world of work and management, people have a real stake in the choices they make. There, given diverse bureaucratic knowledges, each of which knows in its own way, human dynamics are difficult and the knowledge results unclear. Most instructors know that the classroom should make contact with a world in which it is harder to define a problem than to solve one, but many are at a loss about how to make this happen.

Of course, there is value in having students learn in safe environments where they can reflect upon the turbulent world of practice. The traditional classroom is good for this purpose. In fact, one of the best features of public management education for practicing administrators is to serve as a space in which they can step back from putting out the latest fire and reflect on the deeper and longer-term dimensions and patterns of their work. Still, this arena for reflection is not the same as the working reality. How, then can it be made useful?

It is plain that tension between two types of knowledge—worker knowledge and manager knowledge—has haunted ideas about management reform *and* management education, biasing them toward abstract knowledge and away from experiential knowledge. In Part I, we described the dynamics of experiential knowledge, including its philosophical essence. This was necessary because this form of knowledge is not only theoretically underdeveloped within public administration but has been rejected as inferior to science. This rejection is misguided. The fundamental importance of knowledge based in experience indicts orthodox public administration curricula and classroom practices as skewed toward abstractions that the practitioner has to figure out how (or whether) to apply, and away from knowledge gained in practice itself, either directly or in the process of sharing experiences, stories, and lessons with others, looking for patterns and gaining a felt sense for narrative plausibility (Hummel, 1991).

A second reason for articulating working knowledge in detail is this: It has not been adequately appreciated in the actual management of organizations. We have explained how power and knowledge intertwine in the modern era and how appeals to idealist reason and science are power exercises disguised as neutral knowledge. We have outlined how all these factors come together in reductionist and mechano-morphic ways to inform management thinking about people, knowledge, and work at least since the beginning of the twentieth century.

In the following discussion, we address the pragmatic implications of our theory for the teaching of public management and for the actual administration of organizations.

Pedagogy v. Andragogy

Typical university-based courses are taught according to the pedagogical instruction model, based on a physics that rewards instructors more than students and tends to treat adult students, even experienced practitioners, as if they were beginners. The decisions about what to teach and in what order, what is relevant, what is not, are made by the instructor, a method akin to pouring knowledge from vessels found in the front of the room into the empty brains of students. The learner is required to adjust to an established curriculum determined from the outside in. The knowledge consists of vicarious substitution of someone else's theories for one's own experience. In workaday terms, the structure of learning ignores the experiences of the learner. As Charles Beard, a pioneer in public service education said of the academic approach, "If you know how somebody else did a thing you are entitled to a degree, but if you can only do it yourself you are a barbarian" (Stivers, 2010, p. 250). It is fair to ask whether pumping theories into people is imparting knowledge or simply transferring information, which too often does not last because it fails to connect with real situations and real needs.

In the pedagogical method, students become savvy about what matters in the classroom context, which usually means parroting back lines from the textbook or the lecture. Students expect that academic instructors hold the key to success (good grades and ultimately a degree); their Power Point lectures lay out a set of points of excellence, principles of action, and the best theories about how to handle the nuances of working reality. Admittedly, students do want to know more about how to succeed: not just organizationally, but in terms of career advancement. But the incentives are skewed by the form the pedagogy takes. The "good" students are eager to please the authority figure in the front of the room by producing "right" answers. Going along is getting along.

Andragogy, in contrast, is an adult learning model, in which the student is no longer treated as a child—an empty container who is led to water and enjoined, if not forced, to drink at the fount of learning. In andragogy, the student and the teacher contribute equally to the learning process, which is a dialogue and a collaboration. The mind of the student is understood as actively seeking knowledge and indeed already in possession of a good bit of it. The role of the teacher is to help create and facilitate the conditions in which the student can learn. The goal is for the student to *learn how to learn*, so that he or she can take charge of their own knowledge-acquisition process. This, like many aspects of bureaucratic dynamics, is a circular process.

Imagine a student in a large lecture hall in a class about managing organizational behavior. The student, clearly frustrated, raises his hand to press his concern that his family—or he himself—had paid a small fortune to get educated in order to have a grand future. The professor is not making clear what he should do in this situation as opposed to that one. What was the right answer? What was the winning concept?

The student asks, "What should I do?" In the andragogic classroom, the instructor replies, "It depends." "Depends on what?" says the student. The instructor invites the student to look at all the factors in play and decide what aspects of this situation seem important and what actions might be tried to improve it. There is, the instructor notes, no magic theoretical bullet to fire from the same weapon time and again regardless of the contingencies of the situation.

The student is advised that the best path is perhaps no path at all; linear reasoning and science may offer assistance in diagnosing, but seldom can be counted on to produce the right action. The real goal is to find something in the problem situation that, when revealed, helps in *this* situation at *this* time. It is good enough in this case, for the time being, but not necessarily in the next one. Problems have personalities of sorts and the best way to resolve difficulties may well call for different prescriptions over time. There is no one best way. Nevertheless, the reflective practitioner does learn from experiences. They do add up, but not the way numbers do. Expert practitioners learn how to judge the nature of situations, rather than which formula to apply.

Authentic public management education, simply put, encourages teachers not to waste time preparing students to operate in a fictional organizational world. No organization is a machine that runs on a single fuel: rational, calculated knowledge. Students of management need to prepare themselves to take up or expand their responsibilities in organizations that often feel like snake pits. A first step in management teaching is to validate the proposition that students know a lot before they ever enter the classroom—as proven by the fact that they have gotten this far in life, are making their way in society and in most cases are already doing public work. In other words, they are adults. This is especially true in the case of the many public administration students who are already seasoned managers in pursuit of an advanced degree. These practitioner-students already know that problem-solving does not entail applying a formula, that no problem situation is exactly like any other, and that what they need is not a rule-book of so-called solutions but rather the further development of insight and judgment, along with some fresh ideas and the opportunity to get some distance on daily challenges. Handing them abstractions and generalizations not only fails to meet their needs, but disrespects the hard-won knowledge they already have.

Human aims and intentions show themselves in life and work. This is what is meant by "joining purpose to practice" (Adams, et al., 1990). Each side of the equation needs the other. Each is influenced by the presence of the other. Recognizing the truth of this paradox helps in locating the true position of the manager as caught in a cognitive and psychological middle: the "in-between" or the play of intention and emergence—again, a circular process.

The paradox of management education, or management in general, lies in the tension between human intent and the emerging reality of work. At the level of organization design, it lies in the difference between the off-the-shelf organization and the learning organization. It is the difference between the learning manager and the manager enframed by his or her own objectifying view of the world, which casts everything into clearly defined objects to be manipulated. It is the tension also between teaching management as a learning experience and teaching management as a passing on of objectified "truths." Surely the last thing that teachers of management should want to aim at is the passing on of theories and findings of organization design and behavior as if the judgment involved in application were the easiest thing in the world. Judgment does not need to be taught, and in fact *cannot* be taught—but it *can* be learned.

Democracy in the Classroom

Perhaps the most pressing case for greater andragogy in public management education is that it serves, rather than sidelines, democracy. What public administration needs today is not professional experts who approach their duties like benevolent despots showing the one best way to a "muddled, befogged 'people'" (Follett, 1924, p. 3). Rather, contemporary governance requires practitioners who see democracy as a worthy aim rather than a threat. Despite all the emphasis today on inter-institutional collaboration, public management curricula give little attention to developing the skills that foster it: for example, how to involve citizens in developing policy-relevant knowledge, how to deal with conflict, and how to establish and maintain relationships with people and organizations in the community. These *how* questions are the much-talked about "black box" of implementation—much talked about, but little studied and less taught, because they do not lend themselves to the kind of scientific analysis that is now the gold standard.

Andragogy fosters democracy in ways that "the expert at the front of the room" model does not. John Dewey, whose education theories fit the andragogical approach, believed whole-heartedly in science, but not because he favored turning knowledge development over to a class of experts. To the contrary, he saw lived experience as the "ends and means" of democracy, generating knowledge that was usable because it was connected to real life. He saw danger in the unreflective worship of the idol of objectivity. He argued: "Many persons seem to suppose that facts carry their meaning along with themselves on their face. Accumulate enough of them, and their interpretation stares out at you" (Dewey, 1998, p. 343). In Dewey's view, governance starts with the bedrock of what ordinary people know from their daily lives, and each person's contribution is taken seriously by everyone involved. The educational process, he argued, is similarly democratic and collaborative, beginning with the assumption that, like citizens in a policy process, students in the classroom are experts on the conditions of their lives and work. They don't know all they need to know, but what they do know has the validity that comes out of living. They can add to that knowledge—that is, they can learn. Knowledge acquisition has to start there, and proceed in a collaborative process.

Today's instructors confuse the authority of knowledge with their own authority. They assume that because a manager with a decade or more of experience is in the classroom, all of a sudden that manager is a blank slate to be written on. Or worse, the manager slate has a lot of "anecdotal" stuff written on it that needs to be erased so that scientific declarations can be inscribed. So much for democracy.

Paolo Freire's (2000) *Pedagogy of the Oppressed* reinforces Dewey's critical message. He describes conventional pedagogy as a series of seemingly inexorable steps:

a the teacher talks and the students listen—meekly;
b the teacher disciplines and the students are disciplined;
c the teacher chooses and enforces his choice, and the students comply;
d the teacher acts and the students have the illusion of acting through the action of the teacher;
e the teacher chooses the program content, and the students (who were not consulted) adapt to it;
f the teacher confuses the authority of knowledge with his or her own professional authority, which she or he sets in opposition to the freedom of the students;
g the teacher is the subject of the learning process, while the pupils are mere objects.

These "learning" methods school students, including graduate students, in *obedience*, in the habits of compliance that lie at the heart of oppression. Few authoritarian regimes could last purely on the basis of brute force. The authoritarian ruler doesn't need so many guns if the people can be disciplined not to question orders and to accept that the power of the regime is "normal" (see Foucault, 1979).

Students socialized into public service by the "pedagogy of the oppressed" will, in turn, try to *impose* the organization ideal. They will *command* and try to control workers and citizens. They will prize *conformity* to an abstract ideal, such as "performance." They will be *intolerant* of different points of view and try to root out the causes of all conflict. They will not trust any experience that does not match their model of the world. They will blame colleagues and subordinates for not living up to the ideal. They will stifle learning and kill the spirit of the workplace. They will, in short, become the classic American manager, pursuing the "escape from freedom" (Fromm, 1965).

Political freedom does not consist simply of voting. Democracy, as Dewey (1916, p. 87) said, is "a mode of associated living." The roots of democracy lie in the cultivation of democratic attitudes in individual human beings. The classroom, from pre-kindergarten through graduate school, is potentially one of the most crucial settings for the cultivation of democratic attitudes. The classroom can empower students not only by giving them information but also by giving them opportunities to take charge of their own learning—such as by teaching them how to seek out and test the usefulness of the information for themselves.

Democratic administrators need democratic education. The learning process must be cooperative, with many occasions for group learning. The classroom must encourage the development of self-awareness about where various social values and ways of thinking come from and what interests they support. The teacher becomes a citizen-participant who learns with and through the same processes in which students are learning. Authority is contextual and earned, rather than positional. Through these practices, we can prepare public servants and teachers alike to find moments and ways to enact and strengthen democracy in their work and in their lives and the lives of others (Adams, et al., 1990).

To Sum Up

There is no simple prescription for the education problem. Like many of our colleagues everywhere, we have wrestled with the problem of getting students ready for (further) practice. There are practices that do provide guidance for how public management education should evolve.

(1) Many students are already in practice. They know something about the real world. Many have participated in reform efforts of some kind. Therefore, it is useful not to operate classrooms in ways that deny the relevance of their experience to real learning. Their stories are indeed as valid as science and need to be given real weight (Hummel, 1987, 1991).

(2) Teachers need to encourage people to value their own experience. Students need to understand that they do know something. They have theories-of-action that work even if they haven't mastered the textbook labels for those theories. There is certainly more they can learn about theory that adds value and expands their repertoire, but they are not without their own resources.

(3) Students should be encouraged to think critically, to reframe their experience, to engage in what is known as "double-loop" learning (Argyris and Schön, 1978). They need to become critically self-reflective, which means learning a "process of testing the justification or validity of taken-for-granted premises" (Mezirow, 1990, p. 354). This kind of thinking is subversive of the power inside dominant knowledge systems that mask reality.

(4) Public servants get some of their learning on the job doing something real. For pre-service students, practicums and internships are ways of learning through experience. Apprenticeships are even better in our view. For practitioners who already have years in public service, "learning from life" projects can be vehicles

for deliberate reflection on practice that get academic credit when they are written up.

Interestingly, one of our students recently did a study comparing the work effectiveness and promotion rates between military people who had been educated in traditional schools and so-called "strikers" who got part of their education in traditional classrooms and part from chief petty officers who mentored them on the job. The strikers did better overall than their traditionally educated counterparts. We think the reason is clear. Strikers were able to learn more effectively because they had reality as a check on the idealized knowledge they were picking up in the classroom. The point is that the combination of theory and practice makes a real difference in the effectiveness of the overall education experience. If programs in public management are serious about learning, they will move the teacher out of the classroom for a stint in the public agency.

(5) Specialization is not necessarily a good way to learn to tolerate knowledge differences at work. The specialist becomes more dug-in to one way of knowing. It is the old story of the person who knows how to hammer and sees every problem as a nail. There is virtue in mobility assignments, cross-training, and generalized career development. There ought to be more of it.

(6) Classrooms should be highly interactive, participatory, and involve more team projects. Developing people atomistically for their roles as facilitators of group work is ineffective. Judging people on their individual performance fosters individualism and competitiveness rather than cooperation. Hence, the unhappy phenomenon of students unwilling to help others, share information, and participate in group projects because they fear losing some sort of test advantage or resent "free riders" in the group. In the workplace, such attitudes block cooperation which is often highly desirable, even necessary. There are very few jobs in public service that rely solely on isolated individual effort.

To conclude, what are we looking for in the way of public service education, in a world where permanent whitewater prevails (Vaill, 1989), where the reality of working in and running human work systems demands processes and attitudes of continuous learning? What do we do in face of the reality that learning requires not top-down instructional regimens of the pedagogical kind, but rather circular, collaborative processes? Learning opportunities for adults are interactive "circles of learning" that empower and energize the successful public organization (Vaill, 1996; Vaill, 1998; Senge, 1990; Hummel, 1990).

Pedagogy encourages people to deny their own experiences and to follow orders (Schön, 1983; Schön, 1987). Andragogy is "dialogical: assertiveness coupled with active listening become the new rules for learning, shared and otherwise" (Carnevale, 2003, pp. 99–112). In the latter, the education process, the work process, and the political process all serve the growth of democracy, joining purpose to practice in the interests of freedom. Human will and judgment prevail not just for the self, but in concert with others.

References

Adams, Guy B., Priscilla Bowerman, Kenneth M. Dolbeare, & Camilla Stivers. 1990. Joining purpose to practice: A democratic identity for the public service. Pp. 219–240 in *Images and Identities in Public Administration* (eds. H.D. Kass & B.L. Catron). Newbury Park, Calif.: Sage Publications.

Argyris, Chris, & Donald Schön. 1978. *Educating for the Reflective Practitioner: Toward a New Design for Teaching and Learning in the Professions.* San Francisco: Jossey-Bass.

Carnevale, David G. 2003. *Organizational Development in the Public Sector.* Boulder, Colo.: Westview Press.

Dewey, John. 1916. *Democracy and Education.* New York: MacMillan.

Dewey, John. 1998. Search for the public. Pp. 281–292 in *The Essential Dewey*, Vol. I (eds. L.A. Hickman & T.M. Alexander). Bloomington & Indianapolis: Indiana University Press. Original work published 1927.

Fay, Brian. 1975. *Social Theory and Political Practice.* London: Unwin Hyman.

Follett, Mary Parker. 1924. *Creative Experience.* New York: Longmans, Green.

Foucault, Michel. 1979. *Discipline and Punish: The Birth of the Prison.* New York: Vintage.

Foucault, Michel. 1984. What is enlightenment? Pp. 32–50 in *The Foucault Reader* (ed. P. Rabinow). New York: Pantheon Books.

Freire, Paolo. 2000. *Pedagogy of the Oppressed.* New York: Continuum.

Fromm, Erich. 1965. *Escape from Freedom.* New York: Avon Books.

Hummel, Ralph P. 1987. Behind quality management: What workers and a few philosophers have always known and how it adds up to excellence in production. *Organizational Dynamics* 16:1 (Summer), 71–78.

Hummel, Ralph P. 1990. Circle managers and pyramid managers: Icons for the postmodern public administrator.Pp. 202–218 in *Images and Identities in Public Administration: Discourses on Governance* (eds. H.D. Kass & B.L. Catron). Newbury Park, Calif.: Sage Publications.

Hummel, Ralph P. 1991. Stories managers tell: Why they are as valid as science. *Public Administration Review* 31:1 (January-February), 31–41.

Johnson, Peter. 1975. *The Progressive movement, municipal reform, and the founding of the Maxwell School.* Photocopy, Institute for Public Administration Archives. Syracuse, N.Y.: Maxwell School of Syracuse University.

Mezirow, Jack. 1990. How critical reflection triggers transformative learning. Pp. 1–20 in *Fostering Critical Reflection in Adulthood: A Guide to Transformative and Emancipatory Learning* (ed. J. Mezirow). San Francisco: Jossey-Bass.

Schön, Donald. 1983. *The Reflective Practitioner.* New York: Basic Books.

Schön, Donald A. 1987. *Educating the Reflective Practitioner.* San Francisco: Jossey Bass.

Senge, Peter. 1990. *The Art and Practice of the Learning Organization.* New York: Doubleday.

Stivers, Camilla. 2010. Democratic knowledge: The task before us. *Administration & Society* 41:2, 248–259.

Vaill, Peter B. 1989. *Managing as a Performing Art: New Ideas for a World of Chaotic Change.* San Francisco: Jossey-Bass.

Vaill, Peter B. 1996. *Learning as a Way of Being.* San Francisco: Jossey-Bass.

Vaill, Peter B. 1998. *Spirit Leading and Learning: Process Wisdom for a New Age.* San Francisco: Jossey-Bass.

Wilson, Woodrow. 1887. The study of administration. *Political Science Quarterly* 2 (June), 197–222.

INDEX

Note: Page numbers in *italic* type refer to figures Page numbers followed 'n' refer to notes

Abernathy, W. J., and Wayne, K. 24
abstract knowledge 204
accommodation 169
accountability 4, 83, 102, 180, 198–199; career bureaucrats 102; circular 199; executives 96; performance 96; political 98, 103; public sector 190
accounting procedures 95
Ackoff, R. 154, 155
action 36; ethical 191, 192; informed 192
administration 70–71, 82, 83, 172; capacities 105; decisions 162; demands 103; officials 89; and politics 17, 90, 106; power 82, 202; practice 158; science of 94; systems 90; teaching 203–205
administration-by-concept 17
administrative discretion 160; bureaucrats 190, 191
administrative knowledge 201–202
administrative politicians 101
administrative power 82, 202
administrative practice, situational 192
administrators 160, 164; and clients 48
agency authority 102
American Federation of Government Employees (AFGE) 126
American presidents 90, 95
American Society of Mechanical Engineering (ASME) 15
andragogy 210

andragogy vs. pedagogy 205–207
anti-government feeling 170–171
anticipation 55, 57
anxiety 192
Appleby, P. 90, 103–104
application 161
appointees 98–99; political 99, 100–102
apprenticeships 209
Arendt, H. 70, 147, 164
Argyris, C. 21
Aristotle 159, 160, 161, 162, 191, 197
art 76
as-structure 37
assembly line production 72, 95
assertiveness 167, 168, *168*, 169, 178
attunement 50, 57, 62
austerity 27
Australia, government agencies 80
authentic ethics 190–201
authenticity 192–193, 194, 196; frontline workers 67; and trust 194–196
authoritarian work systems 187
authority 3, 74, 82, 154, 183, 191, 208, 209; agencies 102; bureaucrats 71; hierarchical 44; management 4, 74; transfer 72–73
autocracy 148, 164
avoiding 169

Bacevich, A. 100
back-talk 50, 62
bargaining: collective 4, 170–172; distributive 181
Barley, S. R. 48
Barnard, C. 100–101, 103
Barrett, W. 172
Barzun, J. 30
Bauman, Z. 147
Beard, C. 205
beat cops 61–62
being-in-the-world 37, 40, 150, 192, 195, 198
being-with: clients 55–56; nursing homes 56–58; as regulation 64–67
benchmarks 28
Bender, F. L. 192, 196
Bendix, R. 20, 72, 73, 102
Berger, P. L. 70; and Luckmann, T. 41, 42
Bergin, C. 74
Bernstein, R. J. 150, 166–167
best practices 114, 117, 128, 133
Bittner, E. 61–62
black box 152, 207
blaming culture 180
Blue Ribbon Panel 117
blueprints 38
border patrol 64–65, 66
border-crossers 48–49
Braverman, H. 14, 15
Brown, R. H. 149
Brownlow Committee 17–18
Brownlow Report (1937) 17–18, 19
Budget Act (1921) 93
budgetary process 92, 93
building inspectors 65
bureaucracy 3, 35, 149; characteristics 196; dialogue 164; features 184; government 44, 90; ideal-typical 135; modern 39, 71; service 111–127; theory 44
bureaucratic decision-making 162
bureaucratic pyramid 3
bureaucratization 44–45, 61, 73
bureaucrats 148, 198, 200n2; administrative discretion 190, 191; authority 71; career 98, 99; duty 89; and executives 102–103; power 81–82; street-level 60, 63
Bush, President G. W. 27
business: and government 17; ideology 148

capacity, flawed 123
capital: accumulation 72; human 25
capitalism 72, 147, 147–148

care 34, 39, 59
care-givers, and patients 57
care-work, cop-work 61–64
career bureaucrats 98, 99, 102
career civil servants 71, 90
caring 56
Carnevale, D. G. 113, 184–185, 210; and Hummel, R. P. 1, 11
casework, as solicitude 58–61
centralization-by-numbers 95
chain of command 3, 181–182, 184, 190, 191, 199
Chalkley, T. 174, 175
Challenger space shuttle 84–85, 86n1
Chamber of Commerce 92
Champy, J., and Hammer, M. 25
Chandler, S. M., and Pratt, R. C. 99
change 151; knowledge 134–135; organizational 124, 187; productive 151; social 15
Charity Organization Society (COS) 92
Chia, R., and Holt, R. 76
chief executive officers (CEOs) 79
Choice Program 123, 126
circle 149–151, 183; hermeneutic 149–150; of learning 210; managers 148–149; quality 154; trust 174–189, 183; within hierarchy 182–183
circle vs. pyramid 135–136
circular accountability 199
circular causality 38
circular dialogue 172
circular framework 6
circular organizations 154–156
circular practices 186
circular processes 149, 206
circular responses 151–153, 168
circular thinking 149
circularity 167, *168*
citizens 83, 148, 162, 166; involvement 148, 185, 207
city: government 92, 93; management 16
civil service 98, 99
Clark, C. S. 116
classrooms 204, 210; democracy 207–209
Clelland, D. A., Lynxweiler, J. and Shover, N. 65
Cleveland, F. A. 17, 82, 93–94, 95
clients: and administrators 48; being-with 55–56; bureaucratization 61; satisfaction 24; social work 59
Clinton, President B. 27, 123
codes of ethics 190, 198

cognitive skills 74
Cold War 18
collaboration 29, 85, 99, 130, 152, 155, 169, 186; inter-institutional 207
collective bargaining 4, 170–172
collective knowledge 52
collective learning 171
collective schema 58
Colon-Christensen, J. 117
Commission on Care 122–124
Commission on Economy and Efficiency 93
commissioners 105–106
communication 101
community: groups 166; needs 162
compassion, social work 59
competency 81
competition 29, 169
competitiveness 23–24
compliance 208
compromising 169
concepts 2, 3, 50, 70–88; management 77–79
conceptual knowledge 41, 74, 77, 85, 149; power of 44–46
conceptual-scientific knowledge 3, 44
concerned coping 53
conflict 21, 22, 151, 152–153, 172, 195, 207; resolution 167–170, 173n1
conformism 193
conformity 194, 208
Congress 90, 93, 94, 114, 127
consciousness raising 135
Constitution 17, 90
consumers 24
continuous improvement 25
contracting-out 29
control 147, 184; and knowledge 147; managerial 28; social 73; top-down 151
controversy 105
Cook, D., and Wagenaar, H. 160–161
Cooke, M. 16
Cooper, T. L., and Wright, N. D. 101, 104, 105
cooperation 72, 73, 154
coordination 29
cop-work, as care-work 61–64
coping: concerned 53; everyday 49–50, 52–55
Copley, F. B., and Taylor, F. W. 24
corporations 17
cost control 96
cost-effectiveness 29
craft knowledge 85, 98; executives 100; workers 12

craftsmanship 15, 73; police 62–63
creativity 24
crisis responders 55, 63
critical thinking 209
culture: blaming 180; learning 187; organizational 20, 23; political party 91
Cunningham, R. B., and Olshfski, D. 103, 105, 106
customer service 28, 94
customers: government 24, 27; satisfaction 24

Dallmayr, F. 55
Dandeker, C. 44–45, 147
data 51, 154, 160
Davies, A., and Thomas, R. 83, 84
Davis, A., and Thomas, R. 61
decision-making 101, 176, 180; administrative 162; bureaucratic 162; executives 106–107; organizational 154
defense of life 64
DeHart-Davis, L. 61, 65, 67
democracy 17, 73, 74, 148, 154, 164, 202; classrooms 207–209; political 148; roots 208–209
democratic politics 164
democratic state 17
democratization 92
Denver Veterans Affairs Summit (2015) 124–126
Denver Veterans Engagement Board 128–137; circular processes 135–136; community process 131, *132*; mission statement 129; origin 128–130; projects 130–131; values 130
deskilling 15
devolution 102
Dewey, J. 150, 153, 160, 192, 207, 208
dialogic circle, bureaucratic pyramid 166–173
dialogue 6, 150, 153, 160, 166–167, 171, 178, 179, 182, 184, 186, 199; bureaucracies 164; circular 172; conflict resolution 167–170; face-to-face 163; vectors *168*
Diamond, T. 56–58
dilettantes 102
dilettantism 148
Dimock, M. E. 102
direct knowledge 45
disclosure 81
discretion 153, 160, 161, 162, 191
discretionary power 63
distributive bargaining 181

division of labor 2, 3, 40, 42, 43, 52, 71, 82
domination 44, 75, 167
double-loop learning 209
downsizing 102
Dreyfus, H. L. 37, 38, 49, 149–150
Drucker, P. 76
dual rationalities 90
due process 29
Duhigg, C. 94, 99
Durant, R. 101–102

education 4; public service 202–211
effectiveness 183
efficiency 12, 16, 17, 30, 71, 72, 74, 78, 91, 92, 148, 183; government 82; hindrances 85; national 13
Eisenhower, President D. D. 94
elections 90
Electronic Waiting List (EWL) 121, 122
Elmers, C. 116
empathy 66
employees 4, 13, 21, 25; public 16, 171–172
employers 13, 14; knowledge 14
enforcement 13
engagement: degrees of 131, 133; workers 2
Engels, F., and Marx, K. 147
engineering 18–19, 75, 84, 92
Enrollment Clerk (EC) 119, 121, 122
entrepreneurialism 27, 94
Environmental Protection Agency (EPA) 105
environments 155; and organizations 48, 118
episteme 197
Epps, C. E., Maynard-Moody, S. and Haider-Markel, D. 63, 64
ethical action 191, 192
ethics: authentic 190–201; public sector 198, 199
everyday coping 49–50; firefighters 52–55
everyday knowledge 42, 43
Excellence strategies 26
executive control 95; government 91–93
executive knowledge 3, 41, 89–108
executives 3, 127, 183; abilities 104; accountability 96; action 91; and bureaucrats 102–103; craft knowledge 100; decision-making 106–107; experience 106; functions 101; political 98; role 144
existence 37
existentialism 191–193, 195, 196, 200
experience 158; lived 207

experience knowledge, philosophy of 49–50
experience-based knowledge 3
experience–concept gap 5
experiential information 80
experiential knowledge 14, 25, 28–29, 85, 112, 122, 149, 158, 159, 171, 184, 204
experiential learning 178
experiential skill 55
experiential-situational learning 118
expert knowledge 90, 185
expertise 49, 54, 58, 85, 176; political 89, 106
exploitation 195

fabrication 70
faceless commitments 185, 186
facework 6, 147–157, 167, 171, 175, 177, 182, 183, 185
fact-finding, executive approach 124, 125
factory production 71–72, 73
Fandos, N. 126
Fayol, H. 76, 78–79
feedback 81
felt sense 14–15, 22–23, 47–69
field office 182
firefighters, everyday coping 52–55
fleeing felon rule 64
Follett, M. P. 85, 151–153, 167–168, 172, 207
foot patrolmen 61–62
Foote, Dr. S. 114
Ford, H. 95
Ford Motor Company 95, 96
Foucault, M. 113–114, 147, 203
Francis, C. 20
Frank, M. 117–118
free market 75
freedom 195, 196; escape from 193–194, 208; political 208
Freire, P. 194, 208
Fromm, E. 194, 208
frontline knowledge 41, 127
frontline workers 14, 48, 50, 51, 100, 125, 172, 179; authenticity 67; felt sense 47–69; middleness 67; power 60–61; public-sector 56

Gadamer, H. -G. 150, 166
Galileo 78
gaming strategies 65, 66
Gane, N. 91
Gendlin, E. 15, 163

General Foods 20
General Motors (GM) 94–96
Giddens, A. 167, 176–177, 185, 186, 187–188
goals 71; organizational 2, 3, 44, 74; political 19
good faith standards 172
Gore, A. 27
governance 153, 160, 207
government 162, 170–171, 197–198, 199; bureaucracies 44, 89, 90; business 17, 93–94; city 92, 93; customers 24, 27; efficiency 82; executive control 91–93; legitimacy 82–83; machinery 16; managerial bias 5; municipal 16, 92; objectives 16; operations 71; power 82–83; reinvention 26
Government Accountability Office (GAO) 113
government agencies 196; Australia 80; systemization 15
Grant, J. D., and Toch, H. 47
Gregorio, D. J. 64
groups: norms 193–194; resistance 196
guidelines, internal 64
Guignon, C. B., and Pereboom, D. 192
Gulick, L. L. 17, 82
gunlocks 131
Gutierrez, C. 94
Guy, M. E., Newman, M. A. and Mastracci, S. H. 47, 55, 63

Haider-Markel, D., Epps, C. E. and Maynard-Moody, S. 63, 64
Hales, C. P. 76–77
Hamilton, A. 16
Hammer, M., and Champy, J. 25
hands-on intelligence 2
hands-on knowledge 41, 52, 74
Harman, K. 80
Hart, D. K., and Scott, W. G. 76
Hawthorne studies 19
head office 175
head teachers 84
headquarters 182
health: care 97; needs 92–93; public 104
health department, fiscal control 92–93
Health Net 111, 123
health services, veterans 6, 111–127
Heclo, H. 90, 98, 100
Heidegger, M. 37–38, 40, 55, 56, 149–150, 192
Herhert, J. R. 86n1

hermeneutic circle 149–150
hermeneutics 149
Heyman, J. 66
hierarchical authority 44
hierarchical roles 181, 182
hierarchical thinking 172
hierarchy 2, 3, 4, 6, 154, 167
Hill, R. 116
Hogan, R. 116
Holden, M. 101
Holt, R., and Chia, R. 76
Hood, C. 29
Hoover Commission 18
Hopper, T., and Macintosh, N. 81
human capital development 25
human relations 18–23, 29
human resources 20, 72, 155
humanism 21, 22
humans: action 67; nature 18, 21, 73
Hummel, R. P. 1–2, 3, 28, 34, 36–39, 47, 60, 67, 70, 96, 112, 113, 128, 147, 148–149, 153, 181; and Carnevale, D. G. 1, 11; and Stivers, C. 19, 171
Husserl, E. 3, 36–37, 96–97

ideal-typical bureaucracy 135
ideas 50, 70, 77, 78
identity 81, 196
ideology 70, 74–75, 85; business 148; management 4, 74, 83; public management 81–84; science-based 11
ignorance 185
imagination 163
immigration 92
Immigration Service 64, 66
in-and-outers 90
inauthenticity 58, 67, 167
incentives 12, 75
individual rights 162
inducements 21
industrial capitalism 72
industrial humanism 22
industrial psychology 21–22
industrial relations 18, 20
Industrial Revolution 71
industrialism 147
inefficiency 148
information: access 183; exchange 154, 172; experiential 80; gathering 51; sharing 171, 210; transfer 205
informed action 192
initiative 12
innovation 24, 180

Institute of Applied Phenomenology in Science and Technology 5
Institute of Medicine (IOM) 117
instrumental rationality 89, 91
integration 151, 154, 167–168
intelligence: hands-on 2; web-based 79
intentionality 3, 36–37
inter-institutional collaboration 207
interactions 166, 167, 184; circle 183; knowledge 6, 133–134
interdependence 155
interests 29, 176
internet therapy program 131
internships 209
interpersonal skills 23
interpretation 149, 150, 153, 160
intolerance 208

Jacques, R. 73, 75
Jehenson, R. 43
job: descriptions 56; and work 152
Johnson, P. 202
Jones, C. 48, 59
judging 153, 159–160, 162
judgment 76, 106, 153, 159, 160, 184, 191, 203; as dialogic 163–164; moral 192

Kahn, L. I. 5
kaizen 25
Kant, I. 191
Kelman, S., Sanders, R. and Pandit, G. 107
Kemmis, S. 162
know-how 53, 54, 57, 74
knowers 80
knowing: public organizations 34–46; theory 35
knowing is being 36–38
knowing-being 150
knowledge 36; claims 187–188; competing 202–211; conceptual-scientific 3, 44; discontinuity 84; forms 2–3, 112, 148, 158, 175; frameworks 112; gaps 4, 144, 149, 175; role-specific 41, 43; sharing 182; social distribution 43; types 5–6; value hierarchy 114
knowledge approach 113–114, 127; research 142–144
knowledges-in-use 6
Kramer, R. 195, 200n2

labor: process 12, 13; protests 18; skilled 16, *see also* division of labor
land surveying 97

Lapinski, T. 111
laws 13, 161
leadership 91, 101
Lean Production approach 24–26
learners 80
learning 28, 176, 187, 209; circles 210; collective 171; double-loop 209; environments 203–204; experiential 178; experiential-situational 118; organizational 155
legal values 29
Lesser, W. 5
life-worlds 2, 39–40, 45, 149
linear rationality 148, 196
Lipsky, M. 60
listening 62, 169, 178
lived experience 207
local knowledge 58, 64
local office 175
logic of rationality 2, 158
logic of reasonableness 2, 128, 153, 158–165
Long, N. 101
Luckmann, T.: and Berger, P. L. 41, 42; and Schutz, A. 39, 42, 43
Lynxweiler, J., Shover, N. and Clelland, D. A. 65

McCarl, R. 52–55
McCarthy, D. J. 80
McCleary, R. 66
McGill, M. E. 23
Macintosh, N., and Hopper, T. 81
McKinlay, A.: and Starkey, K. 94, 95, 96; and Taylor, P. 81
McNamara, R. 95, 96
management 2, 4, 5, 12, 37, 151, 175; advent of 71–75; as art 79; authority 74; concepts 77–79; consultants 22; definition 71, 76; ideology 4, 74, 83; model vs. practice 79–81; power 102–103; principles 76–77; public administration 70; public sector 19; and science 21; as science 79–80; scientific 12–16, 72–73, 75, 85, 95; solicitude 56; values 29
management reforms 1, 147, 178, 184, 186; failures 2, 5, 11–33
managerial power 102–103
managerialism 5, 83, 84, 196; expansion 23–26; public 26–27; resistance 61
managers 1, 2, 3, 12, 74; activities 76–77, 79–80, 82; circle 148–149; control 28;

identity 81; knowledge 11, 45, 70–88, 204; responsibilities 155; role 70, 143; self-image 79; self-understanding 81; social role 74; stories 163; and workers 18, 80, 152–153
Mannheim, K. 74
Marx, K. 148; and Engels, F. 147
mass production 24
Mastracci, S. H., Guy, M. E. and Newman, M. A. 47, 55, 63
material world, and human action 67
mathematics 96
mathematization 97
May, R. 193
Maynard-Moody, S., Haider-Markel, D. and Epps, C. E. 63, 64
mayors 16, 91, 92, 95
mediators 181, 182, 183
members of parliament (MPs) 90
mental health: coaching 131; commissioners 169–170
merit 19
Merleau-Ponty, M. 38, 199
Mezirow, J. 209
Micklethwait, J., and Wooldridge, A. 186–187
military 210
mine inspectors 65
Mintzberg, H. 74, 79–80
mismanagement 114
mistrust 180, 193, 195, 196
Mitchell, Dr. K. 114
MITRE Corporation 113, 117
modernity 22, 147, 148, 187, 196
moral judgments 192
Morgan, G. 20, 34
Mosher, W. E. 202
mothering 57
motivation 36, 37; workers 19–20, 21, 73
municipal government 16, 92
Munoz, C. 115

national efficiency 13
National Performance Review (NPR) 27, 123
negotiating behaviors 169
networks 4, 99, 152
New Public Management (NPM) 6n2, 16, 27–29, 58, 59, 60, 71, 83, 94, 96, 152, 164, 196
New York Bureau of Municipal Research 92, 93, 94
Newman, M. A., Mastracci, S. H. and Guy, M. E. 47, 55, 63

Noble, D. F. 19, 72, 75
norms 64, 114, 176, 192; group 193–194
numbers 94, 95, 96–98, 100, 103
nursing homes 56–58

Obama, President B. 115, 126
obedience 208
objective knowledge 78
obligations 176
officialdom 89
Olshfski, D., and Cunningham, R. B. 103, 105, 106
oppression 172, 194
orders 173, 191, 193
org chart 181
organizations 2, 34–35, 42, 58, 101, 114; change 124, 187; circular 154–156; control 147; culture 20, 23; decision-making 154; development 22, 23; and environment 48, 118; goals 2, 3, 44, 74; humanism 21; as knowledge structures 39–42; learning 155, 176; pyramid 42–44; reforms 184–185, 196; structures 113, 182; successful 155–156; trust 178; values 101
Others 55
outcomes 1, 197
outsourcing 28, 102
overdocumented alien 64–65

pain management intervention 130
Pandit, G., Kelman, S. and Sanders, R. 107
parole officers 66
participation 21, 167
partnerships 187
party politics 106
passive knowledge 52
patient-centered intervention 131
patients, and care-givers 57
patronage 19, 164
Paulson, H. 99
pay-offs 164
pedagogy 208, 210
pedagogy vs. andragogy 205–207
peer review 81
Pentagon 100
people, coping with 38–39
Pereboom, D., and Guignon, C. B. 192
performance 1, 3, 26–27, 49, 96, 154, 180; accountability 96; measurement 4, 28, 29, 83, 96, 100, 115
Person, H. S. 71
person-to-person acuity 56
personal networks 99

personality conflict 21
phenomenology 5, 127
Phillips, D. 97
philosophy 37
phronesis 159, 161, 191, 194, 197
Piccorelli, J., and Zingale, N. 193
piecework 73
plans 3
Platt, C. S. 23
police 61–64, 179; managers 83–84; racism 63, 64; stop and frisk 63; violence 63
policy 60, 71, 82; outcome measurement 100; social work 58, 60
political democracy 148
political parties, power 92
politicians 90; administrative 101; power 89
politics 16, 19, 36, 82, 91, 92, 183–184; accountability 98, 103; and administration 17, 90, 106; appointees 99, 100–102; democratic 164; executives 98; expertise 89, 106; freedom 208; goals 19; leadership 91; non-rationality 89; rationality 91; rules 202; skill 104, 105; threat to 71; values 29, 71, 91, 162
politics-administration dichotomy 164
POSDCORB 82
post-traumatic stress disorder (PTSD) 115
poverty 27
power 3, 6, 16, 100, 172, 175, 187; inflow 101–102; and knowledge 11–12; relations 3–4, 203; sharing 171; struggles 89, 90, 102
power/knowledge 147
practical wisdom 159, 160, 161–162, 191, 194, 196–198; as judgment 163–164
practice makes perfect 54
practices 160–161, 210; as practical wisdom 161–162
practicums 209
practitioner-students 206
practitioners, reflective 206
Pratt, R. C., and Chandler, S. M. 99
precedents 161–162
prescription 194
principles 13; management 76–77; scientific 84–85
privatization 28, 29, 113, 126, 134, 136
probable cause standards 64
probation 64
problem-solving 155, 203, 204, 206
process 25
production 14, 24

productivity 19, 20, 21, 22, 23, 26, 78; maximum 76; trust 176, 177
professional knowledge 102–103
professional socialization 63
professional-scientific knowledge 44
professionalism 63, 64
profits 13, 15, 21, 72, 75, 76, 196
protests, labor 18
protocols 3, 61, 161
psychic prisons 20
psychology, industrial 21–22
public administration 4, 17, 23, 70, 148, 207
public agencies 26, 27
public employees 16, 171–172
public executives 103–107
public good 162, 190, 191
public health 104
public interest 91, 104, 162
public management 23, 81–84
public managerialism 26–27
public organizations 1, 5, 6, 34–46
public power 83
public sector 197; accountability 190; business values 28; entrepreneurialism 27; ethics 199; frontline work 56; knowledge and power 11–12; management practices 19; objectivity 16; unions 4
public service 197, 198, 199–200; education 202–211
public well-being 93
public-private partnerships 28, 102
publicity 105, 106
publicness 197
Pugh, D. S. 76
pyramids 2, 3; organizational 42–44; of power 6; rational knowledge 158; to circle 147–157; trust 181–182; vs. circle 135–136

quality circles 154
quantitative data 160
quit smoking for good 131

racism, police 63, 64
rational knowledge 158; pyramids 158
rational-technical knowledge 44
rationality 136; instrumental 91; linear 148, 196; logic of 2, 158; political 91
re-engineering 25, 26
reaction 151
Reagan, R. 26

reality 151
reasonableness 149; logic of 2, 128, 153, 158–165
records 58
red tape 26, 27
reflective practitioners 206
reforms 148, 156; management 1, 2, 147, 178, 184, 186; organizational 184–185, 196; and trust 179; welfare 59, 60
regulations 161, 162; being-with 64–67
Rein, L. 116–117
Reina, D., and Reina, M. 180
Reinventing Government 16, 27, 28
Reinvention movement 26
res publica 190
research, knowledge approach 142–144
resistance 2, 21, 61, 196
resources 58, 73, 76
responsibility 180
results 1, 2, 5, 16, 29, 30, 49, 102, 142; measurement 27, 94, 136
return on investment (ROI) 95, 96
Richter, A. 199
Ricoeur, P. 74
rights 4, 162, 176
risk 177, 187
Roberts, J. 199
Rogers, C. 195
role-specific knowledge 41, 43
Romme, A. G. 154–155
Roosevelt, President F. 17, 18, 19
Roosevelt, President T. 13
Rosenbloom, D. H. 29
rules 3, 4, 13, 38, 61, 67, 77, 154, 161, 191, 198; discretion 61; knowledge 202; political practice 202

safety, psychological 180
Sanders, R., Pandit, G. and Kelman, S. 107
Sandfort, J. R. 58, 60–61
Sartre, J. -P. 196, 200
Sayre, W. 17, 18
scalability 118
Schmidt, M. R. 51–52
Schön, D. A. 204
Schutz, A. 2; and Luckmann, T. 39, 42, 43
science 5, 30, 36, 76, 94, 161, 202, 207; investigation 158; and management 21; predictions 97; principles 84–85
science-based ideology 11
scientific knowledge 2, 25, 42, 102
scientific management 12–16, 17, 18, 20, 21, 22, 72–73, 75, 85, 95

scientific-technical knowledge 71
Scott, W. G. 22; and Hart, D. K. 76
self-awareness 209
self-government 148
self-interest 4, 17
self-learning 81
self-protection 177, 178
self-reflection 209
sensing 101, 106
service: bureaucracy 111–127; delivery 112, 129
Sherwood, F. 187
Shinseki, E. 115
Shover, N., Clelland, D. A. and Lynxweiler, J. 65
situations 149, 163
sixth sense 57, 101
skill: cognitive 73; experiential 55; political 104, 105; transfer 72
Sloan, A. E. 95, 96
social change 15
social control 73
social relations 36
social sciences 21–22
social services 83
social work 58, 58–61, 83–84
socialism 92
socialization, professional 63
sociology 22
soldiering 13, 73
solicitude 49–50, 55–56; casework 58–61; managerial 56; social work 58–61
Sonneberg, F. 180
specialization 210
specialized knowledge 43
stakeholders 101, 124
standardization 28, 112
standards 3, 28; probable cause 64
Starkey, K., and McKinlay, A. 94, 95, 96
Steiner, G. 38
stereotypes 63–64, 66
Stivers, C. 15, 93, 205; and Hummel, R. P. 19, 171
stop and frisk 63
street-level bureaucrats 60, 63
stress 59, 180
strikes 15
structures 148
suicide 125, 129
suits 175
surplus value 148
surveillance 28, 72
systematizing 118

systems approach 117, 122, 135
systems theory 117–118
systems thinking 117–119

T-groups 23
talking 154
Tammany Hall 91
Taylor, F. W. 12, 13, 14, 18, 29, 72, 77, 84, 85, 162; and Copley, F. B. 24
Taylor, P., and McKinley, A. 81
Taylorism 16, 25, 26, 156
teachers 61, 83–84
teaching administration 203–205
team-building 23, 183
techne 197
technical knowledge 89, 100, 102
technology 5, 30, 51
Tello, M. 116
temps 90
tensions 178
Tester, J. 111
Teton Dam 51–52, 56, 185
Thatcher, M. 26
Thayer, F. 150–151
theory 205, 210
Theory Z programs 26
thinking 78, 172, 203; critical 209; systems 117–119
Thomas, R.: and Davies, A. 83, 84; and Davis, A. 61
Thompson, T. 116
time-and-motion studies 14
Toch, H., and Grant, J. D. 47
top-down control 151
top-down directives 125
total quality management (TQM) 23, 24, 25, 26
Townley, B. 81
traditional knowledge 72
transformation 135, 178
translators 48, 51
transparency 177
traumatic brain injuries (TBIs) 115
Triage 119
trial-and-error 56
Trist, E. 155–156
triumph of numbers 28
trust 28, 99, 125, 193; and authenticity 194–196; building 178, 183–184; circles 174–189; definition 176–177; as learned behavior 177–178; literature 177–178; organizational 178; police 62;

productivity 176, 177; pyramid 181–182; and reforms 179; zones 177
trustworthiness 186
truth 113, 114, 207
typifications 40, 41

ultimate ends 91
understanding 50
unions 15, 18, 22, 28, 72, 92, 126, 127, 171, 172; public sector 4; representatives 169–170, 181; stewards 99
United States Bureau of Reclamation (USBR) 51
United States Department of Veterans Affairs (VA) 6, 97, 111–127; appointment making 119–122, *120*; appointment wait times 114, 115, 119; independent assessment 117–119; Integrated Report 117, 118; Summit (2015) 124–126, 138–141
United States Navy (USN) 15
university classrooms 204

values: legal 29; managerial 29; organizational 101; political 29, 71, 91, 162
Veteran Health Administration (VHA) 123, 129, 133, 134
veterans: deaths 114, 115; health services 111–127
Veterans Access, Choice and Accountability Act (2014) 117
Veterans Advisory Board (VAB) 129
Veterans Health Organization (VHA) 126
Veterans Research Engagement Board 133
vets helping vets pilot 131
Vietnam War (1954–1975) 113, 114
view from 30, 000 feet 135–136
viewpoints 163

Wagenaar, H., and Cook, D. 160–161
wages 13
Waldo, D. 82–83, 148, 164, 172, 191
War on Poverty 27
Watertown Arsenal 15
Watson, T. 80–81
Wayne, K., and Abernathy, W. J. 24
web-based intelligence 79
Weber, M. 3, 4, 9, 44, 71, 83, 89, 98, 135, 147–148, 191
welcome desk 179
welfare reforms 59, 60
Western Electric 100

whistleblowers 114, 116, 117, 119
white-collar workers 16
Wilson, B. 111
Wilson, C. E. 94
Wilson, J. Q. 154
Wilson, W. 17, 82, 148, 202
wisdom: in practice 153, *see also* practical wisdom
with-ness 55
wooing 163
Wooldridge, A., and Mickelthwait, J. 186–187
work 1, 2, 14, 36, 38, 67, 73, 74; definition 3, 70; and job 152; organizational definitions 142–143; quantity and quality 30; rationalizing 76
workers 3, 50–51, 142–143; control of 11, 12, 14, 20, 28, 30, 70, 73, 178, 208; cooperation 154; craft knowledge 12; deskilling 15; disciplining 28; economic motivations 18; engagement 2; frontline 50, 51, 60–61, 67; interests 29; knowledge 4, 5, 14, 15, 30, 45, 47–69, 85–86, 143, 184, 204; location 48; and managers 18, 80, 152–153; motivation 19–20, 21, 73; power 49, 63; psyche 20; public organizations 5; resistance 2; rights 4; stereotypes 63–64; white-collar 16
working knowledge 12, 42, 84
workplace 29
worksite: inspection 64; regulations 65
Wright, N. D., and Cooper, T. L. 101, 104, 105

Yanow, D. 48, 49, 58

Zingale, N., and Piccorelli, J. 193
zones of indifference 103
zones of silence 186
zones of trust 177

Made in the USA
Thornton, CO
02/06/23 01:11:53

d34bc520-dba7-4c6b-b3b5-4f43e3f65726R01